GW01396014

FIRST
EXPERT

STUDENT'S RESOURCE BOOK with key

Richard Mann • Nick Kenny • Jan Bell • Roger Gower

Contents

Contents

Section	Vocabulary development 2	Language development 2	Reading
B How do I look?	Clothes; Commonly confused words **Exam practice:** Word formation (pp. 67–68)	Modals: speculation and deduction; Choosing the correct present or past form **Exam practice:** Multiple-choice cloze (pp. 68–69)	**Paper 1 Part 6** Gapped text: *Make your image work for you* (pp. 70–71)
B Hobbies	Word formation; Talking about hobbies; Paraphrasing; Phrasal verbs and expressions (pp. 77–78)	Modals: expressing ability: *can, could, be able to*; Other ways of expressing ability; Key word transformations **Exam practice:** Open cloze (pp. 78–79)	**Paper 1 Part 7** Multiple matching: *Me and my passion* (pp. 80–81)
B Spending money	Ways of shopping; Commonly confused words (p. 87)	Subject–verb agreement: singular and plural verbs; *all, both, neither, none and one; it/there;* Key word transformations (pp. 88–89)	**Paper 1 Part 6** Gapped text: *Why do some shoppers still shy away from the net?* (pp. 90–91)
B Getting around	Transport; Word formation: negative prefixes and suffixes; Key word transformations (pp. 97–98)	Hypothetical situations: *wish* + past simple/past perfect/*would/could; I wish/if only;* Other expressions for hypothetical situations; Key word transformations **Exam practice:** Open cloze (pp. 98–99)	**Paper 1 Part 7** Multiple matching: *A good day out* (pp. 100–101)
B Health and fitness	Commonly confused words; Collocations; Comparing photos (pp. 107–108)	*so/such; too/enough/very; as, like* and *such as;* Key word transformations (pp. 108–109)	**Paper 1 Part 5** Multiple choice: *Fit for fame* (pp. 110–111)
B The media	The media; Phrasal verbs **Exam practice:** Multiple-choice cloze (pp. 117–118)	*need + -ing/to be done; have/get something done;* Key word transformations **Exam practice:** Open cloze (pp. 118–119)	**Paper 1 Part 6** Gapped text: *The influence of television* (pp. 120–121)

Vocabulary development 1

EXPERT STRATEGY

Use a dictionary to expand your vocabulary. You should use a good English–English dictionary (such as the *Longman Exams Dictionary*) when you check your answers to exercises in Paper 1, Reading and Use of English. You will also need to use a dictionary when you write compositions, reports, etc. for Paper 2, Writing. When doing reading tests, however, it is better to try to guess the meanings of words as much as you can.

Understanding your dictionary

1 Look at the dictionary entry below and match the numbered boxes (1–8) with the explanations (a–h).

gen·e·ra·tion AC S2 W2 / ˌdʒenəˈreɪʃən/ *n*
1 [C also + plural verb] *BrE* all people of about the same age: *Like most of my generation, I had never known a war.* | *In my generation the divorce rate is very high.* | *the need to preserve the planet for* **future generations** | [+of] *the post-war generation of writers* | **the younger/older generation** (= the younger or older people in society) *The younger generation don't know what hard work is.* | *The story has been handed down* **from generation to generation**. | *If the gene is passed from father to son through the generations, the disease becomes increasingly severe.*
2 [C] all the members of a family of about the same age: *Friction is common when three generations live together.* | *In some families there is little verbal interchange between the generations.* | **first-generation/second-generation, etc.** (= being a member of the first, second, etc. generation to live or be born in a country) *a third-generation American* | *As many as 40 percent of the fathers were first-generation immigrants.*

a the meaning or definition of the word
b the pronunciation of the word, using the International Phonetic Alphabet
c the word class – verb, noun, adjective, etc.
d a second meaning of the word, shown by a number
e a common expression or set phrase
f British English (not American English) usage
g an example sentence showing how the word is used
h grammatical information (e.g. countable noun)

Using your dictionary

2 Look at these entries and answer the questions.

in·her·it /ɪnˈherɪt/ *v*
1 [T] to receive money, property, etc. from someone after they have died: **inherit sth from sb** *He inherited a fortune from his grandmother.* | *inherited wealth.*
2 [T] if you inherit a situation, especially one in which problems have been caused by other people, you have to deal with it: *The present government inherited a closed, state-dominated economy.* **3** [T] to have the same character or appearance as your parents: **inherit sth from sb** *Mr Grass inherited his work ethic from his father.* | *I inherited my mother's curly hair.*

1 When we say the word *inherit*, do we stress the first, middle or last syllable?
2 Do we pronounce the middle part of *inherit* as *hear*?
3 Does the verb *inherit* take a direct object?

house·hold1 /ˈhaʊshəʊld $-hoʊld/ *n* [C]
all the people who live together in one house **SYN house:** *A growing number of households have at least one computer.* | *Families are classified by the occupation of* **the head of the household** (= the person who earns the most money and is most respected in a house). | *There are seven million single-person households in this country.*
household2 *adj* [only before noun]
1 relating to looking after a house and the people in it **SYN domestic: household goods/products/ items, etc.** *washing powder and other household products* | *household chores* | *The government had set a target of recycling 25 percent of household waste by the end of the 20th century.* **2 be a household name/word** to be very well known: *Coca Cola is a household name around the world.*

4 Do we stress the first or second syllable in *household*?
5 Is the word *household* an adjective as well as a noun?
6 As a noun, is *household* countable or uncountable?
7 Can we say: *I bought some items which are household*?
8 Could we say that Madonna is a *household name*?

Language development 1

> **COURSEBOOK** pages 10–11, **EXPERT GRAMMAR** page 182

Situations and habits: Frequency adverbs

1 Read the examples in the box and complete the rules with *before* or *after*.

I usually go out every Saturday night.

The cat will occasionally disappear for days.

My mother's stories are sometimes very funny.

I often used to play chess with my father and he would always win.

Rules

We put frequency adverbs such as *always*, *often*:

1 _____ simple tenses of the verb *be*.

2 _____ simple tenses of other verbs.

3 _____ the auxiliary verb in complex tenses.

4 _____ *used to* but _____ *would*.

Adverbial phrases such as *every day*, *three times a week*, etc. can go at the beginning or the end of a clause. Initial position is more emphatic.

---

2 Rewrite the sentences, putting the words in brackets in the correct place.

1 Adam leaves for school at seven o'clock in the morning. (always)

   _____

2 He goes to school by bus. (every day)

   _____

3 In the past he used to wait a long time for the bus. (never)

   _____

4 The bus would be two or three minutes late. (sometimes)

   _____

5 Nowadays the bus is late. (often)

   _____

6 As a result, Adam arrives late for school. (frequently)

   _____

7 Fortunately, his teacher doesn't complain. (usually)

   _____

8 Adam does his homework on the bus. (regularly)

   _____

State verbs

3 Complete the sentences with the present simple or present continuous form of the verbs in bold.

1 **have**

   a Sandra _____ a large collection of DVDs.

   b Mum, answer the phone, please. I can't answer it because I _____ a shower.

2 **see**

   a I _____ why your sister gets so annoyed with you. You're always borrowing her things!

   b My brother isn't going out with Stella anymore. These days he _____ Tina instead.

3 **taste**

   a 'Why is your spoon in the saucepan?' 'I _____ the soup to check if there's enough salt.'

   b This sauce _____ strange!

4 **think**

   a You haven't said anything all evening. What _____ (you) about?

   b What _____ (you) about the new history lecturer?

5 **appear**

   a Although my dad _____ to be very strict, he's not, really.

   b Alex Cameron _____ as Hamlet at the Theatre Royal all week.

6 **smell**

   a Why _____ (you) those roses? Don't you know they're made of plastic?

   b The biscuits my sister made this afternoon _____ delicious.

7 **look**

   a Today our family's going on a picnic but it _____ as if it might rain.

   b Why _____ you _____ at me like that? Have I done something wrong?

8 **expect**

   a I _____ you're tired after playing football all afternoon.

   b I can't go out tonight because I _____ a phone call from my aunt in the USA.

Past habit

4 Find and correct the mistakes in some of the sentences. Tick the ones that are correct.

1 When I lived at home, I used to ~~going~~ fishing with my father every Saturday. _go_

2 My mother would make us sandwiches for the day. ✓

3 We would have spent hours waiting for a fish to bite.

4 I used love listening to him talk about nature.

5 Often we didn't used to come home until after dark.

6 I remember how my mother used to look at us when we were late.

EXPERT STRATEGY

For Paper 2, Writing, it's important to vary the grammatical structures and verb forms you use. This makes your writing more interesting for the reader. But you have to be careful. Sometimes, a particular form may not be possible.

Listening (Paper 3 Part 1)

Before you listen

1a Read the instructions for the listening task. How many extracts will you hear? The extracts are not related. (Note that in the exam you will hear eight extracts.)

b For questions 1–6, read the sentence that gives the context of the extract, the question and the three options (A–C). Think about the situation: who will be talking and what they will be talking about. Mark the key words in each question. The first two have been done for you.

Multiple choice

2a 🎧 02 Do the task. Note these steps.
- You will hear each extract twice. As you listen, focus on the speaker's main idea – don't worry if you don't understand every word.
- Choose one of the options after listening the first time. If you don't know an answer, have a guess and go on to the next question.

b 🎧 02 Listen again and check your answers.

EXPERT STRATEGY

Read the questions carefully to know what you're listening for. Each question has a different focus. For example, some questions ask about the speaker's opinions and feelings and others ask about the topic.

➤ HELP

1 You're listening for the main point she's making. Which option matches this?
2 Listen for how he feels now, not how he felt at first.
3 Listen to what she says about shopping. Does she enjoy it?
4 Listen for the name of the programme and what the first listener says about it.

EXPERT LANGUAGE

Look back at the multiple-choice questions. Find an example of a question that is asking about:
1 the present.
2 the past.
3 the future.

EXPERT WORD CHECK

*accountant   compensations
fires up   furnishings   fussy
mindless   mixing desk   passion
swapping   tax forms*

You will hear people talking in six different situations. For questions 1–6, choose the best answer (A, B, or C).

1 You hear a woman talking about her car. What is she describing?
   A what she dislikes about her car
   B how she depends on her car
   C why she needs a new car

2 You hear a sound recording engineer talking about his training. How does he feel about the course he followed?
   A unsure how useful it was
   B sorry that it was only part-time
   C grateful for the basic skills it gave him

3 You hear a woman talking about shopping. What is she doing?
   A disagreeing with some recent research
   B justifying a decision she has made
   C defending an activity she enjoys

4 You hear the beginning of a radio programme. What is the programme going to be about?
   A a way of learning new skills
   B helping people who have no skills
   C keeping your own skills up-to-date

5 You hear a student talking about living and studying in London. What did she find most difficult?
   A managing on a restricted budget
   B keeping a record of her spending
   C being criticised by her parents

6 You hear a man talking about the furnishings in his home. What point is he making about them?
   A They needed to reflect his lifestyle at work.
   B The things he chose were modern in design.
   C He didn't want them to remind him of work.

Writing (Paper 2 Part 2: Informal email)

➤ **COURSEBOOK** pages 12–13, **EXPERT WRITING** page 202

Understand the task

1   Read the writing task and answer the questions.
   1 Who are you writing to?
      a someone you know well
      b someone you know a little
   2 What is the main purpose of the email?
      a to entertain the reader
      b to provide important information
   3 What information MUST you include? Mark the parts of the task that tell you.

You have received this email from your English pen friend, Pat. Write an email to Pat, answering her questions.

> Hi there!
>
> Great to hear that you're coming to stay with us for two weeks this summer and that you're bringing a friend with you – that should be fun! But who is this friend? Write back and tell me when you would like to come, what your friend is like and the sort of things you enjoy doing together.
>
> Pat

*Write your **email** in 140–190 words in an appropriate style.*

Check and improve a sample answer

2a Read a student's answer and look at the parts of the task you marked in Exercise 1. Does the email include the required information?

> **EXPERT STRATEGY**
>
> Always check your work for basic errors when you finish writing. You will lose marks if basic errors make your work unclear or difficult to understand. Double-space your writing so that you have room to make corrections if you need to. Make sure that your handwriting is neat and easy to read.

b   The student's teacher has underlined all the mistakes in the email and used symbols to identify the types of mistakes. Look at the key below to see what the symbols mean.

c   Rewrite the email, correcting the mistakes.

KEY TO CORRECTION SYMBOLS

P = punctuation	Ww = wrong word
Sp = spelling	Wo = word order
Gr = grammar	St = style
T = verb tense	

Home 🏠   **Previous** ❮   **Next** ❯   **Search** 🔍

Hi Pat,

Thank you, ⁽ᴾ⁾ for inviting me and my friend to stay with your family this summer. We would both love to come. We can come ⁽ᵂᵒ⁾ for two weeks in August?

I know that you never have met ⁽ᵂᵒ⁾ my friend Angela but I'm sure you'll like her very much. She's a very easy-going person. She's two years smaller ⁽ᵂʷ⁾ than me and studies ⁽ᵀ⁾ to be doctor ⁽ᴳʳ⁾.

Like me ⁽ᴾ⁾ Angela likes walking and horse-riding. She's also very good in ⁽ᴳʳ⁾ tennis. There's one only ⁽ᵂᵒ⁾ thing that Angela isn't very keen on: swiming ⁽ˢᵖ⁾. Its ⁽ᴾ⁾ rather strange because we were used ⁽ᴳʳ⁾ to go with our families to Lake Balaton every year when we were children. Her family even has a house their ⁽ˢᵖ⁾ now.

I won't write any more, Pat, because I take ⁽ᵀ⁾ exams at the moment and I'm very occupied ⁽ᵂʷ⁾. Thank you again for your invitation. I'm looking forward to see you ⁽ᴳʳ⁾ and your family this summer. I've told Angela all about you! Please let me know if we can come in August, won't you. ⁽ᴾ⁾

Yours faithfully, ⁽ˢᵗ⁾

Anna

Vocabulary development 2

▸ COURSEBOOK pages 14–15

Special occasions

1   Match the words/phrases in the box with the photos and write them in the correct column.

athletes   degree   graduate   medals   olive leaves
shake someone's hand   sports event   university

Photo A	Photo B
_____	_____
_____	_____
_____	_____
_____	_____

Comparing photos

EXPERT STRATEGY

When you talk about photos, you may not know what something is called in English. Try to describe it using words you do know. Useful phrases for doing this include *It's like ...* and *It's a kind/sort of ...*

2a   Read how one student compared the two photos and complete the text. Use only one word in each space.

b   What phrases does the student use to:
1 talk about similarities?
2 talk about differences?
3 express an opinion?
4 paraphrase an unknown word?

Both these photos **(1)** _____ special occasions or ceremonies.

The first picture was obviously **(2)** _____ at the Olympic Games. I can see three **(3)** _____ who are holding their **(4)** _____ and looking very happy. In the second photograph a university student is holding some kind of document – I think it's called a(n) **(5)** _____ certificate in English – and shaking an older man's hand. **(6)** _____ the people in the first photo, she also looks very happy. Both the ceremony in the first picture **(7)** _____ the ceremony in the second picture are very formal occasions. People have been given a prize or an award for what they have achieved.

The main difference **(8)** _____ the two photographs is that these athletes have done well in a sports **(9)** _____ at the Olympics, **(10)** _____ the student here has just – what's the word – graduated? – from a university. She is now called a(n) **(11)** _____ , I think. It's interesting that the athletes are wearing olive **(12)** _____ on their heads. The student and the other people in the second picture are also wearing a sort of hat on their heads.

I really love sport, so I think I'd prefer to attend the ceremony in this photograph, at the Olympic Games. I think it must be a very happy time for everyone there – and incredibly exciting.

Language development 2

➤ COURSEBOOK page 17, EXPERT GRAMMAR pages 182–183

Modifying adjectives and adverbs

1a Look at the table comparing the Olympic Games which were held in Athens, Beijing and London. Are the statements below *True* (T) or *False* (F)?

Number of:	Athens 2004	Beijing 2008	London 2012
athletes (total)	11,099	10,942	10,568
athletes (women)	4,306	4,637	4,676
athletes (men)	6,793	6,305	5,892
events	301	302	302
Greek gold medallists	6	0	0
Chinese gold medallists	32	51	38
UK gold medallists	9	19	29
seats in Olympic Stadium	72,000	91,000	60,000

1 Slightly more athletes took part in the Olympic Games in London than in Beijing. _____
2 A far larger number of women than men took part in the London Olympics. _____
3 In Athens and Beijing, China won by far the most gold medals. _____
4 There were not quite as many events in London as there were in Athens. _____
5 The UK won a lot more gold medals in London than in Athens. _____
6 There weren't nearly as many Chinese gold medallists in Athens as in Beijing. _____
7 At the Athens Olympics, there were almost five times as many men athletes as women athletes. _____

b Which phrases in the statements above express:
1 a big difference?
2 a small difference?

c Use the information in the table and these prompts to write more correct sentences comparing the three Olympic Games. Choose one expression only from the words in brackets.

1 large / number of athletes / take part / Athens Olympics / London Olympics (slightly / much)
   A much larger number of athletes took part in the Athens Olympics than in the London Olympics.
2 the number of women / take part / Beijing Olympics / small / London Olympics (a bit / a lot)
3 Beijing / organise / more / events / Athens (slightly / a lot)

4 Athens / not organise / many / events / London (quite / nearly)
5 UK athletes / successful / Beijing Olympics / London Olympics (not nearly / far)
6 Chinese athletes / do / worse / Athens Olympics / London Olympics (slightly / far)
7 Greek athletes / win / many / gold medals / Beijing / London (nearly / exactly)
8 Olympic Stadium / London / big / Olympic Stadium / Beijing (nowhere near / a lot)
9 Olympic Stadium / Athens / small / Olympic Stadium / Beijing (slightly / a lot)

Comparatives and superlatives

2 Find and correct the mistakes in some of the sentences. Tick the ones that are correct.

1 The food I ate at that restaurant in Beijing was the most spiciest I have ever eaten.
2 The first event we saw was far better one than the others.
3 The opening ceremony in London was much more exciting that the ceremonies in Beijing or Sydney.
4 The fireworks for the London Olympics were by far the best I have ever seen.
5 He is a more faster sprinter than all the other athletes.
6 The people in the town were not nearly as much friendly as the villagers.
7 The stadium they are building must be just about the biggest stadium ever built.
8 Unfortunately, we didn't have nowhere near as much time to spend shopping in London as in Beijing.

Reading (Paper 1 Part 7)

Before you read

1 Read the title of the text on page 13 and look at the photo below. What information do you think the text will contain?

  a what gifts you can give in different countries
  b how to behave towards foreign visitors

Skimming and scanning

2 Skim the text and answer the questions.

  1 Which country seems to have the strictest rules about gifts?
  2 In which country are gifts least important?

Multiple matching

3a Look at the example (0) in the exam task below. The key words in the question are highlighted. Mark the part of paragraph 1 which tells you that the answer is A.

b Look at question 1 and follow these steps.

  1 Mark the key words in the question.
  2 Scan the text and mark the part which expresses the same idea.
  3 Read this section carefully and mark the place where you find the answer.
  4 Check that the text you have found exactly matches the question.

c Now continue with questions 2–10. (Note that in the exam there will be 10 questions.)

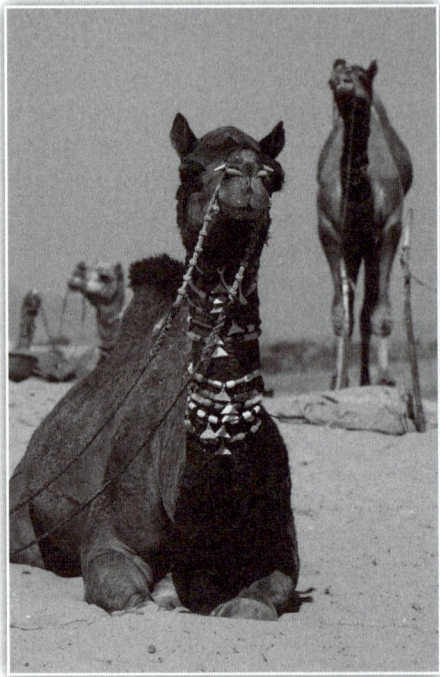

You are going to read an extract from a book which gives businesspeople advice about social customs in different parts of the world. For questions 1–10, choose from the countries (A–D). The countries may be chosen more than once.

According to the writer, in which country:

did a politician receive an unexpected gift?	0	A
is the price of the gift unimportant?	1	
are you expected to give a gift as large as the one you've received?	2	
are most gifts specially made to celebrate a particular event?	3	
have the rules of gift-giving been established for generations?	4	
is it common not to open gifts in front of the giver?	5	
is it unwise to say you like someone else's possessions?	6	
are there rules about how different types of gifts must be presented?	7	
might people be unimpressed by a large gift?	8	
is it important not to damage the packaging of a gift?	9	
will you be forgiven if you get the details of gift-giving wrong?	10	

EXPERT STRATEGY

Always read the questions first in this task. You should then read the text carefully with the questions in mind.

➤ HELP

1 Look for the word *value*. It means the same as *price*.
2 Look for references to the size of the gift.
3 Look for words that mean 'to help you remember'.

EXPERT LANGUAGE

Look back at the text. Find four nouns ending in the suffix *-ity*.

EXPERT WORD CHECK

manners   memento   nicety
ornament   paperweight
pretentious   protocol   reciprocate
ribbon   ritual   sculpture   wrap

The art of giving

In many countries it is customary to give gifts to your guests and hosts but different cultures have different customs. How does the foreign visitor know what to do where?

A Egypt

When the US president Jimmy Carter visited Egypt in 1978, a camel trader was asked to show him round a camel market. The trader was so honoured that he
5 not only gave the tour but also presented the president with a six-year-old camel, a pink ribbon tied around its neck. The camel trader's action was typical of the hospitality and generosity shown in many parts of the Arab world, where good manners are an essential
10 ingredient in a person's character and generosity to guests is essential to a good reputation.
Because there are accepted rules of behaviour in gift-giving, the foreign businessperson must be careful. For example, admiring a painting or ornament in a
15 client's home or office might oblige them to present you with it as a gift. What's more, your Egyptian colleague will probably begin a round of gift-giving and will expect you to reciprocate – if not immediately, then on the next possible occasion – and the gift
20 should match theirs in size and cost, if possible.

B Japan

And the Arab world is not the only place where gift-giving follows set rules. In Japan they are even stricter. As an American who volunteered to teach English to
25 a Japanese woman reported, 'Before each lesson and on each and every visit, the Japanese lady brought me a gift – a book, some paper sculpture or flowers.' Unknowingly, this American was experiencing a ritual rooted centuries deep in Japanese culture. According
30 to Business Tokyo magazine, among the Japanese, 'gift-giving is a necessity, not merely a nicety as it is in the West.' In Japan the proper gift is thought to express the giver's true friendship, gratitude and respect far better than words can. And specific gift-
35 giving rules have prevailed in Japanese society for centuries. They spell out the type of gift to give and how the various types of gifts should be wrapped. So if you plan to visit Japan, be prepared. But don't worry about getting the protocol wrong – foreigners
40 are not expected to know all the rules!

C Thailand

Another country which takes gifts seriously is Thailand. When visiting a home in this country, take flowers or a box of chocolates from the local
45 market. The value is not important; it is the thought and the act that count. It is the tradition in Thailand to wrap gifts beautifully with colourful ribbons and the custom has long been to put the gift aside to be opened later, so don't be offended if the gift seems
50 to go unappreciated. But this custom is not as rigid today as it was and you may be invited to open a gift in front of the giver. But in this case do avoid ripping open the beautiful wrapping as this is considered rude.

55 ## D Australia

And of course, there are countries where businesspeople rarely exchange gifts and Australia is an example of this. Modest gifts such as a business diary, a paperweight or a coffee mug might be
60 presented as a memento of a visit or business meeting, and sales conferences and trade shows often give out T-shirts, ties or baseball caps bearing the date and location of the event. However, anything more than these types of gifts could
65 cause embarrassment in a society known for its friendly informality as people might regard them as pretentious.

Vocabulary development 1

> **COURSEBOOK** page 21

EXPERT STRATEGY

For Paper 4, Speaking, Part 1, be prepared to talk about the job you do or hope to do in the future. You may be asked to describe what you enjoy most about your job or to say what kind of job you would most like to do.

Job factors

1 Look at the list of factors people consider important in a job. Tick the three factors which are the most important for you.

- the salary
- the location (e.g. town, region) of the job
- opportunities for promotion
- a friendly working environment
- good facilities (e.g. car park, canteen, gym)
- long holidays
- opportunities to work independently
- a company car
- opportunities for creativity
- a company pension
- flexible working hours
- opportunities for travel

Describing jobs

2a Read what six people say about their work. What job does each person do? Write the correct job from the box under each person. There are four jobs you do not need to use.

accountant   actor   architect   bank clerk   engineer
journalist   lawyer   lecturer   musician   scientist

I'm very good at maths and statistics. I like my job because I can work on my own a lot. It's also creative. I love testing my theories in the laboratory to see if they are right.

1 _____

I enjoy working with figures. Some people might think that my job is boring but they're quite wrong. Looking after so much money is actually really interesting.

2 _____

I've always been good at persuading people to do or believe things. Now I do it every day in court. My salary is excellent, of course, and there are good career opportunities.

3 _____

My job is very creative. I have to practise a lot, of course, and being on tour with an orchestra can be rather tiring. However, I can take long holidays if I want to.

4 _____

I've always been keen on designing and building things. Now I'm well paid for doing what I enjoy. It's a creative job because you combine theory and practice. You also need to know a lot about different materials.

5 _____

For my job, you need to have a good command of English. You work on your own a lot, particularly when you're following up a big story. The salary's not great but it's an interesting, rewarding job.

6 _____

b Read the comments again. Underline the advantages of each job, according to the six people.

c Write a short paragraph describing your own job or the job you would like to do. Use some of the ideas and language above.

Verb + noun collocations

3 Read the text and decide which answer (A, B or C) best fits each gap.

My career

My name is Helena. Although I did well at school and managed to **(1)** _____ all my exams when I was 18, I decided not to go to university. I wanted to make lots of money instead. I **(2)** _____ for three jobs with large international companies and **(3)** _____ an interview with one of them the following week. They offered me the job. I was now Helena Roberts, Assistant Marketing Manager!

For the first two years I **(4)** _____ very little money but I worked conscientiously. As a result, I soon **(5)** _____ promoted. My dream was to become Managing Director. That was my first big mistake. The company closed down a month later and I was **(6)** _____ redundant!

In my next job, the working conditions were awful. I wanted to **(7)** _____ and look for something else. My colleagues, however, persuaded me to **(8)** _____ on strike with them for better pay. That, of course, was my second big mistake. The boss immediately **(9)** _____ us the sack! It was six months before I found another job.

I've been with my present company for five years now. I'm extremely happy and intend to stay here until I **(10)** _____ at 65. I no longer dream of being Managing Director. Having a job is enough for me.

	A	B	C
1	A pass	B take	C succeed
2	A looked	B applied	C offered
3	A went	B attended	C made
4	A gained	B won	C earned
5	A became	B got	C took
6	A made	B become	C told
7	A resign	B dismiss	C release
8	A make	B go	C put
9	A put	B showed	C gave
10	A retire	B graduate	C withdraw

Pronunciation

4a Say these past simple verbs aloud. Is the *-ed* ending pronounced /t/, /d/ or /ɪd/?

wanted	worked	persuaded	promoted
passed	attended	closed	
applied	gained	offered	

b 🎧 03 Listen and check your answers. Write the verbs in the correct column.

/t/	/d/	/ɪd/

➤ COURSEBOOK pages 24–25, EXPERT GRAMMAR pages 184–185

Past simple and present perfect simple

1 Complete the email with the past simple or present perfect form of the verbs in brackets. Mark the time expressions which help you to decide.

Hi Maria,

I've just read your email. Yes, I'd love to come and help you at your office. I **(1)** _____ (take) my final exams last week and I **(2)** _____ (not have) anything to do since then. Some work would be great! I still **(3)** _____ (not learn) to type, I'm afraid, but I could put your files in order. In January I **(4)** _____ (organise) all the files for the Students' Union. Up to now nobody **(5)** _____ (complain), I'm proud to say! I know you **(6)** _____ (not find) a receptionist yet, so I could do that job as well. The other day I **(7)** _____ (answer) some phone calls from college applicants and I really **(8)** _____ (enjoy) it. So you see, Maria, I have already had lots of experience!
Love,
Alexia

yet, still, already, just

2a Complete the sentences with *yet*, *still*, *already* or *just*. Use the explanations in brackets to help you.

1 I have _____ received an email from my mobile phone company. Do you want to see it? (a short time ago)
2 We've written to him three times and he _____ hasn't replied. (up to now but we expected it to happen by now)
3 Mr Smith is looking for you. Has he spoken to you _____ ? (up to now but we expect it to happen)
4 There's no need for you to phone the bank – I've _____ done it. (before now/earlier than expected)

b Now complete these sentences in the same way.

1 I can't give Mrs Hudson my report because I haven't finished it _____ .
2 We've _____ heard that Sally's been promoted. It's great news, isn't it?
3 My car broke down last week and the garage _____ hasn't fixed it.
4 You don't need to write to Mr Jones – I've _____ written to him.

Present perfect simple and continuous

3a Choose the correct answers.
1 Have you *lived / been living* in Vienna all your life?
2 I'm exhausted! I've *studied / been studying* for my accounting exams all day.
3 Oh dear! We've *missed / been missing* the bus!
4 My boss is away at the moment, so I've *worked / been working* overtime.
5 Can you phone Maria urgently? She's *phoned / been phoning* for you four times this afternoon.
6 Stephen's *tried / been trying* to contact you all day. Where have you been?

b Use the prompts to write complete sentences in the present perfect simple or continuous.
1 I / just / write / my application letter / Can you check it?
_____
2 George / work on / his CV / all day / but / he still / not finish / it
_____
3 Joanna / still / not arrive. / Do you think she / get / lost?
_____
4 although I / learn / English / for over five years / I / never / go / to England
_____
5 Help! / Someone / steal / the money from the safe!
_____
6 I / try / to phone Sue / all afternoon / but I / not be able / get through / yet
_____

Key word transformations

4 Complete the second sentence so that it has a similar meaning to the first sentence, using the word given. Do not change the word given. You must use between two and five words, including the word given.
1 I've never been to the National Museum.
   STILL
   I _____ the National Museum.
2 The last time I saw Jenny was ten years ago.
   FOR
   I _____ ten years.
3 John can still remember how nervous he felt on his first day at work.
   NEVER
   John _____ how nervous he felt on his first day at work.
4 She began working here when she was 18.
   BEEN
   She _____ here since she was 18.
5 Mr Thomas phoned a moment ago to say he will be late.
   JUST
   Mr Thomas _____ to say he will be late.
6 It's been a long time since our last meeting.
   MET
   We _____ a long time.

Listening (Paper 3 Part 3)

Multiple matching

> **EXPERT STRATEGY**
>
> In this task, you're listening for each speaker's main idea. Read the instructions carefully. Make sure you know what you're listening for.

Before you listen

1a Read the instructions for the listening task and answer the questions.
1 How many speakers will you hear?
2 What do they all have in common?

b Mark the key words in the statements (A–E). The first two have been done for you. (Note that in the exam there will be three extra options that you do not need to use.)

c Think of other ways of expressing the information in the statements.

Listening for gist

2 🎧 04 Listen once and decide which speaker mentions the ideas you've marked.

Listening for specific information

3 🎧 04 Listen again and check that the ideas expressed exactly match the wording in the statements.

You will hear five short extracts in which people who have given up stressful jobs in the city are talking about their decisions. For questions 1–5, choose from the list (A–E) what each speaker says.

A I'm not absolutely sure I've done the right thing.	Speaker 1 [1]
B I find I can manage on a much lower income.	Speaker 2 [2]
C A sudden change led me to make my decision.	Speaker 3 [3]
D I had some money to invest in a new career.	Speaker 4 [4]
E I realised that my way of life was making me miserable.	Speaker 5 [5]

> **EXPERT WORD CHECK**
>
> *burning out   city trader   interior design   life coach*
> *public-relations company   redundant   self-sufficient*

Writing (Paper 2 Part 2: Formal email)

➤ **COURSEBOOK** pages 26–27, **EXPERT WRITING** page 203

> **EXPERT STRATEGY**
>
> In Paper 2, Writing, it's important to organise your ideas clearly and divide them into paragraphs. You will lose marks in the exam otherwise. Making a paragraph plan before you write will help you to do this.

Understand the task

1 Read the writing task and answer the questions.
  1 Who are you writing to?
  2 What is the purpose of your email?
  3 What style should you use?
  4 What information MUST you include? Mark the parts of the task that tell you.

You have seen this advertisement in a student magazine. You are interested in applying for the job.

Tour guide needed!

Would you like to work as a tour guide this summer, taking groups of English-speaking tourists to see the attractions of your town? Full training provided!

Write an email to Peter Harlow, giving details of previous work experience and explaining why you are the person we need.

*Write your **email** in 140–190 words applying for the job in an appropriate style. Do not give any postal addresses.*

Plan your email

2a Tick the points you should include in your email.
  1 details about your present job
  2 what you hate about your present job
  3 details about any relevant knowledge/skills
  4 what kind of person you are
  5 your reason for writing/where you heard about the job
  6 names and addresses of people who can recommend you
  7 details about yourself/qualifications/previous experience
  8 details about your home and family
  9 availability for interview/concluding remarks
  10 the kind of clothes you usually wear
  11 why you want the job/why you are suitable for the job

b How will you organise the points? Make a paragraph plan for the points you ticked.
Paragraph 1: _____
Paragraph 2: _____
Paragraph 3: _____
Paragraph 4: _____

Check and complete a sample answer

3a Read a student's answer and complete it with one word or phrase in each space.

(1) _____ , I would like (2) _____ tour guide, which I saw advertised in our student magazine. I am 23 years old and have just completed a first degree in history at Szeged University. (3) _____ , I am thinking of continuing my studies at postgraduate level next year. Although I am not actually from Szeged, I have lived here for many years and know the town and surrounding area very well. I have (4) _____ English and German, and have been learning Spanish for the past two years. Last summer, I worked for three months as a receptionist in a hotel in Budapest. This job involved giving foreign tourists information about the city. I feel (5) _____ for the job you describe in the advertisement because
I know a lot about Szeged and its history.
I think it is a beautiful town and I would enjoy showing tourists its attractions. It would also be a wonderful (6) _____ for me to meet people from other countries. I hope you will (7) _____ seriously. I am (8) _____ whenever it is convenient.

(9) _____ ,
János Kelemen

b Does the email include all the relevant information? Compare it to your list in Exercise 2.

c The email has no paragraphs. Mark where each new paragraph should begin.

Vocabulary development 2

> **COURSEBOOK** pages 28–29

> **COURSEBOOK** pages 28–29

EXPERT STRATEGY

For Paper 4, Speaking, Part 1, you may be asked about your studies and what you enjoy/enjoyed most about them. For Paper 2, Writing, you may have to write a letter or report on the topic of education in your country, for example. Make sure you are familiar with the vocabulary you need.

Education

1a Read the statements about the educational system in the UK and tick the ones which are also true for your country.

1 Education is compulsory until the age of 18.
2 Education in state schools is free.
3 Children start primary school at around the age of five.
4 Children in primary and secondary schools take national tests to monitor their progress.
5 At the age of 16, students usually take important exams in several different subjects.
6 Students who want to continue their studies take advanced level exams at the age of 18.
7 About 40 percent of young people go to college or university after school.
8 For most subjects, an undergraduate university course (leading to a bachelor's degree) lasts three or four years.
9 Some sandwich courses at college or university include a certain amount of work experience.
10 Nowadays, many colleges and universities have a system of continuous assessment rather than formal exams.
11 If a student does very well at university, he or she will be awarded a first-class degree. Weaker students will receive a second-class, third-class or pass degree.
12 A postgraduate course leading to a master's degree usually lasts one year. It may take longer if students have to carry out some research.

b Rewrite any statements you did not tick and make them true for your country.

Commonly confused words

2 Complete the sentences with the words in *italics*.

1 *professor / teacher*
   a When I was 12, my English _____ encouraged me to write stories.
   b Our _____ at university was more interested in his research than in teaching.

2 *check / control*
   a The children in Mr Adam's class are so naughty that he cannot _____ them.
   b Before you hand in written work, you should _____ it carefully for mistakes.

3 *career / course*
   a Dr Jenkins ruined his _____ when he gave several patients the wrong drug.
   b They sent him on a two-week _____ to learn how to use the new computer.

4 *subject / lesson*
   a Monday's French _____ was so boring I thought it would never end.
   b I think physics is a difficult _____ to study at university level.

5 *educate / train*
   a I'm sure your company will _____ you to use the new equipment.
   b Many people feel that schools do not _____ children very well these days.

6 *degree / grade*
   a I think this composition deserves a better _____ than C, don't you?
   b Although my _____ was in chemistry, the headmaster still let me teach biology.

Agreeing and disagreeing

3 Two students are discussing the question 'Do schools prepare children for the real world?' Complete the conversation with the phrases in the box.

*couldn't agree   don't you think   quite true   suppose so
up to a point   what about   you think so   you're right*

Alan: I'm sure that what you study at school is very useful when you start work.

Jane: Do (1) _____ ? Some subjects you study don't prepare you for work at all, I'd say. (2) _____ Latin?

Alan: Well, perhaps (3) _____ about Latin. But other subjects help you when you leave school. (4) _____ that mathematics is useful?

Jane: I (5) _____ . But they could have made it more relevant to everyday life.

Alan: I (6) _____ more. Perhaps the problem is not the subjects we learn but the way they are taught. Take geography – they could make it really interesting.

Jane: I agree (7) _____ but not entirely. You probably learn more about geography when you start to travel. I don't see why it's useful to study it at school.

Alan: That's (8) _____ . But some people may not have the opportunity to travel when they leave school.

Language development 2

➤ **COURSEBOOK** page 32, **EXPERT GRAMMAR** page 185

Articles

1 Choose the correct answers.

1 My brother wants to join *army / the army* when he leaves *school / the school*.
2 I have *degree / a degree* in *chemistry / the chemistry* from *University / the University* of York.
3 Twice *a week / the week* we have *lecture / a lecture* by *Professor / the Professor* Hawking.
4 Do you want to go to *cinema / the cinema* tonight or would you rather go to *theatre / the theatre*?
5 When did *Poland / the Poland* join *European Union / the European Union*?
6 I'd like to come out for *drink / a drink* this evening but I have to revise for *end-of-semester / the end-of-semester* German exam.
7 Although my brother had *good / a good* school education, he didn't know that *River / the River* Danube flows through Budapest.
8 *A computer / The computer* has changed *way / the way* many people live and work.
9 My little sister is making *excellent / the excellent* progress at *school / the school* she goes to.
10 Although people say that *English / the English* are very reserved, I have *English / an English* girlfriend who is just the opposite!

some / any, something / anything

2 Find and correct the mistakes in some of the sentences. Tick the ones that are correct.

1 My flatmate, Mark, wanted to do anything special last night.
2 He had just heard some good news and wanted to go out to celebrate.
3 He phoned any friends of his to ask them if they'd like to come as well.
4 It took Mark's friends some time to arrive, so we didn't leave the flat until after 10 o'clock.
5 We went to three or four different restaurants but didn't like any of them. In the end, we decided to go for a pizza.
6 Mark was in a good mood. In the local pizza restaurant he said, 'You can have anything you like – I'll pay!'
7 Unfortunately, it was late and the owner said that he had hardly some pizzas left.
8 'Give us something you have then. It doesn't matter what it is!' Mark told the owner in desperation.
9 The owner returned with two sad-looking pizzas and half a dozen sandwiches. Some them looked distinctly stale.
10 'Next time we'll stay at home and make the food ourselves. Something's better than this!' Mark groaned.

Extra word

3 Find and cross out the extra word in some of the sentences. Tick the ones that are correct.

1 In the UK some ~~of~~ teenagers leave school at the age of 18.
2 Undergraduate courses in the USA usually last longer than in the UK. ✓
3 My brother doesn't have hardly any homework to do during the summer holidays.
4 I went to the school my father went to when he was a boy.
5 Almost all the countries in the world regard the education as extremely important.
6 My brother got the high grades in every subject when he was at school.
7 I had a bad cough, so I had to spend a couple of days at the home.
8 My friend wanted to study medicine at the University of Birmingham but there weren't any of places available.
9 I couldn't answer some of the questions in the history exam I took yesterday.
10 Even with a good degree, it is sometimes difficult to find a work these days.

Key word transformations

4 Complete the second sentence so that it has a similar meaning to the first sentence, using the word given. Do not change the word given. You must use between two and five words, including the word given.

1 Do you have a computer in your house?
   GOT
   Have _____ home?
2 We went to Paris by train.
   ON
   We went _____ Paris.
3 My little cousin wants to drive a bus when he leaves school.
   DRIVER
   My little cousin wants _____ when he leaves school.
4 Is he a good pianist?
   PLAY
   Does _____ well?
5 We watched a television documentary about Scotland last night.
   ON
   We watched a documentary _____ last night.
6 How about going to see a film this evening?
   CINEMA
   Why don't _____ this evening?
7 I think she is lying about what happened.
   TRUTH
   I don't think she _____ about what happened.
8 Germany is well known for making very good cars.
   REPUTATION
   Germany _____ for making very good cars.

Reading (Paper 1 Part 5)

Before you read

1a Read the instructions for the reading task. What do they tell you about the text? Think about these questions.

1 Where would you read a text like this?
2 Who is the writer?
3 What style do you expect it to be in?
4 What sort of things do you think the text will talk about?

b Now read the title and subheading of the article. What more do you find out? Mark the words which tell you about the writer's attitude.

Skimming

2 Read the text quickly and answer the questions.

1 Were your predictions about the content and the writer's attitude correct?
2 Which of the photos (A–C) do you think shows the writer?

Reading for detail

3 Read the questions (1–6). Don't look at the options (A–D) yet. Which part of the text contains this information? Try to answer the question yourself and mark the relevant part of the text.

Multiple choice

4 Now read the options (A–D) and choose the one closest to your answer. Read the relevant part of the text again to check that your answer is right and that the other options are wrong. Look for parallel words and phrases in the text and the option you have chosen. The first one has been done for you.

EXPERT STRATEGY

The questions come in the same order as the information in the text. You need to read each section of the text carefully and answer the question that relates to it.

➤ **HELP**

2 Find the words *access course* in the text. How did June find out about it?
3 Read the sentences before and after the word and try to work out what it means.
4 Look for the word *tutors* – it means the same as *teachers*.

EXPERT WORD CHECK

*a second bite art appreciation crèche journal
module needlework open evening toddlers*

You are going to read a magazine article written by a woman who has returned to studying in retirement. For questions 1–6, choose the answer (A, B, C or D) which you think fits best according to the text.

1 What did June discover when she first retired?
  A She had more free time than she expected.
  B She had not really been very happy in her job.
  C She needed activities she could do on her own.
  D She no longer found her old hobbies satisfying.

2 What first attracted June to the 'access course'?
  A Some of her friends were doing it.
  B She knew somebody who taught on it.
  C She'd decided she wanted to study full-time.
  D Pensioners who did it were offered a discount.

3 The word *clinched* in line 29 means
  A 'made up my mind for me'.
  B 'put me under pressure to decide'.
  C 'made me reconsider my decision'.
  D 'left me unsure what to do next'.

4 What does June say about the teachers on the access course?
  A They are very patient with the more mature students.
  B They need to know a lot about a wide range of subjects.
  C They appear to be genuinely interested in what they teach.
  D They have problems dealing with such a variety of students.

5 What does *one* in line 45 refer to?
  A a subject June has to study
  B a student on the course June is doing
  C a new way of approaching art history
  D an experience June can share with others

6 When June had to write an essay,
  A she wrote about a college she had once attended.
  B she rewrote one she had written years ago.
  C she wasn't allowed to choose the subject.
  D she found it easier than she had expected.

CARRY ON LEARNING

Everyone, whatever their age, can share in the joy and fulfilment of learning, as June Weatherall found out.

When I first retired, I thought I'd love spending more time on the gardening, needlework and other creative activities I'd found so relaxing after my demanding job. But it didn't turn out that way.
5 I found that I didn't want, or need, that kind of relaxation anymore; I wanted to stimulate my mind instead. Also, they're all solitary activities and I missed the company and interests of my old work companions.

10 So, with a couple of friends, I went along to an art appreciation evening class at our local regional college. It was wonderful but only lasted a year. At the end, I asked my tutor, 'What next?' He suggested I attend his history of art access course. 'Whatever's
15 that?' I asked. The college had an open evening coming up, so I went along to find out.

A full-time access course takes one year and gives you access to university if, like me, you left school without any qualifications, and it's free if you do it
20 full-time. I only wanted to do the art history bit but even so, with my pensioner's discount, it would cost a mere £30 per term.

Lyn, who organises the courses for the college, was enthusiastic. 'Why don't you do the whole course?
25 You could start in the spring term with art history, do another module in the summer, then go full-time in the autumn and do all the subjects.' It sounded

wonderful but wasn't I a bit old, at 63, to start being a student? A
30 definite 'no'. One of the students that year was 82. That clinched it. It must be worth having a go.

The art history part of the course, which I've just completed, was
35 stimulating and involved a trip to the Louvre museum in Paris – which was wonderful. The tutors are enthusiasts and infect us all with their enjoyment of the subjects they
40 teach. 'Lively' would be the word to describe the classes. My fellow students, who are also doing subjects like psychology, maths, biology, etc., are good company. They're mainly people in their thirties, with children, taking a second bite at the educational
45 cherry. There's a crèche to help those with toddlers and an excellent library. They're kind enough to say they find the older students offer a lot in experience – they certainly give a lot to us in newer ways of looking at things. One, a nurse, is changing direction and has a
50 place at Anglia University to do a degree course in art history. Another has been accepted to do English.

We have homework and have to do an essay each term for each subject, and sit exams. For art history, I opted to write about the Bauhaus – a college for all
55 the arts set up in Germany in the early 20th century. The last essay I'd written had been a lifetime ago – in 1955 – so I was a bit apprehensive but I managed fine. We also had to produce a journal about all the painters we'd learnt about, which was fun but rather
60 time-consuming. Occasionally, I envy the more typical mature students, who just do courses for pleasure and don't have to do exams or essays as I do but, really, I'm a very happy lady.

Will I go on to university if I'm successful? I'll see how
65 next year goes. Meanwhile, exercising my brain cells is working well for me. I feel alive. The garden's getting a bit out of control but that's the least of my worries!

Vocabulary development 1

➤ **COURSEBOOK** pages 36–37

Cities and culture

1a Look at the diagram and choose the adjective which collocates with the noun.

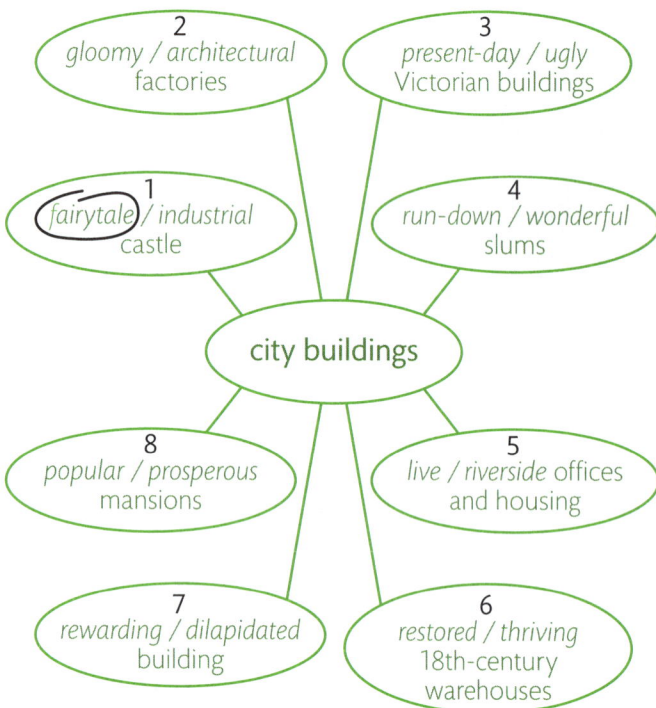

```
        2                              3
  gloomy / architectural        present-day / ugly
      factories                 Victorian buildings

       1                              4
  fairytale / industrial        run-down / wonderful
      castle                         slums

              city buildings

       8                              5
  popular / prosperous          live / riverside offices
      mansions                      and housing

       7                              6
  rewarding / dilapidated       restored / thriving
      building                   18th-century
                                 warehouses
```

b Read the text and check your answers to Exercise 1a. Ignore the gaps at this stage.

c Now complete the text with the adjectives in Exercise 1a which you did not choose.

2 Complete the table.

Forget Edinburgh. Come to Glasgow instead!

It may not have Edinburgh's fairytale castle but Glasgow is a far more **(1)** _____ place to visit. You'll find the people are friendlier too!

Forget those images of gloomy factories, ugly Victorian buildings and abandoned shipyards. Glasgow has changed!

Some people say that Glasgow still seems a little grey and depressing when you first arrive. You still find the occasional dilapidated building in the city centre; there are still run-down slums on the outskirts. But Glasgow is now a proud city – proud of its **(2)** _____ and shipbuilding past, proud of its architectural heritage and proud of its **(3)** _____ role as a leading UK tourist destination.

Four million people visit Glasgow every year. They come as much for the shopping as for the museums and art galleries. There's also a(n) **(4)** _____ theatre scene and **(5)** _____ music events take place almost every night of the week. Then there is the **(6)** _____ architecture; from the restored 18th-century warehouses of the Merchant City to the prosperous mansions around George Square, the **(7)** _____ legacy of Glasgow is among the most striking in the UK.

It's not by accident that £500 million has recently been invested in new riverside offices and housing. Or that the city is one of the most **(8)** _____ conference destinations in Europe. Glasgow has something to offer everyone.

Adjective	Verb	Noun	Adjective	Verb	Noun
strong	strengthen	1 _____	achieved/ achievable	8 _____	achievement
prosperous	2 _____	3 _____	9 _____	–	culture
optimistic	–	4 _____	10 _____	–	architecture
threatening	5 _____	6 _____	declining	decline	11 _____
7 _____	economise	economy	solved/soluble	solve	12 _____

Exam practice: Word formation

(Paper 1 Part 3)

3   Do the task.

*For questions 1–8, read the text below. Use the word given in capitals at the end of some of the lines to form a word that fits in the gap **in the same line**. There is an example at the beginning (0).*

Krakov

In the past, Krakov was a city of great political (0) _importance_ . It was the ancient capital of Poland and the official (1)_____ of the country's kings. The city still has (2)_____ medieval architecture and is listed by UNESCO as a world heritage site because of its great (3)_____ as well as artistic (4)_____ .
Krakov had the largest square in medieval Europe and this is still the (5)_____ centre of the city and the best place to begin your (6)_____ of the winding streets of the old quarter. These streets were home to Poland's greatest artists, writers and thinkers, many of whom studied at the city's famous university. The area still has a (7)_____ atmosphere and it's a pleasure just to wander round. But there is also plenty to do and see as a thriving (8)_____ life continues today.

IMPORTANT

RESIDENT

IMPRESS

HISTORY
SIGNIFICANT

COMMERCE

EXPLORE

ROMANCE

CULTURE

EXPERT STRATEGY

Read the whole text first to get the general meaning before you try to do the task. Think about the type of word that will fit in each gap. Are they nouns, verbs, adjectives, etc?

Language development 1

> **COURSEBOOK** pages 38–39, **EXPERT GRAMMAR** pages 186–187

Adjectives and adverbs

1   Complete the sentences with the words in *italics*.
   1 *good / well*
       a You don't look very _____ . Are you feeling OK?
       b Ask Sue what this word means – her Italian is really _____ .
   2 *steady / steadily*
       a Since 1990, there's been a _____ increase in tourism to this town.
       b Over the past 20 years, the quality of hotels has _____ improved.
   3 *late / lately*
       a There have been a lot of strikes at the airport _____ .
       b The announcement said that the plane would take off _____ .
   4 *hard / hardly*
       a Sarah was so suntanned I could _____ recognise her.
       b I worked extremely _____ to pay for this holiday.
   5 *wide / widely*
       a Can you close the window? It's _____ open at the moment.
       b Mark travelled _____ in Europe when he was a student.
   6 *direct / directly*
       a We can fly _____ to Rome from this airport.
       b If you lose your passport, you should go _____ to the police.

Adverbs of degree

2a   Write the adjectives in the box in the correct column.

~~awful~~ ~~bleak~~ *decisive fantastic fast fragile furious impressive lively marvellous powerful romantic tremendous unique well-known*

Gradable	Ungradable
bleak	*awful*

> **HELP**
1 A 'resident' is a person. You need to make a word that refers to a place.
2 A person is impressed by a place. You need to make a different adjective that describes the place.
3 You need to change one letter and add a suffix to this word.

EXPERT WORD CHECK

ancient   medieval   thriving   wander   winding

b Complete the sentences with *very / extremely* or *absolutely*.

1 When we arrived in Rome, the weather was _____ awful.
2 Many of the monuments of Rome are _____ well known.
3 That porcelain vase you bought looks _____ fragile.
4 Verdi played a(n) _____ decisive role in the development of opera.
5 When my father heard the bad news, he was _____ furious.
6 The service at our hotel was _____ impressive.
7 I found the Colosseum in Rome _____ unique.
8 Anna's two-year-old daughter is _____ lively.
9 With no money and no job, my prospects seemed _____ bleak.
10 Volunteers are making _____ tremendous efforts to rescue artworks threatened by the floods.

Key word transformations

3 Complete the second sentence so that it has a similar meaning to the first sentence, using the word given. Do not change the word given. You must use between two and five words, including the word given.

1 A lot of snow fell yesterday in Vienna.
HARD
It _____ in Vienna yesterday.
2 There has been a steady increase in prices over the last year.
STEADILY
Prices _____ over the last year.
3 My home town is a fairly big industrial city.
QUITE
My home town is _____ industrial city.
4 Prague is rather expensive.
BIT
Prague is _____ expensive city.
5 I have almost no money left after my holiday.
HARDLY
I have _____ money left after my holiday.
6 The number of tourists I saw was really amazing.
ABSOLUTELY
I _____ the number of tourists I saw.
7 Can I fly to Bratislava without having to change planes?
DIRECT
Is there _____ to Bratislava?
8 Keith really lost his temper when they told him to show his passport again.
EXTREMELY
Keith _____ when they told him to show his passport again.

Exam practice: Open cloze
(Paper 1 Part 2)

4 Do the task.

*For questions **1–8**, read the text below and think of the word which best fits each gap. Use only **one** word in each gap. There is an example at the beginning (**0**).*

Every picture tells a story

Venice is built on a lagoon and is therefore highly vulnerable (0) _to_ changing sea levels. High tides often flood the city, threatening its buildings and rich cultural heritage. Instruments were first used to measure sea levels in 1872 and scientists have (1)_____ looking for ways to find (2)_____ what happened before then, as this could help them predict what might happen in future. Then somebody realised that the 18th-century artist Canaletto, unlike most modern painters, painted exactly (3)_____ he saw, so his famous pictures of Venice are almost (4)_____ accurate as photographs. If you look at them closely, you can see a brown-green line on the buildings (5)_____ marks the average high-tide level at the time. The scientists can therefore see that the sea level in Venice (6)_____ risen by about 2.7 millimetres per year (7)_____ Canaletto's day. More (8)_____ 230 years after his death, therefore, the artist's paintings provide a record of sea levels for a period long before modern measurements began.

EXPERT WORD CHECK
average   high tide   lagoon   threatening   vulnerable

Writing (Paper 2 Part 1: Essay)

➤ **COURSEBOOK** pages 40–41, **EXPERT WRITING** pages 199–200

EXAM STRATEGY

In Paper 2, Writing, Part 1, you have to write an essay on a topic that you are given. Two of the points you need to make in the essay are given and you have to write about these points before giving your own ideas as the third point. Read the task carefully and mark key words and phrases. Make sure you discuss the points in the task in your answer or you will lose marks.

Understand the task

1 Read the writing task and answer the questions.
  1 Who are you writing for?
    a someone you know
    b someone you don't know
  2 What style should you use?
    a formal
    b informal
  3 What information MUST you include? Mark the parts of the task that tell you.

In your English class, you have been talking about the importance of museums. Now your English teacher has asked you to write an essay.

*Write an essay using **all** the notes and give reasons for your point of view.*

Some people say that museums would be more exciting if visitors were allowed to touch the exhibits. What do you think?

Notes

Write about:

1 why some people think this
2 why touching the exhibits might be a good or bad idea
3 _____ (your own idea)

*Write your **essay** in 140–190 words in an appropriate style.*

Check and improve a sample answer

2a Read a student's essay. Check the task and tick the points the student has included. Then answer the questions.
    1 What has the student forgotten to include?
    2 What other instruction has the student not followed?

> Some people think that museums are boring places where you're not allowed to touch anything. This is because they have only been to old-fashioned museums where everything is
> 5 behind glass and you're supposed to stand and look at them.
> most of the things, on display are either very old or very valuable. If visitors were allowed to touch them, they could easily get damaged or
> 10 stolen. Also, the exhibits are often very rare. Sometimes the thing you're looking at is the only one in existence and that's why it's in the museum. If everybody could touch it it, would'nt stay in good condition for very long.
> 15 In my opinion, the best type of museums are the one's that have interactive displays, like Science museums where you can press a button and see things actually happening.

b Write sentences to include the missing points from the task and mark where they should go in the essay.

c Find and correct these punctuation mistakes in the essay.
    1 two mistakes with apostrophes
    2 two mistakes with capital letters
    3 two mistakes with commas

d Rewrite the essay.

Listening (Paper 3 Part 2)

Before you listen

1 Read the instructions for the listening task and look at the photos. When do you think they were taken? What can you see?

2 🎧 05 Listen and number the photos (A–E) in order (1–5).

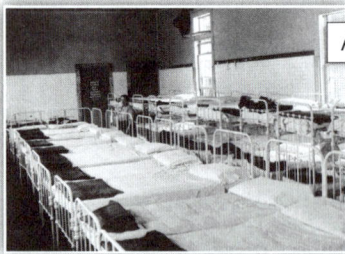

Sentence completion

3a Read the sentences in the task and try to predict what kind of information is missing. Answer the questions.
1 Which answers do you think will be numbers? What type of numbers will they be?
2 Which answers do you think will be proper names?
3 Which answer do you think will be a form of transport?

b 🎧 05 Listen again and do the task. Note the steps below.
Check that:
• your answer fits the gap to make a good sentence
• your answers are single words, numbers or short phrases
• you have written numbers as figures, not words
• your spelling is correct.

EXPERT LANGUAGE

Look at the sentences in the task. Which are about
1 things that happen these days?
2 things that happened in the past?

EXPERT WORD CHECK

baggage guided tour immigration judge oral history possessions

You will hear a tour guide talking to a group of tourists in New York about a visit they will make to the Museum of Immigration on Ellis Island. For questions 1-10, complete the sentences with a word or short phrase.

Museum of Immigration

Ellis Island was busiest between the years (1) _____ and _____ .

The group of tourists will arrive at the museum by (2) _____ .

The first part of the museum you go through used to be the (3) _____ Room.

In the Registry Room, immigrants had both (4) _____ and medical check-ups.

What's called a(n) (5) _____ records the names of immigrants who passed through Ellis Island.

Immigrants staying overnight on the island slept in the (6) _____ Room.

The movie you can see at the museum is called (7) _____ .

The play in Theatre 2 begins at (8) _____ .

Instead of the play, the tourists can visit the (9) _____ .

The *Peopling of America* exhibition is in what used to be a(n) (10) _____ .

Vocabulary development 2

➤ **COURSEBOOK** pages 42–43

EXPERT STRATEGY

For Paper 2, Writing; or Paper 4, Speaking; you may be asked to give your opinions about problems related to the environment and what we can do about them. Make sure you are familiar with the necessary vocabulary.

The environment

1a Read the texts (1–5) quickly and match them with the photos (A–E). More than one answer may be possible. (Ignore the numbered words at this stage.)

b Read the texts again and choose the correct answers.

c List two or three of the most important environmental problems in your country or region and note down possible solutions.

1

The world's rainforests are quickly disappearing. People **(1)** cut *down / up* thousands of trees every day, which is a **(2)** *shame / catastrophe* for the animals and plants that live there. Rainforests are the natural **(3)** *locations / habitats* for thousands of **(4)** *forms / species* of animals, birds and plants. If you **(5)** *destroy / demolish* the rainforests, these creatures will become **(6)** *extinct / vanished*. Governments must **(7)** *take / put* urgent action to save the rainforests.

2

Burning coal and oil releases carbon dioxide (CO_2) into the atmosphere. In large amounts, this gas traps the heat of the sun and causes the **(8)** *hothouse / greenhouse* effect. The problem of global **(9)** *heating / warming* is already affecting the climate of the world. We should start now to look for other forms of energy. Hot countries, for example, could use **(10)** *solar / sun* energy on a larger scale.

3

(11) *Poisoned / Poisonous* gases from cars and factories cause atmospheric pollution and make the air dangerous to breathe. Factories **(12)** *emit / dump* dangerous chemical waste into rivers and seas, causing the death of thousands of fish and sea animals. **(13)** *Atomic / Radioactive* waste is particularly dangerous and has a terrible **(14)** *effect / influence* on the environment. We should **(15)** *abolish / ban* cars from city centres and force factories to be cleaner.

4

Many of the world's natural resources are going to run **(16)** *off / out* in the near future. We should do something about this before it's too late. For example, we could **(17)** *exploit / recycle* paper, metal and glass rather than just throwing them away.

5

Most farmers these days spray their crops with chemical **(18)** *soils / fertilisers* and pesticides. What's more, increasing numbers of farmers are planting genetically **(19)** *modified / changed* crops, even though many people believe that they might be dangerous to our health. Governments should encourage farmers to **(20)** *grow / manufacture* organic crops. Organic fruit and vegetables are much tastier and better for you.

Exam practice: Multiple-choice cloze (Paper 1 Part 1)

2 Do the task.

EXPERT STRATEGY

Read the whole text first to get the general meaning before you try to answer the questions. Read the words before and after each gap.

For questions 1–8, read the text below and decide which answer (A, B, C or D) best fits each gap. There is an example at the beginning (0).

Light pollution

Living on a hill in London, after dark I can see the lights of the city beneath me and also the orange glow they (0) __A__ up into the night sky. But I can (1) _____ see any stars. If light pollution – as this effect is known – continues to increase at its present (2) _____ , our grandchildren will only (3) _____ the chance to see the stars if they visit a remote part of the world. Light pollution is almost (4) _____ for granted in most cities and it is fast spreading into rural areas too. (5) _____ recent research, almost half of all Europeans can no longer see the Milky Way. What's more, this type of pollution doesn't only (6) _____ our view of the night sky, it also wastes money and affects the environment. For example, a single light bulb, (7) _____ on all year, releases around a quarter of a tonne of carbon dioxide into the atmosphere, (8) _____ global warming even worse.

0 A send	B give	C keep	D fill
1 A clearly	B surely	C hardly	D faintly
2 A case	B rank	C grade	D rate
3 A carry	B draw	C get	D catch
4 A brought	B taken	C felt	D passed
5 A According to	B Apart from	C Instead of	D In addition to
6 A destroy	B deny	C defeat	D delay
7 A set	B allowed	C left	D joined
8 A letting	B resulting	C causing	D making

➤ HELP

1 Which word expresses a negative idea?
2 You are looking for a word that describes how quickly something is happening.
8 Only one of the words can be followed by *worse*.

EXPERT LANGUAGE

The options in 5 are linking expressions. Find two more.

Language development 2

➤ **COURSEBOOK** page 46, **EXPERT GRAMMAR** pages 187–188

-*ing* forms and infinitives

1 Find and correct the mistakes with -*ing* forms and infinitives in some of the sentences. Tick the ones that are correct.

1 A few years ago thousands of people in London were astonished when they saw an enormous whale to swim in the River Thames. swimming
2 Millions of TV viewers from around the world found it hard to believe their eyes. _____
3 Onlookers enjoyed to watch the northern bottle-nosed whale as it made its way past Waterloo Bridge.
4 The magnificent creature appeared being lost and very weak. _____
5 Everyone wanted to believe that the whale would find its way back to the sea. _____
6 The two-ton whale was obviously exhausted and injured but people refused giving up hope. _____
7 During the night, rescuers at Battersea Bridge managed lifting Willy (as he was now affectionately called) onto a special boat. _____
8 They hoped to transfer Willy to a bigger ship, which would take him to the Atlantic Ocean. _____
9 Willy was having problems to breathe and suffering from dehydration. _____
10 Willy's condition suddenly got worse, so vets decided to put the animal to sleep with an injection. He died before they could do so. _____
11 Willy, who turned out to be a female whale, made millions of people to feel a sense of wonder for the natural world. _____

EXPERT WORD CHECK

atmosphere   carbon dioxide   glow   light bulb   spreading

Prepositions + -ing forms

2 Complete the sentences with the prepositions in the box.

about (x3)   at   for (x3)   in (x2)   on (x2)   to

1 Rick insisted _____ coming with us to the zoo.
2 I succeeded _____ persuading my father to lend me his new camera.
3 We were really excited _____ seeing the polar bears.
4 I've always been interested _____ learning about animals.
5 We talked _____ going on a safari one day.
6 Rick objected _____ having to pay to visit the aquarium.
7 My sister is good _____ imitating animal sounds.
8 We talked to the man who was responsible _____ feeding the lions.
9 I'm very keen _____ taking photographs of wildlife.
10 I apologised _____ being half an hour late.
11 You don't seem very enthusiastic _____ having a picnic.
12 Dr Tibbet is famous _____ carrying out research on the way dolphins communicate.

Verbs with a change of meaning

3 Choose the correct answers.

1 stop
   a They claim that hunters have **stopped** *killing / to kill* protected animals in the area.
   b On the way to the village, we **stopped** *taking / to take* photographs.
2 remember
   a I hope you **remembered** *bringing / to bring* the camera.
   b I clearly **remember** *putting / to put* our passports in my travel bag.
3 try
   a Why don't you **try** *taking / to take* sleeping pills if you can't sleep?
   b I **tried** *persuading / to persuade* him to come with us but without success.
4 regret
   a I **regret** *telling / to tell* you that the trip tomorrow has been cancelled.
   b I **regret** *paying / to pay* so much for this tent – it's not even waterproof!
5 forget
   a Our guide **forgot** *mentioning / to mention* that the road was full of holes.
   b I have not **forgotten** *seeing / to see* what hunters had done to those elephants.
6 mean
   a The government **means** *taking / to take* action to protect wildlife.
   b Protecting wildlife **means** *changing / to change* the law.

Key word transformations

4 Complete the second sentence so that it has a similar meaning to the first sentence, using the word given. Do not change the word given. You must use between two and five words, including the word given.

1 I really don't like travelling by bus in the morning.
   STAND
   I _____ by bus in the morning.
2 I decided to go to Africa on my own.
   DECISION
   It _____ to go to Africa on my own.
3 I didn't have enough money to go to Rwanda by plane.
   AFFORD
   I _____ to Rwanda by plane.
4 It took me ages to get all the documents I needed.
   SPENT
   I _____ all the documents I needed.
5 It was difficult for me not to smile when they told me the news.
   HELP
   I couldn't _____ heard the news.
6 I can hear laughter coming from the neighbours' flat.
   PEOPLE
   I _____ in the neighbours' flat.
7 They said they would go to the police if we didn't help them.
   THREATENED
   They _____ the police if we didn't help them.
8 I can't wait to visit the new safari park.
   FORWARD
   I'm _____ the new safari park.
9 I'm glad I went to Africa to see animals in their natural environment.
   WORTH
   It _____ Africa to see animals in their natural environment.
10 The idea of waiting for five hours at the airport does not appeal to me.
   KEEN
   I'm not _____ waiting for five hours at the airport.

Extra word

5 Find and cross out the extra word in each sentence.

1 I am thinking of going ~~to~~ bird-watching this weekend.
2 I am taking my daughter with me as she is keen for to learn about the countryside.
3 She is looking forward to be seeing the wild birds she has learnt to recognise.
4 I've told Lorna that it's important to remember taking her binoculars.
5 But, of course, it's also worth to taking a camera so she can keep a record of what she sees.

Reading (Paper 1 Part 7)

Before you read

1 Which of the animals in the box do you expect to be the most intelligent? Tick them.

elephant   fox   leopard   octopus   parrot   pigeon   rat   seal

fox

kea parrot

octopus

Scanning

2 Read the article quickly and find the paragraph (A–F) where each of the animals in Exercise 1 is mentioned. Then read the paragraph about each animal more carefully. Were your predictions right or wrong?

Multiple matching

3a Look at question 1 in the exam task. Mark the part of paragraph B that tells you the answer.

b Look at question 2 and follow these steps.
1 Mark the key words in the question.
2 Scan the text to find the section(s) which may contain the answer.
3 Read this section carefully and mark the place where you find the answer.
4 Check that the text you have found exactly matches the question.

c Now continue with questions 3–10.

> **EXPERT STRATEGY**
>
> Remember to read the questions first in this task. The questions do not come in the same order as the information in the text – you have to find the answers.

> **HELP**
>
> 2 The word *controlled* is in paragraph B but it is not the answer. Which animal has realised what humans were trying to do?
> 5 Look for a period of time in the text.
> 6 Find a word with a similar meaning to *remember*.

> **EXPERT LANGUAGE**
>
> Find three superlative adjectives in the text that have the same meaning.

> **EXPERT WORD CHECK**
>
> *broadcast   die out   locksmiths*
> *pests   prey   tank   to undo*
> *trial and error*

You are going to read an article about animal intelligence. For questions 1–10, choose from the paragraphs (A–F). The paragraphs may be chosen more than once.

Which paragraph mentions:

a type of animal that is now extinct?	1	B
an animal which has prevented humans controlling its behaviour?	2	
an example of intelligence that may not have a positive outcome?	3	
the way the majority of animals react to things?	4	
an animal that managed to solve a problem quickly?	5	
an animal that was able to remember things?	6	
animals that will not appear in the programme?	7	
an animal that exploits aspects of the man-made environment?	8	
environmental problems which are affecting animals?	9	
when you'll be able to see the programme?	10	

Clever Claws

A new wildlife series begins on TV next week

A

What is the world's most intelligent animal? Television producer Mike Beynon and his team of animal experts have searched the world to make the new TV series Clever Claws, which will be broadcast this autumn. You won't find any performing seals among the contenders, however, because all the animals featured use their brains to solve problems encountered in their natural environments. Mike points out that the brainiest creatures are often those that we think of as pests. 'Rats, foxes and pigeons are pretty intelligent,' he says. 'We only call them pests because they have learnt to exploit us, instead of being frightened.'

B

In the last century, animals have had to cope with enormous changes, from pollution to climate shifts. The clever creatures are those that learn to survive by adapting; those that don't, like the dinosaurs, tend to die out as the world around them changes. 'Ninety-nine percent of animal behaviour is controlled by instinct,' says Mike. 'Give most creatures something new and they don't know what to do – it's only the clever ones which accept the challenge.' And the first programme in the series includes a few examples of just that.

C

Can an elephant be as quiet as a mouse? It seems it can! When farmers in Thailand suspected elephants of stealing their banana crops, they hung a bell around each animal's neck so that they'd get warning of an attack. But one elephant has worked out how to stop his bell ringing, so he can get to the bananas undetected. The elephant fills the bell with mud, which stops the sound. But that's not all. By morning, the mud has dried and fallen out and so the locals still can't identify the mystery banana burglar!

D

And it's not only land animals that prove to be quite bright. Octopuses have fantastic eyesight and big brains for their size, so Mike and his team put one in a special tank, designed like a maze with lots of tunnels that led nowhere and choices to make about whether to go left or right at junctions. 'The octopus had a good memory and solved our puzzle by trial and error. After two weeks, it could get out of that maze in under a minute,' says Mike.

E

Just like humans, animals use their intelligence to their own advantage. Sometimes they even use man's inventions to get ahead of the competition. Big cats such as cheetahs and leopards have been spotted standing on safari vehicles, ready and waiting to leap out at their prey. 'Clever but worrying,' says Mike. 'If a cheetah uses a man-made object to gain an advantage over an antelope in an attack, then that is very dangerous because it puts nature out of balance.'

F

And hunger is one of the great motivators of intelligence in animals. New Zealand kea parrots are some of the cleverest. On the programme we see that parrots can actually be very accomplished locksmiths. In order to get at the tasty snack inside a locked box, one such bird had to undo one lock, pull a pin out of a second and then turned a key ten times to open a third. No problem! After only 45 seconds, the kea reached its meal! Now that's what you call intelligence!

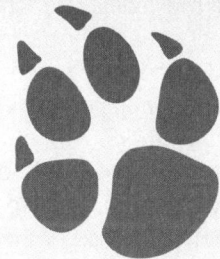

4 Challenges

4A Personal challenges

Vocabulary development 1

> **COURSEBOOK** pages 50–51

Personal life and experience

1 Choose the correct answers.

1 I *have been born / was born* in 1960 in a small town in Wales.
2 When I was five years old, my parents died and I became an *orphan / orphanage*.
3 Life was not easy during my early *childish / childhood* and I was often miserable.
4 As I didn't have many friends, I often felt very *on my own / lonely*.
5 During my teenage years, I was *brought up / grown up* by foster parents.
6 Although my foster parents were not *well-out / well-off*, they looked after me well.
7 In my *final teens / late teens*, I left home and started work in a supermarket.
8 My workmates were all older than me but we *got on / got off* very well.
9 I didn't *win / earn* much money, so it was sometimes difficult to make ends meet.
10 A lot of families lived in *poorly / poverty* in my hometown, so I worked hard and was very ambitious.
11 I managed to *put by / put off* a little money each month.
12 I dreamt of having my own business and living a life of *luxury / luxurious*.
13 One day, I had the *possibility / opportunity* to go on a managerial training course; I loved it.
14 Now I am manager of the supermarket and engaged to a girl from quite a *wealth / wealthy* family.
15 Our *wedding / marriage* ceremony will take place next month.
16 I'll probably never *get / achieve* my ambition of being a millionaire but it doesn't seem so important anymore.

Phrasal verbs

2a Choose the correct answers.

1 As night fell, we set *out / about* on our journey across the desert.
2 Although it was raining heavily, I forced myself to keep *up / on* running.
3 If you want to run the marathon, you'll have to give *over / up* smoking!
4 The expedition ran *into / through* trouble when their jeep broke down.
5 This hot weather really wears me *off / out*. I don't have any energy left at all.
6 'We've lost our map!' 'Well, we'll have to do *without / off* it, won't we?'
7 We need to stop at a garage. We're running *out / up* of petrol.
8 John is always complaining. I don't know how you put up *with / by* him.

b Read the email and replace the words in brackets with phrasal verbs from Exercise 2a in the correct form. Add any other words that are necessary.

Hi Gerry,

I've just reached the midway point on my marathon cycle ride around Australia! I can't believe it! As you know, when I **(1)** _____ (started) on the ride, I was feeling really optimistic. Well, I **(2)** _____ (encountered) difficulties after just a couple of days, when the brake cable on my bike broke. Fortunately, there was no traffic, so I managed to **(3)** _____ (survive without) brakes until I reached the next town and got them fixed! It's been really hard to **(4)** _____ (tolerate) the heat though. It's absolutely **(5)** _____ (exhausted me). When I almost **(6)** _____ (had no water left) in the desert, I got pretty scared – I seriously thought about **(7)** _____ (stopping). But as you can see, I've managed to **(8)** _____ (continue) cycling. Knowing that I'm doing it for charity keeps me going.

More news soon!
Thomas

Exam practice: Word formation

(Paper 1 Part 3)

3 Do the task.

For questions 1–8, read the text below. Use the word given in capitals at the end of some of the lines to form a word that fits in the gap in the same line. There is an example at the beginning (0).

Ultra marathons

If you've ever run a marathon like those held (0) _annually_ in places like London and New York, then you'll know that this is an extremely (1) _____ thing to do. If you're going to finish the 26-mile course, then you need to do months of (2) _____ to ensure the necessary level of (3) _____ . Spare a thought then for people who go in for what are known as ultra marathons. These are longer than (4) _____ city marathons and are run over difficult terrain, often in (5) _____ places like deserts where (6) _____ may have to run across sand or stones, in weather conditions ranging from baking (7) _____ to torrential rain. For example, the 135-mile Badwater Marathon is a real test of (8) _____ , taking runners from the lowest point in North America to the highest, passing through Death Valley on the way.

ANNUAL

CHALLENGE

PREPARE
FIT

TRADITION

HOSPITABLE
COMPETE

HOT

ENDURE

EXPERT STRATEGY

Read the whole text first to get the general meaning before you try to do the task. Think about how the words on the right can be changed.

➤ HELP

2 Change one letter and add a suffix to this word.
5 You need to add a negative prefix to this word.
7 Make a noun from this adjective.

EXPERT LANGUAGE

Find two examples of conditional sentences in the text.

EXPERT WORD CHECK

extremely go in for passing through terrain torrential

Language development 1

Narrative forms

➤ **COURSEBOOK** pages 52–53, **EXPERT GRAMMAR** page 188

1 Put the story in the correct order (1–10). Then choose the correct answers.

1	a	My girlfriend has a lovely black kitten called Max.
	b	I *went / was going* to her house, of course, to help her find Max.
	c	There was Max! He *lay / was lying* fast asleep in his basket!
	d	When she opened the door, I could see from her eyes that she *had cried / had been crying*.
	e	She phoned me yesterday to say that she *lost / had lost* him.
	f	We *had / were having* a hot chocolate when we heard a sound.
	g	Twenty minutes later, we still *didn't find / hadn't found* Max, so we went back inside.
	h	She told me on the phone that she *looked / had looked* everywhere.
	i	It was cold in the garden and it *rained / was raining* heavily.
	j	We *went out / had gone out* into the garden to look for Max together.

Time conjunctions

2a Match the sentence halves to make a short story.

1 One day I was leaving the house when
2 By the time Sue arrived,
3 As soon as I saw her face,
4 The postman arrived with a letter as
5 She didn't continue her story until
6 I began to laugh once

a she was telling me about her boyfriend, Robert.
b I had opened the letter.
c I had recovered from the shock of reading Sue's wedding invitation.
d I had been waiting impatiently for an hour.
e my sister Sue phoned to say she was on her way to see me.
f I knew she had something to tell me.

b Join the sentence pairs using the time conjunctions in bold. Put the verbs in brackets in the correct form. Do not change the order of the sentences.

1 We (arrive) at the party. Everyone (go) home. **by the time**
_____

2 I (watch) a horror film on television. The lights suddenly (go) out. **when**
_____

3 The air hostess (count) all the passengers. The plane (take) off. **once**
_____

4 I (never / live) on my own. I (go) to university. **before**
_____

5 Peter (hear) the good news. He (telephone) his wife. **as soon as**
_____

6 We (wait) for an hour. The train eventually (arrive). **when**
_____

7 The customs officer (search) all our luggage. He (allow) us to go. **after**
_____

8 I (stay) at my grandfather's house. I (discover) an old photograph album. **while**
_____

9 Sarah (not go) back to work. She (recover) from the flu. **until**
_____

10 My sister (read) her exam results. She (burst) out laughing. **when**
_____

Key word transformations

3 Complete the second sentence so that it has a similar meaning to the first sentence, using the word given. Do not change the word given. You must use between two and five words, including the word given.

1 We arrived at the cinema too late for the start of the film.
ALREADY
The film _____ the time we arrived at the cinema.

2 On hearing the good news, everyone at the office gave a cheer.
WHEN
Everyone at the office gave a cheer _____ the good news.

3 A fire broke out on board the plane shortly after it left the ground.
JUST
The plane _____ off when a fire broke out on board.

4 James was surprised by their friendliness.
EXPECTED
James _____ be so friendly.

5 I had hardly opened the front door when the phone rang.
SOON
The phone rang _____ the front door.

6 We didn't set off for the mountains until midday.
WHEN
It _____ off for the mountains.

7 He read the whole letter before saying anything.
UNTIL
He didn't say _____ the whole letter.

8 I met somebody I knew on my flight to Athens last week.
WHILE
I met somebody I knew _____ flying to Athens last week.

9 Sue was excited because it was her first visit to India.
NEVER
Sue was excited because _____ India before.

10 The train journey took six hours, so we were really tired when we got to Madrid.
FOR
We were really tired when we got to Madrid because we _____ six hours by train.

Writing (Paper 2 Part 2: Article)

➤ **COURSEBOOK** pages 54–55, **EXPERT WRITING** page 201

EXPERT STRATEGY
Remember to give specific examples to bring your article to life. Finish with a sentence that summarises what you have said.

Understand the task

1   Read the writing task and answer the questions.

   1 Who is going to read the article?
   2 Who and what is the article about?
   3 What main points should you include?

You have seen this advertisement in an international magazine for young people.

What was your greatest ever challenge?

Write an article that will inspire other young people. Your article should say:
- why you decided to do it
- how you prepared for the challenge
- how you felt afterwards.

*Write your **article** in **140–190** words in an appropriate style.*

Check and improve a sample answer

2a Read a student's answer. The article should have four paragraphs. Mark where a new paragraph should begin.

When I stood on the stage and saw the audience, I was almost too nervous to speak. But I knew I had to do it. My challenge had started three weeks before. I do voluntary work for a wildlife charity. When our leader asked for a volunteer to give a talk about our work at a conference, I said 'no' at first. I had never given a speech in my life and the idea terrified me. Nobody else was free that day, however, so I reluctantly agreed. I spent the next three weeks preparing. I had given presentations at school, so I looked at my old notes and started to prepare PowerPoint slides. Once it was all ready, I practised giving my talk in front of the mirror until I felt completely confident. Although I was nervous when I gave my talk, it went very well. I'm glad I agreed to do the presentation. It taught me that you can do the things which seem impossible if you face up to the challenge.

b   Match each paragraph of the article (1–4) with its function (a–d).

Paragraph	Function
_____	a introduces the topic in an interesting way
_____	b develops the article with details of what happened and moves towards the conclusion
_____	c reflects on the events in the article as a whole/how the main character feels about what happened
_____	d explains the background to the events

c   Find examples of the past simple and past perfect simple in the article. Which tense is used:

   1 to give background information? _____
   2 to move the story forward? _____

d   Find words/phrases in the article that match these meanings.

   1 frightened   _____
   2 unpaid   _____
   3 not willingly   _____
   4 visual information_____
   5 sure of myself   _____
   6 satisfied   _____
   7 confront   _____

3   Write your own article.

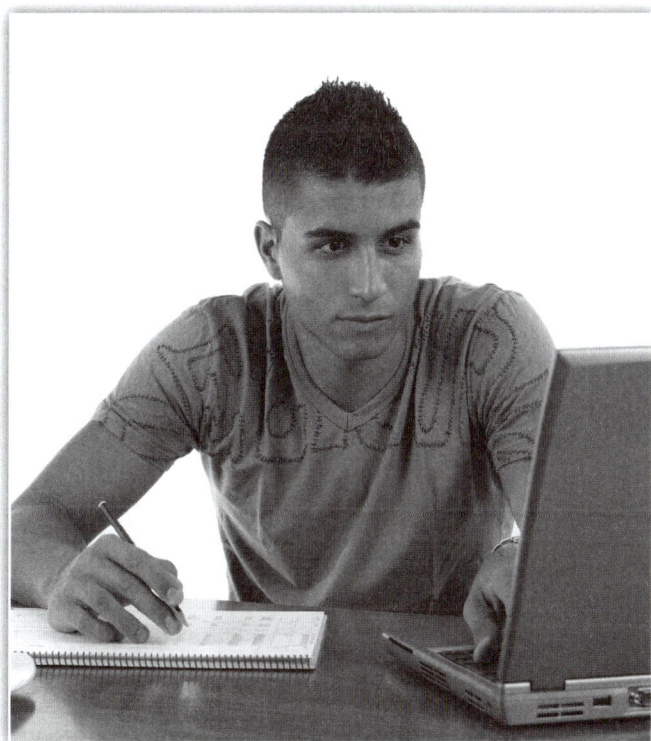

Listening (Paper 3 Part 2)

Before you listen

1a Read the instructions for the listening task and answer the questions.

1 How many speakers will you hear?
2 What is the topic?

b Read the sentences and try to predict the type of information you are listening for to complete each gap. Will any of the answers be:

1 numbers?   2 adjectives?   3 names of sports?

c Mark the main ideas in each sentence. The first one has been done for you. Then think about each sentence. Do you agree or disagree?

Sentence completion

2a 🎧 06 Listen once and complete the sentences.

b 🎧 06 Listen again and check your answers.

EXPERT STRATEGY

Read the words before and after the gap in the sentence. You will probably hear different words that could fit in the gap. Listen carefully to know which one is correct.

➤ HELP

1 You are listening for the word for a person who does the sport.
4 You are listening for a number.
10 You are listening for an adjective that describes how a person feels.

EXPERT LANGUAGE

Which of the sentences are about
1 Martin's opinions?
2 factual information?

EXPERT WORD CHECK

*capabilities   comparable
fundraising   goal   motivation*

*You will hear a well-known sportsman called Malcolm Price talking about training for different physical activities. For questions **1–10**, complete the sentences with a word or short phrase.*

Sports training

Malcolm has achieved sporting success as a(n) **(1)** _____ .

Malcolm says that fundraising for **(2)** _____ can be just as demanding as competitive sport.

Malcolm mentions running and **(3)** _____ as sports requiring training.

Malcolm tells us that his weight is **(4)** _____ .

Malcolm believes that adults can find a comparable level of **(5)** _____ to youngsters.

Malcolm believes having a(n) **(6)** _____ is as important as having a goal.

Malcolm recommends making progress in small stages to avoid feeling **(7)** _____ .

Malcolm says that training becomes boring if it lacks **(8)** _____ .

Malcolm advises us to work towards **(9)** _____ goals in order to enjoy training.

Malcolm admits that training can sometimes be a(n) **(10)** _____ activity.

Vocabulary development 2

➤ **COURSEBOOK** page 56–57

➤ **COURSEBOOK** page 56–57

> **EXPERT STRATEGY**
>
> In Paper 4, Speaking, Part 1, the examiner may ask you what kind of sports you and your friends are interested in. In Parts 3 and 4, you may have to compare different sports and discuss why people do them or what kind of people they might appeal to. Make sure you know the necessary vocabulary.

Describing sports

1a Write the sports in the box in the correct column. Which are team sports (T)? Which are individual sports (I)?

basketball   ~~climbing~~   golf   hang-gliding   high jump ice hockey   karate   parachute jumping   rugby running   scuba diving   snowboarding   tennis water skiing   windsurfing

Category	Sport
Risk (extreme) sports	*climbing (I)*
Track and field events	
Water sports	
Winter sports	
Martial arts	
Ball games	

b Which sports from Exercise 1a are these comments describing? Mark the word(s) which help you decide.

1 The first time I jumped off the side of the hill, I was scared stiff. _____
2 It's hard to keep your balance as the boat pulls you out of the water. At the beginning I was always falling over. _____
3 You need to practise the kicks and punches every day if you want to make progress. _____
4 You don't need a lot of equipment – just a pair of trainers and a good racket. _____
5 It's important to wear a helmet to protect your head from falling rocks. _____
6 The equipment can be expensive – you need a mask, flippers and a wet suit. _____
7 You stand on a kind of ski and use your whole body to make turns and jumps. It's quite difficult to keep your balance at first. _____
8 It's much more dangerous than ice-skating. You have to wear protective clothing like a helmet, knee pads and gloves. _____

2 Do the quiz. Choose the correct answer (A, B, C or D).

Sports quiz

1 What word is used to describe the area where a game of tennis is played?

A *pitch*   B *court*   C *course*   D *ring*

2 What word is used in football results to mean that a team didn't score any goals?

A *zero*   B *nought*   C *nil*   D *nothing*

3 The main difference between badminton and tennis is that in badminton

A there is no net in between the players.
B the players do not use rackets.
C the players do not use a ball.
D the players wear protective masks.

4 A regatta is an event where there are races between

A teams of climbers.
B rowing or sailing boats.
C light aircraft.
D vintage cars.

5 What is the name of the sport in which a bow is used to shoot arrows at a target?

A fencing   B archery   C wrestling   D judo

6 Which sport was invented in Scotland and involves hitting a ball with a club?

A golf   B cricket   C hockey   D lacrosse

7 In baseball or cricket, one team beats the other by scoring more

A sets.   B goals.   C laps.   D runs.

8 Where are you likely to hear the word *jockey* used?

A a horse race
B a golf championship
C a skiing event
D a boxing match

9 Which word is *not* used in football?

A tackle   B pass   C shoot   D serve

10 What is the name of the person who supervises a game of tennis?

A umpire   B referee   C coach   D spectator

Informal expressions

3 Read the text and decide which answer (A, B or C) best fits each gap.

I'm not really **(1)** _____ sport, but I love skiing. I took it **(2)** _____ while I was living abroad. It was my friends who **(3)** _____ me into doing it; they were all keen skiers. They just kept **(4)** _____ at me until I agreed to **(5)** _____ it a go. I hadn't expected to enjoy it so much – I absolutely loved it from the **(6)** _____ go. The sense of speed is exhilarating and, of course, there's the wonderful scenery. I admit I was **(7)** _____ stiff the first time but pretty soon I just wanted to carry **(8)** _____ skiing all day.

1	A for	B into	C about
2	A up	B on	C down
3	A spoke	B told	C talked
4	A across	B on	C over
5	A give	B put	C have
6	A word	B minute	C time
7	A frightened	B scared	C terrified
8	A on	B in	C through

Language development 2

> **COURSEBOOK** page 59, **EXPERT GRAMMAR** pages 188–189

Quantity

1 Complete the sentences with *a*, *some*, *any* or – (if no article or determiner is needed).

1 a Can I have _____ glass of water, please?
  b Don't drop that vase! It's made of _____ glass, not plastic.
2 a I think it is better to play _____ football than watch it on television.
  b I'm going to buy my little brother _____ football for Christmas.
3 a Could you put _____ chocolate on top of my cappuccino, please?
  b Would you like _____ chocolate? Go on – they're delicious!
4 a Did you enjoy the party? You certainly look as if you had _____ good time!
  b I would like to help you but I don't have _____ free time at all.
5 a Could you buy me _____ paper? I want to see what's going on in the world.
  b They've used a new kind of plastic for the cycle helmet. It's as light as _____ paper but much stronger.

Determiners

2a Find and correct the mistakes with determiners in some of these sentences. Tick the ones that are correct.

1 I don't think there will be much interest in tonight's football match.
2 There is a large number of sports information on the internet.
3 There isn't many news about David Beckham at the moment.
4 We have no money at all for new sports equipment.
5 How much players were injured during the game?
6 Football fans caused a great deal of damage to the stadium.
7 We don't have many time to prepare for the championship.
8 There are always plenty of spectators at the London Marathon.
9 They only have a small amount of tickets left for the final game.
10 How many money will the new tennis courts cost?

b Complete the text with *few/a few* or *little/a little*.

I've been training very hard for the championship and I've had very **(1)** _____ time to relax recently. My trainer is very strict and he insists I train every day. I have managed to get away on **(2)** _____ occasions, though. I think it's important to take **(3)** _____ time off now and then. You can't train all the time, can you?

Last weekend I went shopping in town but I have very **(4)** _____ money to spare. And yesterday, **(5)** _____ fans came to see me. They were impressed when I told them about my training routine. Very **(6)** _____ people realise how difficult training for a big event can be.

Key word transformations

3 Complete the second sentence so that it has a similar meaning to the first sentence, using the word given. Do not change the word given. You must use between two and five words, including the word given.

1 The players spent a lot of time training for the game.
DEAL
The players spent _____ time training for the game.

2 Not many fans attended the match on Saturday.
VERY
The match on Saturday was attended _____ fans.

3 My brother is not very interested in sport.
MUCH
My brother doesn't show _____ sport.

4 First-class sports equipment is often very expensive.
LOTS
You often need to spend _____ to buy first-class sports equipment.

5 There is a complete lack of sports facilities at our college.
NO
Our college has _____ all.

6 The government spends very little money on sports education.
SMALL
The government only spends _____ money on sports education.

Exam practice: Open cloze
(Paper 1 Part 2)

4 Do the task.

*For questions **1–8**, read the text below and think of the word which best fits each gap. Use only **one** word in each gap. There is an example at the beginning (**0**).*

The joy of ice-skating

For many people, ice-skating is remembered as a skill (0) __which__ they tried but failed to master in childhood. Very (1) _____ ever go back and attempt to take (2) _____ the sport again. This is a shame because once you've built (3) _____ a bit of confidence, ice-skating is great exercise as (4) _____ as being enjoyable and fun.

Most major cities in the UK now have ice-skating rinks and most rinks have an introductory package for new ice-skaters, which includes either group (5) _____ individual lessons. There are various types of ice-skating but many newcomers choose ice-dance (6) _____ it is the most sociable activity on ice. Skaters find that the thrill of moving around so gracefully is like (7) _____ else they've ever experienced. Of course, such grace doesn't come overnight. A couple of hours' individual tuition with a teacher, plus five hours' practice each week is roughly the level (8) _____ commitment needed to make progress.

EXPERT STRATEGY
Read the whole text first to get the general meaning before you try to do the task. Think about the type of word that is missing in each gap.

➤ HELP
1 You need a word that means 'a small number of people'.
4 Which word makes a phrase meaning 'in addition to'?
7 You need a negative word here.

EXPERT LANGUAGE
Which two answers are phrasal verbs?

EXPERT WORD CHECK
commitment   gracefully   newcomers   package
rinks   to master

Reading (Paper 1 Part 6)

Before you read

1 Read the instructions for the reading task and the title and subheading of the article. Which of the following topics do you think the article will talk about?

a the future of sponsorship
b the advantages of sponsorship
c how commercial sponsorship of sports started
d the disadvantages of sponsorship

Skimming

2 Skim the article. Match the topics in Exercise 1 (a–d) with the paragraphs (1–6) in the article. Each topic can go with more than one paragraph. Which topic is not mentioned?

Gapped text

3a Read the first paragraph of the article and sentence G. Which words in the text link to these words from sentence G?

1 they = *the organisers of the tennis tournament*
2 the company =
3 the privilege =

b Read the rest of the article carefully and do the task. Note these steps. For each gap, do the following:
• Read the text before and after the gap and think about the type of information which is missing.
• Look for a sentence in the box which talks about this topic area.
• Choose the correct answer by checking the grammatical and lexical links between the base text and the key sentence. Look out for pronouns, synonyms, etc.
• Cross off each sentence as you use it but be prepared to look again when you check your answers.

c Read the article again with your answers to check that it makes sense.

EXPERT STRATEGY

Read the whole text first to get the general meaning before you try to do the task. Look for words before and after the gap that refer to the missing sentence.

➤ HELP

2 Which sentence (A–G) refers to yearly income?
3 What is the main idea in this paragraph? Which sentence (A–G) introduces this topic?
4 What is the topic of this paragraph? Which sentence (A–G) introduces this topic?

EXPERT LANGUAGE

Find three examples of determiners in sentences A–G.

EXPERT WORD CHECK

broadcast clashes harmless merchandise privilege sponsorship to coincide television coverage tournament

You are going to read an article about commercial sponsorship in sport. Six sentences have been removed from the article. Choose from the sentences (A–G) the one that fits each gap (1–6). There is one extra sentence which you do not need to use.

A People also complain that sponsors have too much influence on the sport in return for their financial backing.

B Many loyal local fans also believe that their needs are being ignored in favour of more profitable television audiences.

C Although this may appear harmless, the pressures they face can be intolerable.

D By 1992 this new business had an annual turnover of over £30 million.

E But there is a downside: much is demanded of the top stars in return for their high earnings.

F Increased public awareness of sports has, in turn, helped to stimulate demand for certain products.

G It was only in the 1970s that they realised they could be charging the company for the privilege instead.

BUSINESS CALLS THE SHOTS

Sport has undoubtedly made huge financial gains from business sponsorship. But at what cost to the fans and players?

Many sporting organisations only began to understand how valuable commercial sponsorship might be in the last decades of the 20th century, when individual players and their agents started finding their own sponsors. The organisers of the famous Wimbledon Tennis Tournament, for example, had been paying the sports equipment manufacturer, Slazenger, to supply balls and equipment since 1902. Slazenger had been getting hundreds of thousands of pounds' worth of free publicity from the live television coverage of the event but the organisers of the tennis tournament were getting nothing in return. `1` `G`

Wimbledon also began to put its name on a range of merchandise which it sold to fans, including clothing, towels, china and stationery. `2` Because of their increased overall income, the organisers of the tournament were able to donate millions to the British Lawn Tennis Association and so help develop the sport in the country where the tournament is held.

Sporting agents believe that the injection of money and commercialism into sport from various sources has helped everybody. Players have gained financially, with earnings reflecting the true value of their abilities; sports administrators have cashed in on television's wish to broadcast major events; businesses have gained publicity for their products and found top sports stars willing to promote them and lastly, the public's desire to see top matches and wear a range of sporting goods has been satisfied. `3`
Top tennis players have to play more and more events across the world. Three-times Wimbledon winner Boris Becker was referring to the top ten players at the end of one exhausting season when he said, 'Everyone is badly injured or is having a nervous breakdown.'

Meanwhile, agents are now signing up potential stars at even earlier ages – some are as young as ten years old. `4` Child stars Andrea Jaeger and Tracy Austin were both forced out of the game after receiving permanent injuries while still in their teens. At least Ms Austin had earned $5 million before her injury.

`5` A sportswear manufacturer might, say, insist that a player it sponsors competes in a minor tournament in its home town. Meanwhile, the demands of television often influence sporting decisions. The timing of major sporting events such as cup finals, key matches or Olympic events are set to coincide with peak viewing times or to avoid clashes with popular programmes. In 1994 the football World Cup was held in the USA because it was the country which offered the organisers the best commercial opportunities, even though it had no organised football league and the game was relatively unknown there. US television companies even discussed altering the length of the playing periods in order to get in more advertising.

But whatever the arguments, commercialisation has given many sports a higher profile. `6` Sometimes, of course, the public finds that these goods are also the most expensive, so they end up paying for the sponsorship anyway. But then, as the saying goes, 'You pay your money, you take your choice.'

Vocabulary development 1

➤ **COURSEBOOK** pages 64–65

Word formation

1a Complete the table.

Subject	Person	Adjective
1 _____	2 _____	scientific
3 _____	geneticist	4 _____
5 _____	psychologist	6 _____
7 _____	8 _____	linguistic
9 _____	10 _____	archaeological
astronomy	11 _____	12 _____

b Complete the word formation rules with *subject*, *person* or *adjective*.

1 The suffix *-ist* or *-er* is often used for a(n)
_____ .

2 The suffix *-ics* or *-y* is often used for a(n)
_____ .

3 The suffix *-ic*, or *-ical* is often used for a(n)
_____ .

c Use the word given at the end of the sentences to form a word that fits in the gap.

1 One hundred students were asked to take part in a _____ experiment. **PSYCHOLOGY**
2 The study of _____ has made it possible to clone animals. **GENETIC**
3 Copernicus is one of the most famous _____ who have ever lived. **ASTRONOMY**
4 The speed of a child's _____ development depends on many factors. **LINGUIST**
5 The area around Stonehenge in the southwest of England is of great _____ importance. **ARCHAEOLOGY**
6 Modern _____ theories about the universe often seem strangely similar to the beliefs of ancient cultures. **SCIENCE**

Pronunciation

2a 🎧 07 Listen and mark the stress on the words in Exercise 1a.
scientific

b 🎧 07 Listen again and practise saying the words aloud.

Expressions

3 Replace the words in bold in the sentences with the phrases in the box.

*as a consequence of   at the forefront of
getting better and better   hard to put down
in the widest sense   packed with   the latest
to great effect*

1 According to **the most recent** theories, the universe is expanding rapidly.
2 We understand the genetic code better today **due to** the hard work of many scientists around the world.
3 Stephen Hawking's book *A Brief History of Time* is **full of** interesting facts and theories.
4 *Language Play* by David Crystal is **a book you cannot stop reading**.
5 The Roslin Institute in Scotland is **one of the leading organisations doing** research into cloning.
6 Scientific techniques which tell us the age of archaeological finds are **improving steadily**.
7 Scientific research at many universities benefits the community **generally**: members of the public, artists, writers and academics.
8 Einstein used his knowledge of mathematics and physics **very effectively**.

Adjective + noun collocations

4 Match the adjectives (1–8) with the nouns they collocate with (a–h). Each adjective must collocate with all the nouns in a set.

1 original	a belief/responsibility/experience
2 fascinating	b ideas/news/information
3 eye-catching	c book/insight/discovery
4 influential	d reading/breeze/colour
5 ideal	e idea/design/plan
6 personal	f present/holiday/solution
7 up-to-date	g photo/dress/advertisement
8 light	h theory/scientist/organisation

Exam practice: Multiple-choice cloze (Paper 1 Part 1)

5 Do the task.

*For questions **1–8**, read the text below and decide which answer (**A**, **B**, **C** or **D**) best fits each gap. There is an example at the beginning (**0**).*

The discovery of DNA

One of the (**0**) __A__ moments in science occurred in 1953, when Francis Crick and James Watson at Cambridge University discovered the structure of DNA. They said that DNA was (**1**) _____ to two spiral staircases going up and down at the same time. Scientists all over the world (**2**) _____ this 'double helix' model immediately. The discovery was, of course, the result of years of hard work, and Crick and Watson weren't the only scientists who had been (**3**) _____ out research to find out what DNA (**4**) _____ like. Maurice Wilkins and Rosalind Franklin at King's College, London, had also been (**5**) _____ on the problem. They used X-ray analysis of DNA, (**6**) _____ Crick and Watson preferred to build models. One day, without (**7**) _____ a word to her, Wilkins showed Franklin's results to Watson, and it was those results which helped him to discover the real structure of DNA. In 1962, Watson, Crick and Wilkins were (**8**) _____ the Nobel Prize for their work. Rosalind Franklin, who had died four years earlier, was not even mentioned at the ceremony.

0	A greatest	B largest	C tallest	D broadest
1	A same	B similar	C alike	D resembled
2	A accepted	B agreed	C admitted	D allowed
3	A making	B doing	C holding	D carrying
4	A looked	B appeared	C existed	D compared
5	A thinking	B trying	C working	D seeking
6	A however	B whereas	C unlike	D despite
7	A telling	B dropping	C giving	D saying
8	A presented	B awarded	C donated	D celebrated

EXPERT STRATEGY

Read the whole text again when you've finished to make sure it makes complete sense with the answers you've chosen.

EXPERT WORD CHECK

model   Nobel Prize   research   staircase   X-ray

Language development 1

➤ **COURSEBOOK** pages 66–67, **EXPERT GRAMMAR** pages 189–190

Future forms: Present simple, present continuous, *will* and *be going to*

1 Choose the correct answers.

1 What time *does the bank close / is the bank closing* in the afternoon?
2 'There's no milk in the fridge.' 'OK. *I'm getting / I'll get* some from the supermarket.'
3 Those magazines I ordered arrived a month late. *I'm complaining / I'm going to complain* to the manager of the shop!
4 Get away from that ladder! *It's going to / It'll* fall down – look at the strength of the wind!
5 *Will you do / Are you doing* anything this evening? If not, do you want to go out?
6 I wouldn't go near Julia's dog if I were you. *He's going to / He'll* bite you.
7 I can't go to the cinema with you on Friday because *I meet / I'm meeting* Paul.
8 Haven't you written your essay yet? What *are you telling / are you going to tell* Professor Stevens on Thursday?
9 *Are you going to / Will you* help me? I can't lift this table on my own.
10 I believe that Jerry Bond *will win / is winning* the local elections.

Future simple, future continuous and future perfect

2 Complete the sentences with the correct future form of the verbs in brackets.

1 I am sure that scientists _____ (discover) life on another planet one day.
2 I can't believe I've been promoted! This time next week, I _____ (work) in a smart office in New York.
3 Don't worry, I _____ (finish) writing my report by Friday. I'll give it to you then.
4 Don't call me tomorrow. I _____ (paint) the house all day.
5 On Saturday we _____ (be) married for 20 years. It's amazing, isn't it?
6 Have we run out of coffee? I _____ (go out) now and get some.
7 It's no trouble to take you to the airport – I _____ (go) that way anyway.
8 I don't think you'll see your friends. They _____ (leave) before you get back.

Future time clauses

3 Complete the sentences with the correct form of the verbs in brackets.

1 I promise I _____ (let) you know as soon as I _____ (find out) the answer.
2 After you _____ (finish) classes, _____ (we/go) to the cinema?
3 _____ (you/want) a cup of coffee before you _____ (leave)?
4 As soon as everyone _____ (be) here, we _____ (start) the seminar.
5 When the exams _____ (be) over, my group _____ (have) a big party to celebrate.
6 When the rain _____ (stop), why _____ (we/not go) for a walk?

Degrees of certainty

4 Read the text and decide which future form (A, B or C) best fits each gap.

In 100 years' time, I'm absolutely certain that astronauts **(1)** _____ on Mars. By then, they **(2)** _____ a space colony there as well. Who knows? It's quite likely, of course, that human beings **(3)** _____ other planets as well by that time – Jupiter perhaps. Within a century, it's almost certain that people **(4)** _____ on the moon.

As regards medicine, it **(5)** _____ very different in 100 years from now. We **(6)** _____ a lot more about DNA. I'm sure that doctors **(7)** _____ genetic information to diagnose diseases on an everyday basis. By then, it's possible they **(8)** _____ ways to use the same genetic data to stop people from getting ill. What an absolutely amazing prospect!

1 A will have landed   B might land
  C might have landed
2 A are going to build   B could build
  C might have built
3 A will visit   B are visiting
  C will have visited
4 A will be living   B are going to live
  C are living
5 A will be   B will have been
  C could have been
6 A will have known   B will know
  C could know
7 A are going to use   B are using
  C will be using
8 A may find   B may have found
  C could be finding

Exam practice: Open cloze
(Paper 1 Part 2)

5 Do the task.

*For questions 1–8, read the text below and think of the word which best fits each gap. Use only **one** word in each gap. There is an example at the beginning (0).*

Science as a career

For years, British universities have been worried because fewer (0) _and_ fewer students are choosing to do degrees in scientific subjects. These days students (1) _____ do well at science and maths at school are more attracted (2) _____ careers in areas such (3) _____ information technology and electronics rather (4) _____ in pure scientific research.

Many people think that when they are choosing which course to study, students do a kind of 'cost-benefit analysis'. In (5) _____ words, they ask themselves (6) _____ the effort of doing the course will be matched by future career prospects. But scientists through the ages have rarely been well paid and (7) _____ my opinion, earning lots of money shouldn't really be the motivation for scientists, either.

What attracted me to science was the thought of discovering some new law of nature (8) _____ nobody had ever seen before. In short, catching a glimpse of things that are bigger than humans. That must be much more satisfying than designing computer games or vacuum cleaners, mustn't it?

EXPERT STRATEGY

Read the whole text again when you've finished to make sure it makes complete sense with the answers you've chosen.

➤ HELP

2 You need a preposition here.
3 Which word completes this expression, with a meaning of 'for example'?
5 This word completes the linking expression.

EXPERT LANGUAGE

Find an example of a question tag in the text.

EXPERT WORD CHECK

cost-benefit analysis   degrees   law of nature
pure research   vacuum cleaners

Writing (Paper 2 Part 1: Essay)

➤ **COURSEBOOK** pages 68–69, **EXPERT WRITING** pages 199–200

➤ **COURSEBOOK** pages 68–69, **EXPERT WRITING** pages 199–200

EXAM STRATEGY

In Paper 2, Writing, Part 1, you have to write an essay on a topic that you are given. Two of the points you need to make in the essay are given. You have to write about these points before giving your own ideas as the third point. The wording of the question helps you to plan your essay and organise your ideas. Use the points to help you divide your essay into paragraphs.

Understand the task

1   Read the writing task and answer the questions.

1   Who are you writing for: someone you know or someone you don't know?
2   What style should you use: formal or informal?
3   What should each of the three main paragraphs be about? Mark the parts of the task that tell you.

In your English class, you have been talking about important scientific research. Now your English teacher has asked you to write an essay.

*Write an essay using **all** the notes and give reasons for your point of view.*

A lot of money is spent each year on scientific research. Some people think that medical research is more important than other types and so should receive more money. Do you agree?

Notes

Write about:

1   why medical research is important
2   why other types of research are also important
3   _____ (your own idea)

*Write your **essay** in 140–190 words in an appropriate style.*

EXPERT STRATEGY

Always check your work for basic errors when you finish writing. You will lose marks if basic errors make your work unclear or difficult to understand. Double-space your writing so that you have room to make corrections if you need to. Make sure that your handwriting is neat and easy to read.

Organise a sample answer

2a Read the jumbled sentences (a–i) from a student's essay. Decide which paragraph (2, 3 or 4) each sentence should go in. The introductory paragraph is only one sentence and has been done for you.

1   Introductory sentence:
Scientific research is very important but it is very expensive and somebody has to pay for it.

☐ a In my opinion, the benefits of scientific research can be difficult to predict.
☐ b The scientists who study diseases and find cures for them are obviously doing a very important job and should have financial support.
☐ c Medical research, however, isn't the only important type of scientific research.
☐ d Also, scientists who study things like DNA are likely to find out things about the world that can benefit everybody in the future.
☐ e Another important group of scientists are the ones who develop new drugs.
☐ f The work they do in helping to find new types of treatment for diseases is also very significant.
☐ g Scientists discover many things when they are planning space missions and those things can be useful on Earth too, so in my view, it is worth spending money on them.
☐ h For example, the scientists who develop new types of crops for agriculture help farmers to feed the world's growing population and that is extremely valuable work.
☐ i For example, some people think that exploring outer space is a waste of money but I don't agree.

b   What order should the sentences come in within each paragraph?

Listening (Paper 3 Part 2)

Before you listen

1a Read the instructions for the listening task. What is the topic? Think about what you know about this topic.

b Read the sentences and try to predict what kind of information is missing. Remember to look at the words before and after each gap. Which answer(s) do you think will be:

1 numbers?
2 proper names?
3 parts of the face?

Sentence completion

2a 🎧 08 Listen once and complete the sentences.

b 🎧 08 Listen again and check your answers.

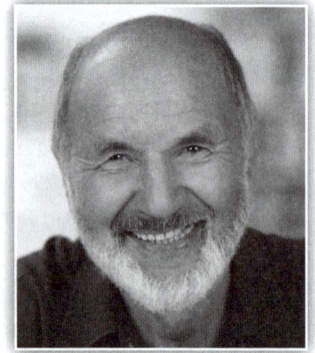

EXPERT STRATEGY

Remember that you won't hear the exact wording of the sentences but you will hear the same information in the same order. Use the sentences to help you follow the recording.

➤ HELP

1 You are listening for the name of a country. Be careful: a number of countries are mentioned.
3 You are listening for a number but it's not the first one you hear.
8 You need to write two words for this answer, linked by *and*.

EXPERT LANGUAGE

Which of the answers are:
1 adjectives?
2 verbs?

EXPERT WORD CHECK

*character traits   cheekbones
muscles   puzzled   tight   unrelaxed*

You will hear a woman called Lillian Scott talking about face-reading, the skill of judging a person's character from the shape of their face. For questions 1–10, complete the sentences with a word or short phrase.

Face reading

The skill of face-reading is believed to have come from (1) _____ originally.

The title of Lillian's book is (2) _____ .

Lillian explains that the face contains approximately (3) _____ muscles.

Lillian says that when people look in a(n) (4) _____ , they usually manage to look their best.

Lillian says that people often feel (5) _____ when they see themselves on video.

Experts say that the left side of the face is regarded as more (6) _____ by most people.

Lillian says that successful (7) _____ are often people with wide cheekbones.

Lillian says that the shape of a person's (8) _____ and _____ may show how determined they are.

Lillian advises women against using too much (9) _____ at interviews.

Lillian suggests (10) _____ and _____ when listening to people at interviews.

Vocabulary development 2

➤ COURSEBOOK pages 70–71

EXPERT STRATEGY

Inventions and their usefulness or importance is a common topic in the Speaking test. In Part 3, for example, you may be asked to talk about a number of different inventions and decide which three you couldn't live without or which have changed our lives the most. Collect useful vocabulary in your vocabulary notebook.

Modern inventions

1a Label the pictures with the words in the box. There are ten extra words which you do not need to use.

broadcast   call   channels   download   DVD player
earphones   focus   images   keyboard   lens
optical mouse   remote control   ringtone   software
text message   viewfinder   website   zap

1 _____
2 _____
3 _____
4 _____
5 _____
6 _____
7 _____
8 _____

b Complete the sentences with words from Exercise 1a.

1 Some people change the _____ of their mobile several times a week.
2 You need the right computer _____ in order to edit digital photos at home.
3 With digital TV, the number of _____ which are available to viewers is enormous.
4 You don't need to _____ my camera. It does it automatically.
5 I found a really good _____ yesterday about sharks and whales. I'll email you the address if you like.
6 Last night's interview with the president was _____ live from the White House.
7 I love listening to music on my phone. I _____ songs from the internet and listen to them on the bus.
8 You can edit the _____ you've taken with your camera using your computer.
9 I'll put my mobile where I can hear it. I'm expecting a(n) _____ from my brother.
10 Using the remote control, it's easy to _____ from channel to channel.

Agreeing and disagreeing

2 Two students are discussing the question 'What do you think is the most important thing ever invented?' Put the sentences from their discussion in the correct order (1–6). Then choose the correct answers.

☐ **a** Peter: I think the computer is the most important thing ever invented. If you have a computer, you can do so many things that you couldn't do before. Computers and the internet have changed the way people live.

☐ **b** Ingrid: Yes, you *are / have* right – I hadn't thought of that. I'm not sure if fire is a thing that we invented, though. It's a natural phenomenon. People discovered it. *Aren't / Don't* you agree?

☐ **c** Ingrid: I couldn't agree *much / more*. Without writing we wouldn't be able to live like we do today. The whole of our civilisation is based on things which are written down. Maybe it is the most important invention.

☐ **d** Ingrid: Yes, that's *true / truth*. But I don't think computers have changed our lives as much as cars. The car is a more important invention, *to / in* my opinion. It's easy to live without a computer but you can't live without a car, can you?

☐ **e** Peter: Yes, I suppose *so / that*. Well, writing then – writing was invented. That was a really important invention, I think.

☐ **f** Peter: No, I suppose *no / not*. Life would be *much / more* slower and more difficult without them. But I think other things are more important. What *for / about* fire, for example? I mean, that's something that changed the history of the whole human race.

Commonly confused words

3 Complete the sentences with the words in *italics*.

1 *machine / engine*
  a This car has a very powerful _____ , so you'll have to drive carefully.
  b To operate the coffee _____ , just put your money in here and press the button.

2 *electric / electrical*
  a We need to buy a new _____ cooker as soon as possible.
  b All the _____ equipment in this room needs to be replaced.

3 *appliance / device*
  a A vacuum cleaner is a(n) _____ which almost every household possesses.
  b My car has a(n) _____ which checks whether everyone is wearing a seat belt.

4 *mechanic / technician*
  a My father works as a _____ in the Microbiology unit of the hospital.
  b A _____ looked at my car the other day and said that I should get a new one.

5 *invent / discover*
  a I am sure that astronomers will _____ much more about distant galaxies in the future.
  b Do you think someone will _____ a flying car one day?

6 *fix / correct*
  a Can we find someone to _____ the TV? It's not working properly.
  b I've noticed a number of errors in this report. Can you _____ them, please?

Exam practice: Word formation
(Paper 1 Part 3)

4 Do the task.

*For questions **1–8**, read the text below. Use the word given in capitals at the end of each line to form a word that fits in the gap **in the same line**. There is an example at the beginning (**0**).*

The risk of new technology

Sometimes a new invention or the (0) _introduction_ of a new piece of technology fails to make the	INTRODUCE
(1) _____ on our lives that people thought it would. Home (2) _____ is one area where there	IMPRESS
	ENTERTAIN
is a constant stream of new (3) _____ , only a few of which will become universally (4) _____	PRODUCE
	SUCCESS
and a part of our everyday lives. This is a cause of great (5) _____ to designers and manufacturers	ANXIOUS
who invest large sums of money in the research and (6) _____ of new technologies. For example, in	DEVELOP
the period (7) _____ after digital television systems	IMMEDIATE
first went on (8) _____ , relatively few people	SELL

bought them. Many people were quite satisfied with their existing television reception and so didn't want to change, especially given that the new system seemed so expensive.

EXPERT STRATEGY

Read the whole text again when you've finished to make sure it makes complete sense with the answers you've chosen.

➤ HELP
3 You need a plural noun here.
4 Add a suffix but don't change the spelling of the root word.

EXPERT LANGUAGE

Find eight examples of adjective + noun collocations in the text.

EXPERT WORD CHECK

research and development   stream   sums of money   universally

Language development 2

Reflexives

> **COURSEBOOK** page 74

1a Find and cross out the extra word in some of the sentences. Tick the ones that are correct.

1 I usually get ~~myself~~ up at seven o'clock in the morning.
2 Nobody came to repair the TV, so I fixed it myself. ✓
3 I wonder myself whether he'll be able to fix my car.
4 You'll hurt by yourself if you're not careful.
5 He went to the dance on his own.
6 They talked to themselves one another all evening.
7 Did you feel yourself nervous during the exam?
8 My brother managed to learn about computers by himself.
9 John and Alice met each one another on holiday last year.
10 I enjoyed myself at the party last night.

b Complete the sentences with the correct form of the verbs in the box. Add any other words that are necessary.

| blame | concentrate | ~~cut~~ | know | like | look at |
| relax | write |

1 This knife is extremely sharp. I've just _cut myself_ .
2 The accident was not your fault. Don't _____ for what happened.
3 I'm not going to help you with your letter. You can _____ .
4 Tom and Simon are very good friends. They've _____ for ages.
5 You look exhausted. Why don't you _____ more?
6 Maria stood in front of the mirror and _____ for over five minutes.
7 Melina's grades are very poor. She really needs to _____ on her schoolwork this term.
8 Alexia and Nick will probably refuse to work together. They don't _____ , I'm afraid.

Structures with question words

2a Match the sentence halves.

1 John didn't know	a how to operate your new tablet.
2 Susan couldn't understand	b what to do when his computer crashed.
3 The instructions explain	c what to say when they asked you about it.
4 The police were not sure	d why her car wouldn't start.
5 I know exactly	e where the robbers they were chasing had gone.
6 I'm surprised you knew	f why you have come to see me.

b Complete the conversations using a structure with a question word and the correct form of the verbs in brackets.

1 A: Do you have a problem?
   B: Yes. I don't know _____ (use) this new coffee machine.
   A: It's easy – let me show you.
2 A: What are you looking for?
   B: I've lost my new pen. I can't remember _____ (put) it.
   A: I think I saw it next to the telephone.
3 A: You look worried.
   B: Yes, I'm not sure _____ (do) about my exam results. They're terrible!
   A: I think you should talk to Professor Thom.
4 A: Are you upset about something?
   B: Yes, I am. Ivan was rude to me this morning. I can't understand _____ (speak) to me like that.
   A: Maybe he was just in a bad mood.

Key word transformations

3 Complete the second sentence so that it has a similar meaning to the first sentence, using the word given. Do not change the word given. You must use between two and five words, including the word given.

1 Was the party enjoyable last night?
   YOURSELF
   Did _____ the party last night?
2 Are you badly hurt?
   HURT
   Have _____ badly?
3 I didn't need any help to repair my bike.
   REPAIRED
   I _____ own.
4 We can't use the new computers.
   KNOW
   We don't _____ the new computers.
5 I can't remember Mike's instructions.
   FORGOTTEN
   I _____ told us to do.
6 Paul didn't know the right person to ask for technical advice.
   SURE
   Paul wasn't _____ for technical advice.
7 Nobody came with me to the cinema yesterday.
   MYSELF
   I _____ to the cinema yesterday.
8 In the interview, I couldn't think of anything to say about my hobbies.
   KNOW
   In the interview, I didn't _____ about my hobbies.
9 Luke and Paul are having a very long conversation.
   TALKING
   Luke and Paul have _____ other for ages.
10 Is this your own drawing or did someone help you?
   YOURSELF
   Did _____ or did someone help you?

Reading (Paper 1 Part 6)

Before you read

1 Read the title and subheading of the article and answer the questions.

1 Does *too clever for their own good* have a positive or negative meaning?
2 What pieces of electronic equipment do you use regularly? Make a list.
3 Which pieces of equipment on your list do you find especially difficult to use? Tick them.

Skimming and scanning

2a Scan the article to find what electronic equipment it mentions. Compare with your list in Exercise 1.

b Skim the article. What is the main message?

1 Companies should pay more attention to what customers want when they design new products.
2 Many new products don't function properly because they are too complicated.

Gapped text

3a Read the first paragraph of the article and sentence G (in gap 1). Which words in sentence G link to the highlighted words in the first paragraph?

1 The emperor = *He*
2 Mozart's new music =
3 sensing this =

b Read the rest of the article carefully and do the task. Note these steps. For each gap, do the following:

• Read the text before and after the gap and think about the type of information which is missing.
• Look for a sentence in the box which talks about this topic area.
• Choose the correct answer by checking the grammatical and lexical links between the base text and the key sentence. Look out for pronouns, synonyms, etc.
• Cross off each sentence as you use it but be prepared to look again when you check your answers.

c Read the article again with your answers to check that it makes sense.

EXPERT STRATEGY

If you are not sure of an answer, move on to the next question. Fill in as many answers as possible, then go back and look again at the questions you could not answer the first time round.

EXPERT LANGUAGE

Find three relative pronouns in sentences A–G.

EXPERT WORD CHECK

*dream up   ethnographers
functions   icons   instruction booklet
software packages   symptom
tense   unknown*

*You are going to read an article about technology. Six sentences have been removed from the article. Choose from the sentences (**A–G**) the one that fits each gap (**1–6**). There is one extra sentence which you do not need to use.*

A   And that's because technological development is led by engineers, whose job involves endlessly dreaming these up and adding them to products.

B   In reality, people say all sorts of things in response to a list of questions but rarely what they really think.

C   And having bought one, which of us actually has the patience to go through the detailed instruction booklet that comes with it?

D   It's probably the same list of essential pieces of equipment, since most of them are difficult to use.

E   There are, however, reasons to be hopeful, if evidence from companies in the airline and motor industries is anything to go by.

F   People who invent useful things are good at solving technical problems but often they are not so good at explaining things to non-technicians.

G   He says he likes it but doesn't seem very convinced – something's not quite right.

IN SEARCH OF SIMPLICITY

Have you ever felt that some pieces of electronic equipment were just too clever for their own good?

In the film *Amadeus*, there's a lovely scene in which Emperor Joseph II of Austria is asked what he thinks of Mozart's music. It's a tense moment for Mozart, the unknown young composer. What does the emperor make of Mozart's new music? [1] [G] 'What do you mean, Sir?' Mozart asks, sensing this. 'Too many notes,' replies the emperor. That feeling, that there is too much to understand all at once, is a familiar one to users of many modern technology products. Think of a software programme with all its detailed menus and screens or e-commerce sites with form after form to fill in or the complicated telephone in your pocket with all those icons and messages. Too many functions, too many screens, too many notes.

The 'too many notes' problem is a symptom of a larger one in technological innovation because a good idea can easily turn into a bad product. For example, think about the products considered to be the great technological successes of the 20th century: the photocopier, fax, video recorder, PC, mobile phone. Now think of the technology that frustrates you as a consumer. [2]

Yet it's not that these products don't function properly. Companies put technical products through all sorts of tests before they come onto the market. Indeed, there's a whole industry sector that specialises in such trials. But what they are testing is whether the product works. What they should be testing is how it works and how it could work better for the consumer. There seems to be some confusion about what makes a good product, as opposed to good technology. People seem to believe that the more a piece of equipment can do, the better it is. Most software packages and most pieces of electronic equipment have too many functions. [3]

In a typical home, for example, there are many devices that tell the time: cookers, radios, answering machines, TVs and hi-fi systems, as well as clocks and wristwatches. Some of them need to know the time to perform their other functions but others don't – the clock was just added for the sake of it.

Another problem is that companies are not good at getting the right information from the people who will use their products. For example, a lot of faith is put in market-research interviews. [4] To understand consumer behaviour, designers of domestic appliances are now getting help from people called ethnographers, who spend their time observing how people actually behave, which can be of great importance in the design of a genuinely useful new product.

A further reason for the failure of technology is the lack of cooperation between the engineers and those who do the marketing in many companies. [5] Marketing staff, therefore, find it hard to follow what engineers are talking about, so tend to put too much emphasis on the familiar aspects of new technology when promoting the products.

Until companies realise that the technology they are producing is not what customers actually want, they'll no doubt continue to persuade us to buy new pieces of equipment which will disappoint us. [6] They have found that when designers and marketing people do talk together at an early stage in the development of a product, then equipment is less likely to end up containing unwanted functions that get in the way.

6 Enjoying yourself

6A Music

Vocabulary development 1

> **COURSEBOOK** pages 78–79

Word formation

1a Use the word given at the end of the sentences to form a word that fits in the gap.

1 Even as a little girl, Madonna's _____ was to become a famous singer. **AMBITIOUS**

2 It wasn't easy to find a _____ for the band's lead singer when she fell ill with a throat infection. **REPLACE**

3 To become a top musician, you need both skill and considerable _____ . **CONFIDENT**

4 World music is steadily gaining in _____ among young people. **POPULAR**

5 Jamie Cullum's _____ to become a great jazz performer was apparent at an early age. **DETERMINE**

6 Many people admired the _____ of singer George Harrison during his final illness. **BRAVE**

7 Björk is well known for her _____ and the originality of her songs. **CREATE**

8 Some great performers often experience feelings of _____ and depression in their personal lives. **LONELY**

b Write the nouns from Exercise 1a in the correct column. Then add two more nouns you know to each column.

-ence	-ity	-ion	-ment	-ness	-ery

Pronunciation

2a 🎧 09 Listen and mark the stress on the words. The first one has been done for you.

1 am<u>bi</u>tion, determination, satisfaction, fascination

2 creativity, popularity, dependability, adaptability

b Choose the correct answer to complete the pronunciation rule.

When a word ends in -tion or -ity, we stress:

A the suffix.

B the second syllable.

C the syllable before the suffix.

Prepositional phrases

3 Choose the correct answers.

1 A year ago, our folk rock group, Train, was *in / under* danger of splitting up.

2 The group's lead guitarist and vocalist, Jack, was *in / at* hospital for over six months.

3 Performing without Jack was *away from / out of* the question.

4 Quite *by / at* chance, we heard of another musician who could replace him.

5 We contacted Luca *at / by* email, asking him if he would like to join the group.

6 Luca's agent telephoned *on / in* his behalf and suggested we organise a jam session.

7 Luca turned out to be a brilliant musician and already knew a lot of our songs *at / by* heart.

8 Two months later, the new band's first performance *in / at* public was a huge success.

Verb + noun collocations

4a Complete the text below with the words in the box.

audition   debut   impact   launch   offer
opportunity   performance   records   role   scholarship

b Mark the verb which is used with each noun you used in Exercise 4a. The first one has been done for you.

J. LO!

Jennifer Lopez was born in 1969 in New York. Having decided at an early age to become a musical theatre actress, she <u>gave</u> her first **(1)** _____ when she was just 16. Then, at 17, she won a(n) **(2)** _____ to a well-known Manhattan dance school.

In 1990 Jennifer went for a(n) **(3)** _____ for a minor part in the TV series *In Living Colour* and was successful. She was then given the **(4)** _____ to appear as a backup dancer in Janet Jackson's video *That's the Way Love Goes*. Five years later, Jennifer Lopez made her big screen **(5)** _____ in *The Money Train* but it was the film *Selena*, in which she played the leading **(6)** _____ , that turned her into a superstar.

In 1999 Jennifer took up a(n) **(7)** _____ from a record company and moved into music. She's made a huge **(8)** _____ on the music scene since then. With record sales of over 75 million, she's considered one of the most influential Hispanic performers in the USA.

Is that all? Well, Jennifer Lopez also owns a clothing line (*J.Lo*) and the **(9)** _____ of her own perfume, *Glow by J.Lo*, saw her break all **(10)** _____ in sales.

Key word transformations

5 Complete the second sentence so that it has a similar meaning to the first sentence, using the word given. Do not change the word given. You must use between two and five words, including the word given.

1 Joanna is now at the top of her profession.
RISEN
Joanna _____ the top of her profession.

2 The lead dancer performed exceptionally well this evening.
GAVE
The lead dancer _____ this evening.

3 Gary is obviously the best singer in the group.
STANDS
Gary _____ the best singer in the group.

4 When on tour, musicians often miss their home.
FEEL
Many musicians tend to _____ when they're on tour.

5 Everyone was surprised at how popular the band's first album was.
BY
Everyone was surprised _____ of the band's first album.

6 Jennifer didn't accept the role in the new musical.
DOWN
Jennifer _____ the role in the new musical.

7 The lead vocalist gets impatient very easily when she's rehearsing a new song.
LACKS
The lead vocalist _____ when she's rehearsing a new song.

8 In April the band left London to begin their world tour.
SET
The band's world tour began when they _____ London in April.

9 Lucas has always been full of ambition.
VERY
Lucas has always _____ person.

10 Despite rumours, the bass guitarist does not intend to leave the band.
HAS
Despite rumours, the bass guitarist _____ the band.

Language development 1

➤ COURSEBOOK pages 80–81, EXPERT GRAMMAR pages 190–191

Defining and non-defining relative clauses

1a Decide if the sentences below contain *defining* (D) or *non-defining* (ND) relative clauses. Then add commas where necessary.

1 The Rolling Stones, who were one of the most popular groups of the 1960s, still give live concerts today. ND

2 We're taking the plane that leaves Heathrow at six o'clock. _____

3 Jennifer Lopez's perfume which was called *Glow* quickly became the number one perfume in over nine countries. _____

4 Look! The pianist who played at the concert last night is sitting over there! _____

5 Where are the tickets for *Cats* that I bought this morning? _____

6 Jennifer Lopez whose success as a singer has been phenomenal has no plans yet to stop acting. _____

7 I'll arrange an interview with someone who can help you. _____

8 The song which we enjoyed most at the Eurovision Song Contest was the Hungarian one. _____

b Find two sentences in Exercise 1a where the relative pronoun can be omitted and cross it out.

2 Rewrite the article, adding the missing information (a–h) in the gaps. Use relative clauses and make any changes necessary.

Karaoke, whose popularity has spread throughout the world in recent years, originated in Japan.

Karaoke (1) _____ originated in Japan. *Kara* is an abbreviation of the word (2) _____ and *oke* is short for *okesutura*, or orchestra. Usually, a recorded song consists of both vocals and a musical accompaniment. However, recordings of songs (3) _____ are called *karaoke*.

For almost 30 years Japanese people (4) _____ have been picking up microphones and singing karaoke. Family karaoke sets (5) _____ are extremely popular in Japan. Apparently, they also help children (6) _____ to learn to read more quickly.

In Japan (7) _____ noise can be a problem. So special places for people (8) _____ started to appear in the towns and the countryside. The first 'karaoke box' appeared in a rice field near Kansai as early as 1984.

a They wanted to sing karaoke.
b Houses and flats are often built very close together there.
c They consist only of the accompaniment.
d They display the words and scenes of a song on a monitor.
e Its popularity has spread throughout the world in recent years.
f They have reading problems.
g It means 'empty' in Japanese (*karappo*).
h They have always enjoyed singing after work and at parties.

Reduced relative clauses

3a Rewrite the sentences to make them shorter, using present or past participles.

1 The people who live in the flat above mine are actors.
   The people living in the flat above mine are actors.

2 The musical, which starred the members of a pop band, was a huge success at the box office.
   _____

3 The singer, who appears first at the festival, will record her next album in London.
   _____

4 One day I saw a busker who played four instruments at the same time.
   _____

5 The band's second album, which featured songs written by the drummer, was fantastic.
   _____

6 The vocalist, who sang in Spanish for the first time, received a standing ovation.
   _____

b Read the extracts from two student articles and mark the relative clauses which can be shortened. Then rewrite these sentences.

A

The rock concert, which was held last night in the college hall, was a great success. I'm sure everyone who went last night will not forget it for a long time. During the performance, Jeff Stone, who was constantly cheered and applauded by his fans, amazed the audience by his skill as a musician. He played a number of old favourites, which included *Red Rose* and *Road to Heaven*, and sang songs from the band's latest album. At one point, the people who were sitting in the front seats jumped up and started to dance in the aisles.

B

The classical concert on 6 April was disappointing. Beethoven's seventh symphony, which was performed by the University Orchestra, lacked passion. In fact, the musicians who were playing in the strings section of the orchestra appeared to be positively bored. The conductor, James Oliver, who has led the orchestra, surprised the audience by his unorthodox interpretation of the symphony.

Relative clauses and prepositions

4 Join each sentence pair in two ways: formal and informal. Use relative clauses.

1 That's the man. I bought the tickets from him.
   Formal: *That's the man from whom I bought the tickets.*
   Informal: *That's the man I bought the tickets from.*

2 That's the person. I spoke to her on the phone earlier.
   Formal: _____
   Informal: _____

3 Bill is the sound technician. We work for him.
   Formal: _____
   Informal: _____

4 They are redecorating the hall. The concert will take place in it.
   Formal: _____
   Informal: _____

5 Is this the CD? You recorded the album on it.
   Formal: _____
   Informal: _____

6 Are these the tickets? We paid so much money for them.
   Formal: _____
   Informal: _____

Exam practice: Open cloze

(Paper 1 Part 2)

5 Do the task.

*For questions **1–8**, read the text below and think of the word which best fits each gap. Use only **one** word in each gap. There is an example at the beginning (**0**).*

An opera director's upbringing

My mother loved music and she influenced me (0) _in_ my choice of career. She had a number (1) _____ records which I played a lot from quite (2) _____ early age. These included classical recordings as (3) _____ as traditional folk music and the current pop songs. I was lucky because I discovered all kinds of music and my mother never gave me the impression that one sort was better (4) _____ another. I just learnt to love each type of music for (5) _____ it was. The thing which really influenced my future career, (6) _____ , was the public lending library near our home. Before the days of downloadable books, everyone in the UK used public libraries. Our local one had a record collection (7) _____ addition to books. I would borrow whole operas which came in boxed sets, complete (8) _____ a booklet containing all the words and the musical score.

➤ **HELP**

1 The missing word is a preposition.
2 You need to use an article here.
6 Look at the punctuation. What type of word goes here?

EXPERT LANGUAGE

Find an example of a reduced relative clause in the text.

EXPERT WORD CHECK

boxed sets   classical   folk   lending library   musical score

Writing (Paper 2 Part 2: Review)

▶ **COURSEBOOK** pages 82–83, **EXPERT WRITING** page 205

EXAM STRATEGY
In Paper 2, Writing, Part 2, you may have to write a review of something you have experienced. For example, it could be a review of a film that you have seen or a book you have read. Make your review as interesting as you can and address your readers directly. It is very important to express your personal opinion of what you experienced.

Understand the task

1 Read the writing task and answer the questions.
   1 Where will the review appear? Who will read it?
   2 What is the aim of the review?
   3 What MUST you include?
   4 What style will you use?

You have seen this advertisement in a student magazine.

Reviews needed!

Could you write us a review of a concert you went to recently? Pop, rock, folk, classical – it doesn't matter! Write about the concert, including information about who the musicians were and what they played. Say whether the concert was a success or not.

The best reviews will be published in this magazine next month.

*Write your **review** in 140–190 words in an appropriate style.*

Compare two sample answers

2 Look at the features of a good review. Read the two reviews and decide which features they have. Which review is better?

A good review:

1 has an eye-catching title.

2 has an interesting opening paragraph, which tells the reader what exactly is being reviewed.

3 is divided into paragraphs, each focusing on one aspect of the subject of the review.

4 is written in an appropriate style and involves the reader by addressing him/her directly.

5 describes clearly what the writer experienced, including important details.

6 gives the reader a clear impression of the personal opinion (good or bad) of the writer.

7 uses varied and interesting language.

8 finishes with a strong sentence, which summarises what has been said.

Correct two sample answers

3a Correct the errors the teacher has identified in each review. (See Unit 1, page 9 for a key to the correction symbols.)

b Write your own review.

Review 1
The Flaming Lips don't disappoint their British fans

It was obvious from the start that the Flaming Lips concert at the Brighton Centre was going to be different. When Wayne Coyle floated over the heads of the audience inside a huge plastic bubble, everyone knew this is ^T^ a night to remember.

The Flaming Lips are putting ^T^ on shows like this since the band was formed in 1983 in Oklahoma. They love to surprise their fans with special effects and surrealistic costumes. Wayne Coyle, the band's charismatic vocalist, loves to give people a good time.

In Brighton, the Flaming Lips played that old favourite *Yoshimi Battles the Pink Robots*, as well as *The Yeah Yeah Yeah Song*. The audience danced and sang along with the band, going wild with excitement when the Flaming Lips began to play *Mr Ambulance Man*.

The concert was a huge success. When I left, it seemed that the world had suddenly become more interesting – and more fun. If you love rock music, go and see them. They won't be in the UK for long!

[178 words]

Review 2

I like music and I love going to concerts. Last month I went to two concerts.

A band I really like is called Blue Dream. You have heard ^Gr^ of them? They are an exciting band from the USA. Blue Dream play back-to-basics blues. They have a hugely ^Ww^ number of rock fans from all over the world. The band consists of Tom and Sylvie Gray, and they are using ^T^ just guitar and drums to accompany the most ^Gr^ their songs. They suddenly became famous two years ago. Before that, nobody knew anything about them. Tom and Sylvie always wear blue and black clothes when they perform. Three of the best Blue Dream songs were recently rewritten for performance with an orchestra. I read at ^Ww^ a student magazine that a ballet company is going to dance to these songs at an opera house. I'm wondering ^T^ what the audience will think. They normally go and see *Swan Lake*! I would like to go to that concert.

[162 words]

Listening (Paper 3 Part 4)

Before you listen

1a Read the listening task. Mark the key words and think about what the speaker will be talking about.

b What do you think the subject and purpose of the TV programme was?

Multiple choice

2a 🎧 10 Listen once and note the answer to each question as you listen. Then choose the best answer (A, B or C). (The questions follow the order of the listening.)

b 🎧 10 Listen again and check your answers. Make sure the options you did not choose are not possible.

c Was your prediction in Exercise 1b correct?

EXPERT STRATEGY

Read the questions and options before you listen and mark the key words.

➤ HELP

2 Listen to what Peter says after the words *to be honest*; it tells you his opinion.

3 Listen for when Peter says, 'But the worst bit was.' What is he talking about?

4 Listen to what Peter says about the artists.

EXPERT LANGUAGE

Look at the adjectives in the options. Which express
1 positive ideas?
2 negative ideas?

EXPERT WORD CHECK

*abstract art   decorator   gallery
panel of experts   reduced to tears
volunteer   wheelchair*

You will hear an interview with Peter Harris, a painter and decorator who took part in a television programme in which he learnt to be an artist. For questions 1–7, choose the best answer (A, B or C).

1 How did Peter become involved in the television programme?
   A   His employer told him about it.
   B   A television company approached him.
   C   Some friends suggested it to him.

2 How did Peter feel when he went to the local art gallery?
   A   foolish in front of his friends
   B   unimpressed by the quality of the things he saw
   C   confident that he'd be able to produce some abstract art

3 What did Peter find most difficult about his training?
   A   There was no fixed programme.
   B   His lessons were filmed for television.
   C   He had to comment on it afterwards.

4 What did Peter discover about abstract art?
   A   It's not so serious as people think.
   B   Some of it is actually not very good.
   C   It's not meant to be easy to understand.

5 How did Peter feel when he realised he'd painted a wheelchair?
   A   It affected him quite deeply.
   B   He became angry with himself.
   C   The experience was rather frightening.

6 How did Peter feel about the final programme in the series?
   A   surprised to have fooled the experts
   B   satisfied with what he had achieved
   C   disappointed not to have done better

7 What does Peter say about selling his paintings?
   A   He dislikes some of the buyers.
   B   Other painters were jealous of him.
   C   His family doesn't approve of the idea.

Vocabulary: Idiomatic expressions

3 🎧 10 Listen again and complete the phrases.
   1 … and that's when I realised it was _____ .
   2 To be honest, I thought it was all _____ .
   3 But the worst _____ was having to film what's called a video diary.
   4 The artist wants you to think, you know, which can be _____ !
   5 It reduced me _____ .
   6 … three out of four experts failed _____ which paintings were mine.

Vocabulary development 2

➤ **COURSEBOOK** pages 84–85

> **EXPERT STRATEGY**
>
> In Paper 4, Speaking, Part 2, you may be asked to compare two photographs showing different types of art or music and say which you prefer. It is important to use relevant vocabulary and to say as much as you can about the topic. You won't make a good impression if you cannot speak for one minute.

Talking about the arts

1 Read the descriptions. What kind of art is each person describing? Complete the sentences with the words and phrases in the box. Then mark the words which helped you to decide. There are two extra words which you do not need to use.

art exhibition   ballet   film   musical   play
street performance   TV show

1 'The first picture was taken at a(n) _____ .
   I can see a lot of paintings on the walls and in the middle of the room there are some statues as well. Some people are looking at the works of art on display. The man in the foreground looks very serious and he seems to be writing things in a notebook. Maybe he is an art critic or something like that.'

2 'In this picture I can see some people who are doing some kind of _____ . They are in the town square, I think. They are wearing very colourful clothes. One of them is playing a violin and the woman in the foreground looks as if she is reading something aloud – or perhaps she is singing, I don't know. There is a hat on the ground in front of them, where people are putting money.'

3 'This photo shows a(n) _____ but it's strange because the photo wasn't taken in a theatre. The actors are performing in a big old building – it's a kind of warehouse, I think. There is no stage and the lighting is not very good. The audience is really big though and they seem to be having a good time.'

4 'These two photos both show different kinds of _____ . In the first photo there are some people in a TV studio chatting to the presenter about something – maybe politics or current affairs. They look very serious! In the other photo I can see two teams in the studio, so it's probably a quiz show. I hate quiz shows – usually, I change the channel!'

5 'Personally, I would prefer to see the _____ , especially if the director is well known and there are some big names in the cast. I do go to the theatre now and then but I prefer the cinema. When the plot is exciting, you just forget all your problems.'

Definitions

2 Find words in the word square that match the definitions below.

C	O	M	P	O	S	E	R
A	E	E	L	M	I	V	E
S	O	Q	C	W	S	N	V
T	S	I	H	N	T	B	I
V	C	L	A	P	A	H	E
O	R	M	P	U	G	P	W
D	I	E	T	C	E	L	X
U	P	B	E	P	R	O	S
P	T	E	R	F	O	T	T

1 the names of all the actors in a film or play _____
2 the words of a film an actor has to learn _____
3 the writer of a piece of classical music _____
4 an article written by a critic, giving his/her opinion of a film or play _____
5 the story of a film or novel _____
6 the audience do this to show they have enjoyed a performance _____
7 a book is divided into a number of these _____
8 a raised platform in a theatre where plays are performed _____

Adjective + noun collocations

3a Match the adjectives (1–8) with the nouns they collocate with (a–h). Each noun must collocate with all the nouns in a set.

1 detective/romantic/historical   a plot
2 talented/young/eccentric   b statue
3 live/open-air/free   c painting
4 ethnic/commercial/abstract   d novel
5 oil/famous/valuable   e concert
6 huge/marble/bronze   f soap opera
7 complicated/clever/gripping   g art
8 Brazilian/popular/low-budget   h artist

b Complete the sentences with adjectives from Exercise 3a.

1 I read _____ novels because I like trying to guess who the murderer is.
2 The plot of his last novel was so _____ that I got really confused.
3 I don't know why soap operas are so _____ in my country. They're always dubbed as well!
4 I'm not keen on _____ art because it doesn't represent the real world.
5 The state should encourage _____ young artists.
6 I go to _____ rock concerts in the summer.
7 I prefer watercolours to _____ paintings.

Exam practice: Multiple-choice cloze (Paper 1 Part 1)

4 Do the task.

For questions 1–8, read the text below and decide which answer (A, B, C or D) best fits each gap. There is an example at the beginning (0).

Art online

At one (0) _A_ , only the largest, most powerful companies had real works of art hanging in their boardrooms. These were usually expensive paintings by well-known artists whose work smaller companies couldn't (1) _____ . If a smaller company wanted to (2) _____ in a more modest work of art, this could (3) _____ up a lot of staff time as it involved visits to art galleries and somebody making a choice in the (4) _____ that their colleagues would like it. But things have changed because now art has (5) _____ online. These days there are websites to help companies find the right picture or piece of sculpture. Most employees who buy art for their workplaces don't know a great (6) _____ about it. So one of the main aims of the website is to (7) _____ them in their choice. Details of the type of artwork they want and their budget are entered into a search engine, and a selection of art (8) _____ up on screen for all to see.

0	A	time	B	day	C	date	D	age
1	A	assist	B	appeal	C	achieve	D	afford
2	A	bargain	B	purchase	C	invest	D	profit
3	A	keep	B	take	C	hold	D	run
4	A	hope	B	trust	C	aim	D	wish
5	A	joined	B	gained	C	turned	D	gone
6	A	load	B	deal	C	lot	D	extent
7	A	show	B	teach	C	guide	D	learn
8	A	comes	B	brings	C	bears	D	lays

EXPERT STRATEGY

Look at the four options and decide which one goes with the words before and after the gap.

➤ **HELP**

1 The option you need is related to money.
3 Which word completes the phrasal verb meaning 'to use'?
7 Look at the words after the gap – only one of the options can fit with them.

EXPERT LANGUAGE

Which answer is part of a common determiner?

EXPERT WORD CHECK

boardrooms   budget   sculpture   search engine   staff time workplaces

Language development 2

➤ **COURSEBOOK** page 88

Key word transformations

1 Complete the second sentence so that it has a similar meaning to the first sentence, using the word given. Do not change the word given. You must use between two and five words, including the word given.

1 Opera does not interest Tania.
INTERESTED
Tania _____ opera.

2 He has the ability to become a great musician.
CAPABLE
He _____ a great musician.

3 The Institute of Art and the College of Art are not connected.
CONNECTION
There _____ the Institute of Art and the College of Art.

4 Whose job is it to choose the actors' costumes?
RESPONSIBLE
Who _____ the actors' costumes?

5 We need to solve this problem quickly.
SOLUTION
We need to find _____ this problem.

6 Charles never forgets people's names.
GOOD
Charles is very _____ people's names.

7 You cannot compare these two artists.
COMPARISON
There _____ these two artists.

8 The number of students at the college suddenly increased.
INCREASE
There was _____ the number of students at the college.

9 I find it very difficult to understand the work of that artist.
DIFFICULTY
I have great _____ the work of that artist.

10 I am sure it was a disappointment to you that you missed the concert.
DISAPPOINTED
I'm sure you _____ the concert.

be / get used to + -ing

TV magician and street entertainer David Blaine once spent two and a half days in a block of ice. On another occasion, he lived for 44 days without food in an acrylic glass pod in London.

2a Match the sentence halves to make sentences about David Blaine's life.

1 When David Blaine was a child, he
2 When he was only 19, his mother died. David couldn't
3 He moved to Manhattan, where he
4 In David Blaine's TV show *Street Magic*, he
5 Before his 'ice performance', he trained hard so that his body
6 Although most magicians still wear formal evening clothes when they perform, David Blaine
7 Although he eats meat, he

a usually prefers to eat fish.
b used to perform his tricks for ordinary people on the pavements of Manhattan.
c used to live with his mother in a very poor part of New York.
d used to do card tricks for celebrities in nightclubs.
e usually wears a simple jacket and T-shirt.
f get used to living on his own afterwards.
g would get used to being in a very cold environment.

b Find and correct the mistakes with *used to* in the sentences.

1 Since David Blaine is now a celebrity, he is used to be approached by people on the street in the USA.
2 He stopped appearing in public with his friend Leonardo DiCaprio because he couldn't to get used to the way people always called him 'Leo's friend'.
3 David Blaine is used to be spending a lot of time preparing for his difficult and often dangerous feats.
4 He once tried to hold his breath underwater for longer than the world record of 8 minutes 58 seconds. In training for this, he had to getting used to slowing down his heartbeat so that his body used less oxygen.
5 Although it was very unpleasant at first, David Blaine is now use to being attacked in the press by other illusionists and entertainers.

Exam practice: Open cloze
(Paper 1 Part 2)

3 Do the task.

For questions 1–8, read the text below and think of the word which best fits each gap. Use only one word in each gap. There is an example at the beginning (0).

THE APPEAL OF ART

I was never very interested (0) _in_ art as a teenager. The famous paintings by classical artists of the past were obviously quite good but the subject matter didn't appeal (1) _____ me. In our local art gallery, (2) _____ instance, they had lots of portraits of people looking very stiff and formal. I'd never heard of most of these people, so they didn't really hold (3) _____ attention.
There was also one room full of modern art. We used to laugh at the paintings in there because they seemed (4) _____ be things any child could do. We couldn't make any sense of them at (5) _____ . So when I started going out with a girl (6) _____ was studying at art college, it came as quite a pleasant surprise (7) _____ she told me that she didn't like the stuff in our art gallery either. She made sculptures out (8) _____ everyday objects like old bicycle frames and saucepan lids. Now this may sound strange, but at that point art suddenly started to mean something to me!

EXPERT STRATEGY

Remember to write only one word in each gap.

➤ HELP

1 Which preposition always comes after *appeal*?
3 Look back in the sentence to see which personal pronoun is needed here.
8 Look back at the verb in the sentence – this word is linked to it.

EXPERT LANGUAGE

Which answer is a relative pronoun?

EXPERT WORD CHECK

*bicycle frames   saucepan lids   stiff and formal
subject matter*

Reading (Paper 1 Part 5)

Before you read 1 Read the instructions for the reading task and the title of the article. Think about what the article might be about.

Skimming 2 Skim the text. Answer these questions, which focus on the main idea of each paragraph.

Paragraph 1: What is unusual about the museum described in the article?
Paragraph 2: How has the museum and the local area changed?
Paragraph 3: What happened two years ago and why?
Paragraph 4: What is the aim of the evening events at the museum?
Paragraph 5: What was the result of introducing these events?

Multiple choice 3 Do the task. Follow these steps.

- Read the questions. Don't look at the options yet.
- Find the place in the text where the information is contained. Find your own answer to each question and mark the relevant piece of text.
- Now read the options and choose the one closest to your answer.
- Read the piece of text carefully to check that your answer is right and that the other options are definitely wrong. Look for phrases in the text and in the option that express the same idea.

EXPERT STRATEGY

Only one of the four options will match the question exactly. Read carefully to know which one it is.

➤ HELP

1 Bryan says, 'I have to be there.' What is he referring to?
3 The answer comes in the next sentence.
5 Find the place where he says, 'The great thing for me'.

EXPERT LANGUAGE

Find an example of an adjective + preposition collocation in the first paragraph.

EXPERT WORD CHECK

*free of charge   guidebooks
handcuffed   hide-and-seek
puppet show   reggae   toughest*

You are going to read a newspaper article about a museum in New York. For questions 1–6, choose the answer (A, B, C or D) which you think fits best according to the text.

1 What has attracted the man called Bryan to the museum this evening?
   A the chance to meet new people
   B the type of music being played
   C the range of entertainment on offer
   D the fact that it costs nothing to get in

2 In the past the museum attracted few visitors because of
   A the poor quality of the exhibitions it put on.
   B the negative way it was described in reviews.
   C the part of the city where it was located.
   D the limited space it had for exhibitions.

3 What does *them* in line 27 refer to?
   A museums
   B guidebooks
   C visitors
   D exhibitions

4 What did Arnold Lehman decide to do when he became director of the museum?
   A concentrate on art from Brooklyn
   B change the type of things exhibited
   C improve the appearance of the building
   D get local people interested in the museum

5 What has pleased Arnold Lehman most about 'First Saturdays'?
   A Young people are showing an interest in art.
   B Other museums are now trying to copy the idea.
   C The idea has made money for the museum.
   D The music and dancing has been particularly popular.

6 In the last paragraph, the writer shows that she
   A is unsure about the real value of 'First Saturdays'.
   B admires what the museum has managed to do.
   C doubts that the scheme will have long-term success.
   D is surprised by the way visitors have reacted to the art.

It is Saturday night at the Brooklyn Museum of Art in New York, a large important-looking 19th-century building. Since six o'clock, entry to the museum has been free of charge. People are shouting in the galleries but the guards, who seem to be unusually relaxed, take no notice. On the ground floor, in the galleries devoted to African art, children are playing hide-and-seek while their parents sip beer from plastic cups. Some teenage girls wander by, leaving a trail of perfume, and head through the sculpture exhibition to a temporary dance floor where a DJ is playing reggae music. Watching the scene is Bryan, a young teacher from a local school. What brings him out tonight? 'I'm here for the reggae, of course,' he says. 'When I heard they were playing that, I thought, "I have to be there," and obviously, a lot of people feel the same way.' Besides the DJ, the museum has laid on gallery talks, a Martin Scorsese film, a puppet show and a samba band.

The Brooklyn Museum of Art wasn't always so trendy. For decades, it put on excellent exhibitions that few came to see. Guidebooks described the enormous building as 'an undiscovered treat'. Had it been over in the city's fashionable Upper East Side, of course, the museum would have been packing them in. Even when they put on dull exhibitions, New York's top museums can count on a steady stream of visitors – mostly tourists. But Brooklyn, one of New York's toughest districts, isn't on the standard tourist route. When the museum was built, it was in a wealthy suburb but these days the surrounding streets are home to recent immigrants – mostly poor folk from the Caribbean.

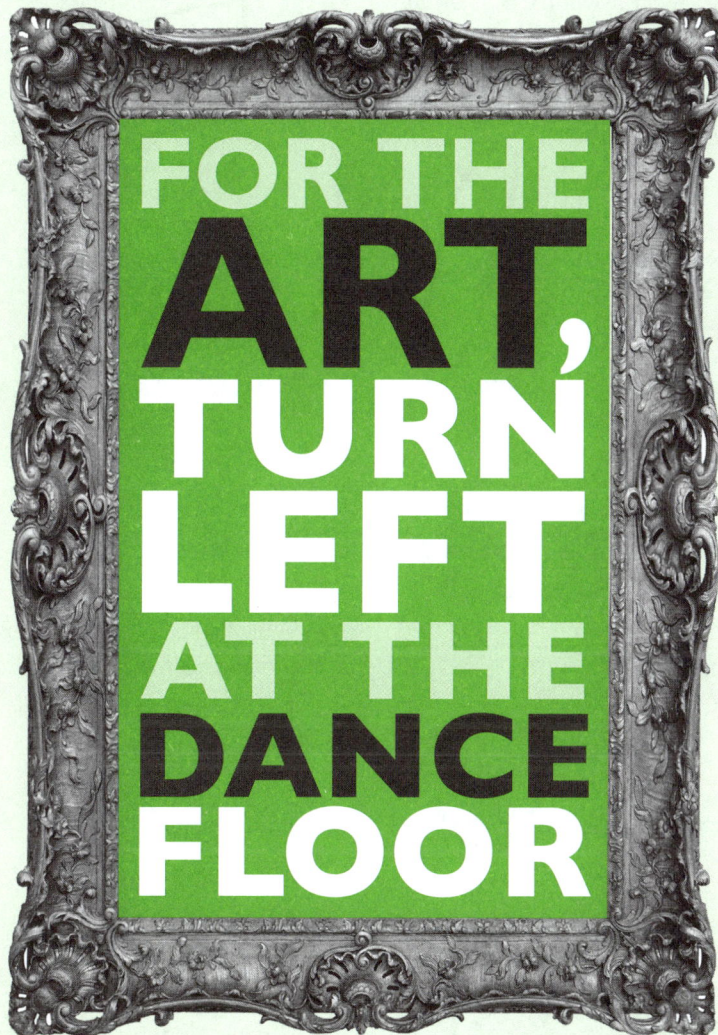

Two years ago, in an effort to revive itself, the museum appointed a new director, Arnold Lehman, who was born in Brooklyn. Lehman was convinced that the museum should forget about trying to attract visitors from the other side of town and try to appeal instead to people from the surrounding area. 'The neighbourhood's changed,' he explains, 'but this is where the museum is and we can't – and won't – pretend we're somewhere else.'

The free evening events, called 'First Saturdays', are Lehman's way of reaching out to people. They are certainly popular: the crush of visitors has forced the museum to move the dance floor from the entrance hall to the car park. Lehman is delighted with the result: 'It's remarkable to hear people say, "I live four blocks away and I've never been in this building before". The great thing for me is when you see teenage boys looking at art in the galleries without being handcuffed to their parents,' he says. What's more, the annual number of visitors to the museum has roughly doubled – from 250,000 to half a million – since the scheme was introduced. Similar institutions across the country are now calling, wanting to know how much it costs 'to throw a good party'. The answer, incidentally, is about $25,000 per event. 'And worth every dime,' says Lehman.

The real achievement of 'First Saturdays' is both more significant and more profound than the increased visitor numbers suggest. Most people visit art museums because they want to have a special 'artistic' experience. The Brooklyn Museum of Art has introduced thousands of ordinary people to the idea that museum-going can be a perfectly normal part of their lives.

FOR THE ART, TURN LEFT AT THE DANCE FLOOR

Vocabulary development 1

> COURSEBOOK pages 92–93

Food quiz

1 Do the quiz. Choose the correct answer (A, B, C or D).

What do you know about food?

1 What word is used to describe rubbing cheese, fruit, etc. against a rough surface in order to break it into small pieces?

A *slice*   B *chop*   C *grate*   D *shred*

2 What word is used to mean that food is cooked slowly in water that is gently boiling?

A *roast*   C *bake*
B *simmer*   D *fry*

3 What do you add to food when a recipe tells you to season it?

A salt and pepper   C tomato ketchup
B olive oil   D vinegar

4 If you eat a *dessert* after your main course, you eat something

A sweet.   C sour.
B bitter.   D spicy.

5 When you are eating food, what should you do before you swallow it?

A digest it
B sip it carefully
C gobble it up
D chew it well

6 Which of these kinds of food is rich in vitamin C?

A meat and poultry
B rice and pasta
C fruit and vegetables
D oil, butter and margarine

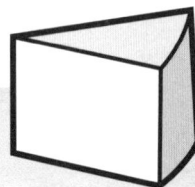

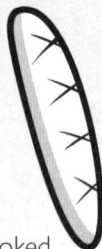

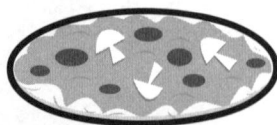

7 Why would you say that you need to *count your calories*?

A You have to heat the oven to a certain temperature.
B You need to calculate the weight of some meat.
C You are on a diet.
D You have to boil an egg.

8 Which word is used to describe old bread which has become hard?

A *rancid*   C *rotten*
B *mouldy*   D *stale*

9 Which spice is used to make Indian and Mexican food hot?

A cinnamon   C nutmeg
B chilli   D saffron

10 What would someone mean if they said that some meat had *gone off*?

A It is undercooked.
B It is overcooked.
C It has just been taken out of the oven.
D It is bad and cannot be eaten.

11 What is the substance which makes bread rise called?

A yeast   B starch   C calcium   D flour

12 Which ingredients might you find in a fresh salad?

A beef, pork or chicken
B lettuce, cucumber and tomatoes
C lentils or beans
D rice or noodles

Phrasal verbs and verb phrases

2a Match the verbs (1–8) with the phrases (a–h).

1 come across	a something you don't want
2 find a way round	b something different
3 come up with	c weight
4 run	d something unexpectedly
5 get rid of	e the amount of food you eat
6 turn to	f a solution or idea
7 cut down on	g a business
8 put on	h a problem or difficulty

b Two students are discussing the value of fast food. Complete the conversation with the correct form of the verbs in Exercise 2a.

Yvonne: I don't think fast food is good for you at all. I'm sure that if we (1) _____ fast-food restaurants, we'd be much healthier. Nobody would miss them.

Pablo: I don't agree, Yvonne. My father (2) _____ a small fast-food restaurant and people go there every day to eat. Teenagers meet their friends there for lunch.

Yvonne: Exactly. They're in fashion at the moment. People will (3) _____ something else when they think that burger restaurants are not cool places to be anymore. Maybe salad bars.

Pablo: No. I think that fast food restaurants are here to stay. Someone will have to (4) _____ a really brilliant idea if they want young people to stop eating hamburgers. Anyway, I don't see why they are so bad.

Yvonne: They're bad for you because they don't contain healthy ingredients. I (5) _____ an article in a magazine the other day which said that they only put poor-quality meat in hamburgers. Also, if you eat a lot of junk food, you (6) _____ a lot of weight. It's a big problem today. Researchers are trying to (7) _____ it by going to schools and encouraging children to (8) _____ the amount of fast food they eat.

Exam practice: Multiple-choice cloze (Paper 1 Part 1)

3 Do the task.

*For questions **1–8**, read the text below and decide which answer (**A**, **B**, **C** or **D**) best fits each gap. There is an example at the beginning (**0**).*

Tomatoes: the perfect fruit

High in the Andes mountains of modern-day Peru, the local inhabitants have been cultivating and eating tomatoes since prehistoric (0) __C__ but the food has only become popular in the rest of the world (1) _____ recently. These days the bright red fruit (2) _____ an important role in the cooking of many cultures and is a key ingredient in many types of fast food, providing both taste and colour to dishes that (3) _____ would be rather ordinary.

The tomato (4) _____ to the nightshade family of plants, many members of which are poisonous. When they were first (5) _____ into North America, therefore, tomatoes were viewed with (6) _____ and people tended to use them as table decorations (7) _____ than as food. In Europe the tomato was first grown in Italy in 1555, although it wasn't (8) _____ with pasta until much later. These days, far from being harmful, tomatoes are known to contain substances which are good for our health.

	A	B	C	D
0	A ages	B periods	C times	D dates
1	A effectively	B relatively	C apparently	D eventually
2	A forms	B meets	C does	D plays
3	A nonetheless	B instead	C otherwise	D meanwhile
4	A admits	B fits	C possesses	D belongs
5	A imported	B arrived	C appeared	D presented
6	A doubt	B threat	C suspicion	D danger
7	A except	B better	C apart	D rather
8	A combined	B joined	C added	D accompanied

EXPERT STRATEGY

Keep reading the words before and after the gap when choosing your answer.

EXPERT LANGUAGE

Find an example of the present perfect continuous in the text.

EXPERT WORD CHECK

ingredient   inhabitants   poisonous   prehistoric   substances

Language development 1

→ **COURSEBOOK** pages 94–95, **EXPERT GRAMMAR** pages 191–193

Permission, necessity, advice and recommendations

1a Rewrite the sentences using the correct form of *can*, *must*, *have to*, *should* and *ought to*.

1 It's a good idea to eat lots of fresh fruit and vegetables.
   You ought to eat lots of fresh fruit and vegetables.
2 You are allowed to take your own wine to that restaurant.
3 It's not a good idea to eat junk food every day.
4 The table is reserved so we aren't allowed to sit here.
5 It isn't necessary for Alice to come with us if she doesn't want to.
6 I think you had better leave your coat in the cloakroom.
7 Is it necessary for us to book a table at that restaurant?
8 It's advisable not to eat too much before going to bed.
9 Parking your car outside the restaurant is prohibited.
10 Are we permitted to sit at any table we want?

b Complete the text. Use only one word in each gap. More than one answer may be possible.

I saw Dr Ingrims last week and he said that I **(1)** _____ to lose at least ten kilos. Since then, I've been on a strict diet. I **(2)** _____ eat chicken and fish in small amounts but I am not **(3)** _____ to eat red meat at all. He also told me that I **(4)** _____ avoid cheese, although it didn't matter if I ate a little now and then. I suppose I had **(5)** _____ get used to living on fresh salads, hadn't I? Actually, I forgot my diet yesterday and ordered a Chinese takeaway. I know that I **(6)** _____ not have eaten takeaway food but I felt I **(7)** _____ to eat something I really liked. Perhaps I needn't **(8)** _____ felt so guilty – it was a chicken dish, after all – but I think I **(9)** _____ to have been a bit more sensible. From now on, it's just lettuce and carrots!

Key word transformations

2 Complete the second sentence so that it has a similar meaning to the first sentence, using the word given. Do not change the word given. Use between two and five words, including the word given.

1 It wasn't necessary for us to take a taxi.
   HAVE
   We _____ a taxi.
2 You can't smoke in the non-smoking area.
   ALLOWED
   You _____ in the non-smoking area.
3 You really should wear a warmer coat.
   BETTER
   You _____ a warmer coat.
4 It's very important to remember to tip the waiter.
   NOT
   You _____ to tip the waiter.
5 You are under no obligation to accept his offer.
   HAVE
   You _____ his offer.
6 It was a mistake going to that restaurant last night.
   SHOULD
   We _____ to that restaurant last night.
7 They made me book the table a week in advance.
   HAD
   I _____ the table a week in advance.
8 Don't go to that part of town after dark!
   MUST
   You _____ to that part of town after dark!

Exam practice: Open cloze
(Paper 1 Part 2)

3 Do the task.

*For questions 1–8, read the text below and think of the word which best fits each gap. Use only **one** word in each gap. There is an example at the beginning (0).*

Irn-Bru

Scotland is unusual in having a locally made soft drink that **(0)** _manages_ to compete with the big international brands. Irn-Bru is a sweet, brightly coloured fizzy drink **(1)** _____ a taste that reminds some people of bubble gum and **(2)** _____ of the pink mouthwash you get at the dentist. **(3)** _____ so many other fast-food products, you either love it or you hate it. Yet at the time of **(4)** _____ conception, over 100 years ago, there was nothing particularly original about 'Iron-Brew', as it was then called. There were many similar soft drinks **(5)** _____ the market but Barr's Irn-Bru had the big advantage of **(6)** _____ manufactured in Glasgow, a city which had a population of one million, and it quickly became extremely popular. What's more, Barr was one of the first businessmen to understand **(7)** _____ value of celebrity endorsement. As early as 1905, the world champion wrestler Alex Munro was advertising the drink and it continues to benefit **(8)** _____ clever marketing today.

EXPERT WORD CHECK

brands   *bubble gum*   *endorsment*   *fizzy drink*
mouthwash   *wrestler*

Writing (Paper 2 Part 2: Report)

➤ **COURSEBOOK** pages 96–97, **EXPERT WRITING** page 204

EXPERT STRATEGY

You should provide the reader with factual information in a neutral style. The points should be ordered logically under headings so that the reader can find the information quickly.

Understand the task

1 Read the writing task and answer the questions.

1 What is your role?

2 Who are you writing the report for? What style will you use?

3 How many parts are there to the question? Mark the parts of the task that tell you what to include in your report.

Your English teacher has asked you to write a report about the best places to go shopping for clothes in your area. You should include information that will be useful for people of different ages and levels of income, and you should recommend one place for whole families to visit.

*Write your **report** in **140–190** words.*

2 Choose four of these headings to use in your report. What order will you put them in?

- My favourite clothes shop
- A good place for families to go shopping
- Shops for older and younger people
- Why designer shops are best
- Where to get the best bargains
- Shops in different price ranges
- Introduction: the main local shopping centres

Improve a sample answer

3 Which phrase in each pair is i) in a neutral informative style and ii) in another style?

1 a This is the place to get the coolest stuff.
  b The shops in this area stock the latest fashions.
2 a This shopping centre offers good value for money.
  b The clothes in this place are really cheap.

3 a This shop has clothes to suit a wide range of tastes.
  b You can find all sorts of stuff in this shop.
4 a This area is popular with older consumers who prefer traditional styles.
  b The clothes in the shops are really boring and old-fashioned.
5 a You don't pay much but let's face it: most of the stuff's rubbish.
  b Although the prices are low, the clothes are not always very good quality.
6 a The parking's easy and there's a brilliant play area for kids.
  b The large car park and children's play area are good for families.

4 Read a student's report and tick the points in the task which have been included. Is all the information under the correct heading? What important information is missing?

Untitled – Notepad   _ ▢ X

File Edit View Insert Format Table Help

Report on clothes shopping in my city

Introduction
There are many places to buy clothes in my city. In the city centre, there are traditional clothes shops and designer shops. In the suburbs, there are shopping malls where you can find large chain stores.

Shops for different ages
In the city centre, the best shops are the designer shops, where you can buy all the latest fashions. I would buy all my clothes in these shops if I had enough money but they are really expensive, so mostly I just go window-shopping there.

Shops for different income levels
If you want to find cheaper shops, you should head for the malls in the suburbs. These have really good clothes for young people, similar to the designer stuff, but much cheaper. There are also good markets in the city, where you can sometimes find a bargain.

Recommendation for families
There's a shopping mall called Fairview which is really good for families. At Fairview, you can find chain stores selling things like baby clothes and the clothes children wear for school, as well as sports clothes for their free-time activities. It's the best place for families to go.

Listening (Paper 3 Part 1)

Before you listen

1a Read the instructions. How many extracts will you hear?

b For questions 1–8, read the sentence that gives the context of the extract, the question and the three options (A–C). Think about the situation. Mark the key words in each question.

Multiple choice

2a 🎧 11 Do the task. Note these steps.
- You will hear each extract twice. As you listen, focus on the speaker's main idea – don't worry if you don't understand every word.
- Choose one of the options after listening the first time. If you don't know an answer, have a guess and go on to the next question.

b 🎧 11 Listen again and check your answers.

> **EXPERT STRATEGY**
>
> Remember that you hear each extract twice. Use the second time to check your answer.

> **HELP**
> 1 The answer comes at the end of the recording.
> 2 Listen to everything the woman says to know the answer.
> 4 Listen to what the man says about the photography in the book.
> 6 Listen to the first thing the woman says; it will help you rule out one of the options.

> **EXPERT LANGUAGE**
>
> Which of the questions are asking about the speakers' opinions?

> **EXPERT WORD CHECK**
>
> *constructive criticism   helpings*
> *organic food   processed   recipes*
> *supermarket chain   vegetarianism*

*You will hear people talking in eight different situations. For questions 1–8, choose the best answer (**A**, **B**, or **C**).*

1 You hear the beginning of a radio programme about food. What does the presenter say is most surprising about the website he's describing?
A the number of recipes available
B the way that different flavours have been combined
C the fact that one ingredient appears in so many of the recipes

2 You hear a woman talking about vegetarianism. What is she doing when she speaks?
A supporting the principles of vegetarianism
B doubting the seriousness of many vegetarians
C explaining why she has become a vegetarian

3 You hear part of an interview with a woman who is in favour of organically-grown food. What opinion is she expressing?
A Only food grown locally should be labelled as organic.
B It's best to avoid the organic sections of supermarkets.
C Even commercially-produced organic food is a good thing.

4 You hear part of a radio discussion about travel guidebooks. What does the man find disappointing about the book called *The Ultimate Guide*?
A the range of information included
B the quality of the illustrations
C the clarity of the descriptions

5 In a radio play, you hear two people talking about pizza. Where is this scene taking place?
A in their home   B in a restaurant   C in a supermarket

6 You hear part of a radio programme about looking for a job on the internet. Which group of people is being described?
A unemployed people
B people dissatisfied with their jobs
C part-time workers looking for full-time jobs

7 You hear a radio news report about a scientific conference. What is the main aim of the experiment described?
A to attract attention to an idea for a new product
B to demonstrate the power of marketing
C to get funding for a new area of research

8 You hear the owner of a large restaurant talking about her work. What is her main aim in running the restaurant?
A encouraging competition between the chefs
B ensuring a standardised product for the customers
C involving all the staff in checking the quality of the food

Vocabulary development 2

➤ **COURSEBOOK** pages 98–99

Clothes

1 Read the comments different people made about what they usually wear and choose the correct answer (A, B or C).

a 'I tend to wear fairly elegant clothes during the week – **(1)** _____ jackets, straight skirts or trouser suits. The first **(2)** _____ my clients get of me is very important. Now I don't feel right in **(3)** _____ clothes, so even at the weekends I still wear the same kind of thing.'

1 A fitted	B shaped	C created
2 A appearance	B impression	C picture
3 A easy	B relaxing	C casual

b 'When I'm not at school, there's no point in dressing up in **(1)** _____ clothes. They just get dirty. I wear **(2)** _____ bottoms and a T-shirt. I've also got three different football **(3)** _____ – Manchester United, England and Barcelona.'

1 A smart	B sharp	C official
2 A tracksuit	B trouser	C suit
3 A uniforms	B kits	C costumes

c 'At the moment the **(1)** _____ is to wear very short or very long skirts with trainers or shoes with **(2)** _____ heels. Interesting or unusual patterns in **(3)** _____ colours are popular this season too. I wouldn't dream of wearing anything that wasn't **(4)** _____ fashion. I wear patterned or **(5)** _____ tights with my school uniform.'

1 A habit	B design	C trend
2 A high	B tall	C extended
3 A bright	B full	C powerful
4 A on	B at	C in
5 A wrinkled	B striped	C lined

d 'I like clothes but I'm not a fashion victim. Now I've got kids I want to be comfortable, so I don't wear **(1)** _____ skirts anymore. However, that doesn't mean that I live in jeans and baggy **(2)** _____ all the time. I don't like **(3)** _____ clothes. I go for well-cut clothes in **(4)** _____ like silk or cotton.'

1 A firm	B close	C tight
2 A scarves	B hats	C sweaters
3 A careless	B scruffy	C disordered
4 A fabrics	B substances	C cloths

Commonly confused words

2 Complete the sentences with the words in *italics*.

1 *number / size / figure*
   a Yes, we have that dress in black. What _____ are you?
   b We only have a limited _____ of tracksuits in stock.
   c She has such a wonderful _____ because she's always at the gym.

2 *suit / fit / match*
   a That hat doesn't _____ you. It's too old-fashioned.
   b I need a white handbag to _____ my new white dress.
   c I must have put on weight. These trousers don't _____ me anymore.

3 *dress / get dressed / wear*
   a Come on, _____ ! You can't stay in bed all day!
   b How do you normally _____ for work?
   c You can't possibly _____ that skirt to the party! It's dirty.

4 *try on / put on / have on*
   a It's raining heavily outside, so _____ your raincoat.
   b Can I _____ the coat in the shop window? How much is it?
   c Are you sure you saw Peter? What kind of jacket did he _____ ?

5 *take off / undo / loosen*
   a Do you want to _____ your coat and put it over there?
   b In the summer I have to keep my tie on. I usually _____ it a bit, though.
   c Can you help me _____ the buttons on the back of my dress?

6 *uniform / costume / suit*
   a What _____ are you going to wear to the fancy-dress party?
   b As a soldier, you have to wear a _____ at all times.
   c When I worked for that company, I refused to wear a _____ .

Exam practice: Word formation
(Paper 1 Part 3)

3 Do the task.

For questions 1–8, read the text below. Use the word given in capitals at the end of some of the lines to form a word that fits in the gap in the same line. There is an example at the beginning (0).

Fancy dress

At some point in our lives, most of us will receive an (0) <u>invitation</u> to a fancy-dress party. What would your reaction be? Clearly, some people get very excited at the prospect of dressing up in (1) _____ clothes and they will immediately start thinking about their (2) _____ of costume. These people will probably invest quite a lot of money and effort in making sure that they make the best possible (3) _____ on the night. Others are likely to be less (4) _____ with the idea of changing their normal appearance and these people might get (5) _____ about what to wear for quite different reasons. Nobody wants to look (6) _____ , so don't go as James Bond if you don't have the style and (7) _____ to carry it off. Much better to wear the silliest (8) _____ imaginable and go prepared to join in the fun.

INVITE

USUAL

CHOOSE

IMPRESS

COMFORT

ANXIETY

FOOL

ELEGANT

FIT

EXPERT STRATEGY
Check the rest of the sentence when changing the word to fit the gap.

➤ HELP
1 You need a negative prefix here .
2 What is the noun of this verb?
7 Add a suffix to make a noun here.

EXPERT LANGUAGE
Find three phrasal verbs in the text.

EXPERT WORD CHECK
costume   invest   silliest   the prospect of

Language development 2
➤ **COURSEBOOK** page 101

Speculation and deduction

1a For each sentence, decide if the speaker means:

A 'I'm certain it's true.'
B 'I'm certain it's not true.'
C 'I'm not sure if it's true.'

1 I think the library might be closed today. <u>C</u>
2 That dress you want must be very expensive if it has a designer label. _____
3 She hasn't answered the phone, so she might not be at home. _____
4 He must be Greek because his name is Papadopoulos. _____
5 They didn't come tonight. They could be watching TV, I suppose. _____
6 Peter can't be ill because I saw him playing tennis this morning. _____
7 They are laughing a lot next door. They must be having a good time. _____
8 The ticket couldn't be that expensive. I expect they've made a mistake. _____

b Complete the sentences with the correct form of *might / might not, may / may not, must* or *can't* and the verbs in brackets.

1 John didn't come to class today. He <u>might be</u> (be) ill, I suppose, or just bored.
2 This scarf _____ (belong) to Stella. She hates black.
3 Tell Maria which restaurant you plan to go to on her birthday. She _____ (like) Chinese food.
4 You've been working hard all day. You _____ (be) exhausted!
5 John _____ (have) that book already. Why don't you give him a ring to check?
6 This bag is very cheap. It _____ (be) a genuine Gucci handbag.
7 There's a lot of music and laughter coming from next door. They _____ (have) a party.
8 I wonder why they are so late. They _____ (try) to find somewhere to park, I suppose.

2 Rewrite the sentences using *might (not) have, must have* or *can't have*.

1 I'm sure Claudia was upset when she discovered that someone from the party had taken her coat.
Claudia _____ .

2 It's possible that the person who took it didn't realise it was the wrong one.
The person who took it _____ .

3 I'm quite sure Anna didn't take it because I saw her go home early.
Anna _____ .

4 Rachel is the same size as Claudia, so maybe she took it.
Rachel is the same size as Claudia, so she _____ .

5 It was a fur coat, so it's certain it was worth a lot of money.
It was a fur coat, so it _____ .

6 I'm sure her father wasn't very pleased when she told him about it.
Her father _____ .

Choosing the correct present or past form

3 Find and correct the mistakes with modal verbs in some of the sentences. Tick the correct ones.

1 Why is Peter wearing a pullover on such a hot day? He must to be very hot.

2 You shouldn't phone Alex at this time because he could be asleep.

3 Mr Dickens looks very smart these days. He must find a new job.

4 Simon's car is not here, so he must have left for work.

5 Tina can't have been paid £200 for that dress – it doesn't even fit her!

6 The neighbours are shouting at each other again. They must have another argument!

7 It can't have been raining all night because the road is almost dry.

8 Keith is late, isn't he? He may be do overtime at the office, I suppose.

9 Emma looks very unhappy after her shopping trip. She may not found a wedding dress that she liked.

Exam practice: Multiple-choice cloze
(Paper 1 Part 1)

4 Do the task.

For questions 1–8, read the text below and decide which answer (A, B, C or D) best fits each gap. There is an example at the beginning (0).

A designer's taste

I am a fashion designer by (0) __A__ . Each year I produce my own (1) _____ of new clothes for young people to wear, which I present to the world in a fashion show in London. Although I like the outfits that I design and I feel very proud when my shows get good (2) _____ in the press, the clothes are quite (3) _____ the things I would choose to wear myself. (4) _____ , some people think it's surprising that the clothes I find most comfortable are not currently fashionable at all. I get (5) _____ pleasure, for example, out of what are (6) _____ 'vintage clothes', especially those designed by the great fashion houses of the past. I (7) _____ a big thrill from imagining who might have worn them when they were new and what their history may be. Some of my coats and dresses are quite valuable, so they must have been worn by quite famous people, but I don't know this for (8) _____ .

0	A profession	B work	C employment	D job
1	A arrangement	B collection	C gathering	D composition
2	A replies	B revisions	C reviews	D receipts
3	A unlike	B dissimilar	C different	D opposite
4	A Elsewhere	B Despite	C Otherwise	D Indeed
5	A large	B great	C wide	D deep
6	A titled	B known	C called	D referred
7	A have	B take	C find	D get
8	A sure	B real	C true	D fact

> **EXPERT STRATEGY**
> Keep reading the words before and after the gap when choosing your answer.

> ➤ **HELP**
> 3 Only one of these words can take a direct object.
> 4 The linker you need is stressing an idea that has already been introduced.
> 8 Which option expresses a degree of certainty?

> **EXPERT LANGUAGE**
> Find three modal verbs expressing degrees of certainty in the text.

> **EXPERT WORD CHECK**
> *a big thrill   outfits   the press   vintage*

Reading (Paper 1 Part 6)

Before you read **1** Read the title and subheading of the article. Think about the topic and decide if these statements are *True* (T) or *False* (F) for you.

1 We judge other people according to the way they look. _____
2 It's a good idea to look at people in magazines and try to dress the same way. _____
3 It's important to choose the right clothes for different occasions. _____
4 Most people have a favourite style of clothing. _____
5 We should not be frightened to try new colours even if we are not sure we like them. _____
6 It doesn't matter if our clothes are a size too big. _____
7 What we say is more important than how we look. _____

Skimming **2** Skim the text and look at your answers in Exercise 1 again. Did you agree with the writer of the article?

Gapped text **3a** Read the second paragraph and look at gap 1. Follow these steps.

1 Look at the highlighted words before and after the gap.
2 Now look at sentence B. How does it refer to these words?

b Read the rest of the article carefully and do the task. Note these steps. For each gap, do the following:
- Read the text before and after the gap and think about the type of information which is missing.
- Look for a sentence in the box which talks about this topic area.
- Choose the correct answer by checking the grammatical and lexical links between the base text and the key sentence. Look out for pronouns, synonyms, etc.
- Cross off each sentence as you use it but be prepared to look again when you check your answers.

c Read the article again with your answers to check that it makes sense.

> **EXPERT STRATEGY**
> Underline any pronouns (e.g. *this, these*) in the sentences and think about what they refer to.

> **HELP**
> A Look for what *these items* could be.
> E Look in the text for something which you *cross*.

> **EXPERT LANGUAGE**
> Find a reflexive pronoun in sentences A–G.

> **EXPERT WORD CHECK**
> *convey a message   reappraising*
> *washed-out   wrong signals*

> *You are going to read an article about personal appearance. Six sentences have been removed from the article. Choose from the sentences (**A–G**) the one that fits each gap (**1–6**). There is one extra sentence which you do not need to use.*
>
> A Look at these items and ask yourself what they have in common.
> B A better idea is to stand in front of a full-length mirror and be honest with yourself about what you see.
> C Sometimes we buy these ill-fitting clothes without thinking.
> D But once you've got used to this change, it will be easier to make those difficult decisions.
> E It may be fun to cross these sometimes but do take care not to go too far all at once.
> F However, there's no need to abandon your individual taste completely.
> G You'll look better and you'll feel a better person all round.

Vocabulary: Phrasal verbs and idiomatic expressions

4 Match the verbs and expressions (1–4) from the text with their definitions (a–d).

1 dwell on (line 12)
2 dictate (line 21)
3 catch someone's eye (line 35)
4 grab (line 51)

a take or choose something quickly
b influence or control
c think or talk for too long about something unpleasant
d make someone notice something

Make your **image** work for you

Our appearance conveys a message to everyone we come into contact with. Maybe it's time to pay a bit more attention to it.

When we meet people for the first time, we often make decisions about them based entirely on how they look. And of course, we too are being judged on our appearance. Undoubtedly, it's what's inside that's important but sometimes we can send out the wrong signals and so get a negative reaction, simply by wearing inappropriate clothing.

For example, people often make the mistake of trying to look like someone else – perhaps someone they've seen in a magazine – but this is usually a disaster as we all have our own characteristics. 1 B There's no need to dwell on your faults when you do this – we all have good points and bad points – think instead about the best way to emphasise the good ones.

When selecting your clothes each day, think about who you're likely to meet, where you're going to be spending most of your time and what tasks you're likely to perform. Clearly, on a practical level, some outfits will be more appropriate to different sorts of activity and this will dictate your choice to an extent. 2 After all, if you dress to please somebody else's idea of what looks good, you may end up feeling uncomfortable and not quite yourself.

But to know your own mind, you have to get to know yourself. What do you truly feel good in? There are probably a few favourite clothes that you wear a lot – most people wear 20 percent of their wardrobe 80 percent of the time. 3 Are they neat and tidy, loose and flowing? Then look at the things hanging in your wardrobe that you don't wear and ask yourself why. Go through a few magazines and catalogues and mark the things that catch your eye. Is there a common theme?

Some colours bring your natural colouring to life and others can give us a washed-out appearance. Try out new ones by all means, but remember that dressing in bright colours when you really like subtle neutral tones or vice versa will make you feel self-conscious and uncomfortable. You know deep down where your own taste boundaries lie. 4

So, you've chosen an outfit that matches your style, your personality, your shape and your colouring. But is it really the right size? If something is too tight or too loose, you won't achieve the desired effect and no matter what other qualities it has, it won't improve your appearance or your confidence. 5 For example, some people who dislike shopping grab the first thing they see or prefer to use mail-order or the internet. In all cases, if it doesn't fit perfectly, don't buy it because the finer details are just as important as the overall style.

Reappraising your image isn't selfish because everyone who comes into contact with you will benefit. 6 And if in doubt, you only need to read Professor Albert Mehrabian's book Silent Messages to remind yourself how important outward appearances are. His research showed that the impact we make on each other depends 55 percent on how we look and behave, 38 percent on how we speak and only seven percent on what we actually say.

8A Relationships

Vocabulary development 1

> **COURSEBOOK** pages 106–107

Vivid vocabulary

1a Complete the diagrams with the words and expressions in the box. They are all from the text on page 107 of the Coursebook.

clutch something   dash   get to your feet
give someone a nod   give something a kick
push something into someone's hand
slip (on a wet surface)   stare at someone
tap someone on the shoulder

You do this with your eyes.

You do this with your hands.

You do this with your feet.

You do this with your head.

b Now add these words and expressions to the diagrams in Exercise 1a.

glance at someone   grab something   jump up
shake someone's …   shake your …   tap your …
trip over something   wave at someone
wink at someone

Collocations

2 Match the verbs in the box with the words they collocate with. Each verb must collocate with all the words in a set.

be   break   celebrate   fall   get   go   have   make

1 _____ engaged/married/divorced/on well with someone
2 _____ in love/excited/happy/confused
3 _____ in love/asleep/out with a friend (over something)
4 _____ a wedding anniversary/a birthday/an engagement

5 _____ a date/a relationship/a baby/an argument/problems
6 _____ friends/up with someone (after an argument)/plans/a mistake
7 _____ out with someone/on a date/on a honeymoon
8 _____ off an engagement/up a relationship/up with someone

Relationships

3a Complete the sentences with the words/phrases in the box. Use plural forms where necessary.

acquaintance   best friend   colleague   fiancée
flatmate   partner   relative   workmate

1 My family is very big – two brothers, three sisters and lots of cousins. I have some _____ in Australia but *we're not very close*. We send each other cards on special occasions, that's all.
2 I share an apartment with another student from the university. My _____ is a bit older than me but *we have a lot in common*. I don't think I could share with someone who was totally different from me.
3 I don't know Sue very well, so she's a(n) _____ rather than a friend. I get the impression that *she looks down on me* because my family isn't as well-off as hers.
4 I've known my _____ ever since we were children. *I've always adored her*. I felt so happy when we got engaged six months ago. The wedding's going to be next month.
5 I work in a small office. I've known most of my _____ for over five years and *we see eye to eye on most things*.
6 Yvonne was my _____ at school. We did absolutely everything together. *I really admired her* – she knew exactly what she wanted in life and was willing to work hard to get it.
7 Dennis was my _____ in yesterday's tennis match. *I can't stand him* – he's so rude and uncooperative. Roger and Bill beat us really easily.
8 During the summer holidays I had a job picking fruit on a farm. It was hard work, but my _____ were friendly and *I grew very fond of them*.

b Look at the phrases in *italics* in Exercise 3a. Tick (✓) the ones which describe positive feelings and cross (✗) those that describe negative feelings.

c Write short descriptions of members of your family and friends.

Exam practice: Multiple-choice cloze (Paper 1 Part 1)

4 Do the task.

For questions 1–8, read the text below and decide which answer (A, B, C or D) best fits each gap. There is an example at the beginning (0).

Blind date

Aged 18, I (0) __A__ a job in the offices of a TV company. There was a boy working upstairs who seemed very cool and sophisticated because he got to meet all the stars. All the girls in the office used to try to (1) _____ him up whenever he paid a (2) _____ to our department. Then one day, (3) _____ unexpectedly, he invited me to a big charity dinner at an expensive hotel. I was so excited and (4) _____ spending a fortune on a new dress, shoes and hairstyle.

As we walked into the hotel, cameras were flashing and I felt like a real celebrity. We went up a long, wide flight of stairs, just like in a (5) _____ from the movies. But as we (6) _____ the top, one of my new leather-soled shoes slipped on the red carpet. I fell backwards and went head over (7) _____ down the stairs, landing in a heap at the bottom. I was unhurt but (8) _____ shaken and extremely embarrassed.

0	A got	B held	C set	D joined
1	A speak	B chat	C talk	D gossip
2	A tour	B trip	C stay	D visit
3	A more	B even	C quite	D much
4	A brought about	B called for	C ended up	D went through
5	A part	B scene	C play	D show
6	A managed	B achieved	C arrived	D reached
7	A elbows	B knees	C heels	D feet
8	A badly	B poorly	C toughly	D hardly

EXPERT STRATEGY

If you're not sure, cross out the options which you're sure are incorrect and choose the most likely answer.

➤ HELP

1 The missing word makes a phrasal verb with *up*.
2 Which word collocates with *paid*?
6 The meaning is 'arrived at' but you need a verb you can use without a preposition.

Language development 1

➤ **COURSEBOOK** pages 108–109, **EXPERT GRAMMAR** pages 193–194

Reported speech: Reporting exact words

1 Find and correct the mistakes in the sentences. Say if they are mistakes with the *verb tense* (T), *word order* (WO) or if the *wrong word* is used (WW).

1 Tina told me she ~~has spent~~ three months at a college in the UK last year. __spent (T)__
2 I asked her why had she gone there. _____
3 She replied she wants to improve her English. _____
4 I asked her if she will go to London with me in the summer. _____
5 She said she had spent some time there the last year. _____
6 I asked her why didn't she want to go there again. _____
7 She said me it had rained all the time she was there. _____
8 I said we could bring umbrellas with us. _____

Reporting verbs

2a Choose the correct answers.

1 My teacher *advised / recommended* me to go abroad to study.
2 Peter *told / said* to me that he wanted to get married and settle down.
3 I *denied / refused* to tell Paul what I had done the previous evening.
4 Julia *admitted / informed* that she had been out with Ben.
5 My mother *blamed / accused* me of breaking her favourite vase.
6 My girlfriend *insisted / agreed* to come to the airport with me.
7 Sandra *threatened / warned* to tell Richard what I had said.
8 Tania *suggested / persuaded* going for a pizza after the film.

EXPERT LANGUAGE

Find two examples of words with negative prefixes in the text.

EXPERT WORD CHECK

charity dinner   flight of stairs   in a heap   sophisticated

b   Match the sentences (1–10) with the reporting verbs (a–j). Then rewrite the sentences in reported speech.

a	1	Would you like to come to my house for lunch?
	2	I'm really sorry I missed your birthday party.
	3	I will definitely be at the wedding.
	4	Don't go out with Ken because he's dangerous!
	5	I'll help you write the invitations.
	6	If you go to the Oasis Club again, I'll tell your father.
	7	I really didn't invite your ex-boyfriend to my party.
	8	Why don't you ask Dave out on a date?
	9	I think you should break off your engagement.
	10	You told me a lie!

a Anna invited _me to go to her house for lunch_ .
b Ruth suggested _____ .
c Denise offered _____ .
d Eve denied _____ .
e Keith threatened _____ .
f Maureen advised _____ .
g Sue apologised _____ .
h Rob accused _____ .
i Richard promised _____ .
j Maria warned _____ .

Key word transformations

3   Complete the second sentence so that it has a similar meaning to the first sentence, using the word given. Do not change the word given. Use between two and five words, including the word given.

1 'I won't tell anyone what you did,' George said.
   PROMISED
   George _____ what I had done.

2 'I'll buy the theatre tickets,' Peter said.
   INSISTED
   Peter _____ the theatre tickets.

3 'Can I have another piece of cake?' Doug asked.
   WHETHER
   Doug asked _____ another piece of cake.

4 'Why didn't you arrive on time, John?' Sally asked.
   WHY
   Sally asked John _____ on time.

5 'You've broken my watch, Simon!' Alan said.
   ACCUSED
   Alan _____ watch.

6 'Don't leave the mountain footpath, Paul!' Patricia said.
   WARNED
   Patricia _____ leave the mountain footpath.

7 'Would you like to go to a rock concert this weekend, David?' Maria asked.
   INVITED
   Maria _____ go to a rock concert that weekend.

8 'We haven't reserved you a seat, I'm afraid,' the airline representative said.
   ADMITTED
   The airline representative _____ reserved me a seat.

Exam practice: Open cloze
(Paper 1 Part 2)

4   Do the task.

*For questions 1–8, read the text below and think of the word which best fits each gap. Use only **one** word in each gap. There is an example at the beginning (0).*

Blind date

I first met my girlfriend Charlotte through what (0) _is_ known as online dating. We had each sent in our personal details (1) _____ inclusion in the website's database. The database search results suggested we were a good match (2) _____ principle and we were sent contact details so that we could get in touch with each (3) _____ . Our first meeting took (4) _____ in a restaurant in London. It was (5) _____ people call a blind date and (6) _____ of us had ever been on one before, although we didn't realise this at the time.

My first impression was that Charlotte was smartly dressed and looked much prettier (7) _____ in her photo. She told me she'd come straight from the office and there hadn't been time to change into something more casual. At first, it was quite difficult to find something to talk about apart (8) _____ our jobs. But then Charlotte asked me about my hobbies and we found we had quite a few interests in common. We've been going out ever since.

EXPERT STRATEGY
Remember to read the whole text through once you've filled in all the gaps.

➤ HELP
1 The missing word is a preposition.
6 The word you need is the negative form of *both*.
7 Which word follows a comparative adjective?

EXPERT LANGUAGE
Find fair examples of the past perfect in the text.

EXPERT WORD CHECK
first impression   in common   inclusion   online dating

Writing (Paper 2 Part 1: Essay)

➤ **COURSEBOOK** pages 110–111, **EXPERT WRITING** pages 199–200

EXAM STRATEGY

It's important to plan an essay in advance so that the argument is organised in the most logical way. The wording of the question helps you to do this. Discuss the points in the question and make sure you:
- support your ideas with reasons or examples.
- use linking words to show the connection between your ideas.

Understand the task

1a Read the writing task and answer the questions.
1 Who will read the essay?
2 What style should you use?

b Note down two advantages and two disadvantages of living at home.

Advantages	Disadvantages
_____	_____
_____	_____

In your English class, you have been talking about the advantages and disadvantages of young people living at home with their parents when they are studying at university or starting work in their first jobs. Now your English teacher has asked you to write an essay.

Write an essay using **all** *the notes and give reasons for your point of view.*

Young people should live with their parents for as long as they want.

Notes

Write about:

1 advantages of living with parents
2 disadvantages of living with parents
3 _____ (your own idea)

Write your **essay** *in 140–190 words.*

Read a sample answer

2a Read a student's essay and cross out the option (A, B or C) which is *not* possible.

Nowadays, it's common for young people to continue to live with their parents until their mid-twenties. **(1)** _____ , many people think that this is a bad thing and that young people should be encouraged to leave home earlier.

There are many reasons why young people continue to live with their parents. They may feel comfortable at home. **(2)** _____ , they do not need to cook, wash their clothes or pay rent. This last point is important because life today has become very expensive. **(3)** _____ , it's difficult to live well if you don't earn a high salary.

(4) _____ , many young people say that they only became mature once they left home. Living away from their parents when they went to college or started work forced them to be independent. **(5)** _____ , they had to start to think for themselves and sort out problems on their own.

In my view, young people should stay with their parents if they want to. **(6)** _____ , they should understand that gaining some independence would be beneficial. Travelling independently of their parents in their summer holidays could be a good idea, **(7)** _____ , for those who continue to live at home.

1	A However	B Furthermore	C Nevertheless
2	A Therefore	B For instance	C For example
3	A Despite this	B As a result	C Consequently
4	A However	B On the other hand	C Even so
5	A Similarly	B In other words	C That is to say
6	A Nevertheless	B As a consequence	C On the other hand
7	A otherwise	B for instance	C therefore

b Read the essay again and complete the paragraph plan the student followed.

Paragraph 1: Introduction: _____
Paragraph 2: Advantages of living at home
Advantage(s): _____
Example(s): _____
Paragraph 3: _____
Disadvantage(s): _____
Example(s): _____
Paragraph 4 (my own idea): _____
Example(s): _____

Features of an essay

3 Read the list of features of a good essay. Tick the ones that the essay above has.

A good essay:
1 is divided into three or four main paragraphs.
2 has an introduction that makes a general statement about the topic.
3 supports the main points with details.
4 uses linking words to connect the ideas.
5 states the writer's view in the final paragraph.
6 uses a neutral style consistently.
7 is between 140 and 190 words.

4 Write your own essay.

Listening (Paper 3 Part 3)

Before you listen

1a Read the instructions for the listening task. What are the speakers going to talk about?

b Mark the key words in the statements (A–H).

Multiple matching

2a 🎧 12 Listen once and focus on each speaker's main point. Match the main points with the closest option (A–H).

b 🎧 12 Listen again and check your answers. Make sure the ideas expressed in the recording match the options exactly.

*You will hear five short extracts in which women are talking about what it was like to grow up with a twin sister. For questions **1–5**, choose from the list (**A–H**) what each speaker says. Use the letters only once. There are three extra letters which you do not need to use.*

A The way people regarded us used to annoy me.	Speaker 1	1
B I always felt I was being compared to my sister.	Speaker 2	2
C I had frequent disagreements with my sister.	Speaker 3	3
D My sister and I had very similar tastes.	Speaker 4	4
E I was glad not to spend too much time with my sister.	Speaker 5	5
F I used to get upset when my sister laughed at me.		
G I always felt closer to my older brother than to my twin sister.		
H My sister used to let me down occasionally.		

EXPERT STRATEGY

Read the options A–H. Think about the words and expressions you expect to hear.

➤ HELP

Speaker 3: Listen for the second time Emily's name is mentioned – the answer follows this.
Speaker 4: Listen to what she says about clothes and hair. How did people react?
Speaker 5: Did the twins enjoy being together?

EXPERT LANGUAGE

Find an example of the past continuous in the statements.

EXPERT WORD CHECK

gang up on   identical   in tune   infuriate   misled

Paraphrasing

3 🎧 12 Listen again and complete the phrases from the recording.

Speaker 1
1 people would _____ us up
2 we were both _____ independent
3 which was a(n) _____ for disaster

Speaker 2
4 there was a real _____ between us

Speaker 3
5 Emily is the first person I'll _____ if I'm feeling down

Speaker 4
6 people just _____ us together

Speaker 5
7 it _____ me mad
8 we used to _____ our older brother

Vocabulary development 2

➤ **COURSEBOOK** pages 112–113

Word formation

EXPERT STRATEGY

In the word formation task (Paper 1, Reading and Use of English, Part 3), you should not only decide what part of speech the word is (e.g. adjective, noun, verb) but also whether it is plural or negative.

1 Read the extracts from an article about hobbies. Use the word given at the end of the sentences to form a word that fits in the gap.

1 Reading _____ magazines, you'd think that celebrities like film stars, top models, etc. spend their whole non-working lives at parties. **WEEK**

2 But according to a new book, this is often far from the _____ . **TRUE**

3 We don't expect rock stars to enjoy doing things like collecting stamps, which people generally regard as really _____ hobbies. **BORE**

4 Being a celebrity is all about image and their fans have certain _____ of these people. **EXPECT**

5 Jarvis Cocker, lead singer of rock band Pulp, spends a lot of time bird-watching – and he's not _____ because quite a few rock stars collect things like old coins and matchboxes. **USUAL**

6 During my research, I saw some very _____ film stars doing crossword or jigsaw puzzles. **GLAMOUR**

Talking about hobbies

EXPERT STRATEGY

In Paper 4, Speaking, Part 1, the examiner may ask if you have any hobbies and how you became interested in them. Make sure you are familiar with the vocabulary you would need to describe your hobby effectively.

2a Complete the descriptions with the hobbies in the box. There are two extra hobbies which you do not need to use. Mark the words which help you decide.

*bird-watching   board games   chess   gardening   knitting
making models   stamp collecting   trainspotting*

> I started doing it when I was a child. I used to buy plastic kits. The only thing you needed was a tube of glue and some paints. Nowadays I make all the parts myself from wood or metal.

1 _____

> I've had this hobby all my life. You don't need any special equipment – just albums to put your collection in and a magnifying glass. I love all the different colours and designs from around the world.

2 _____

> It's exciting when you see species you know are rare. You have to try to get as close as you can without making a sound. A good pair of binoculars is essential.

3 _____

> Since we moved to a bigger house, I've been doing a lot of it. It keeps me fit. I have a number of tools, such as forks and spades, and a lawn mower, which I use every weekend.

4 _____

> You have to keep a record of everything that comes into the station. It can get a bit cold waiting on platforms all day, so you need a warm coat or anorak.

5 _____

> My sister and I have six or seven different ones. It's much better than playing cards. I love the moment when you throw the dice – you never know what's going to happen.

6 _____

b Write a short description of a hobby you have, or have had in the past. Make notes about:

1 when you started the hobby.
2 what attracted you to it.
3 what equipment you need.
4 How much time you spend on it.

Paraphrasing

3 What items of clothing or equipment from Exercise 2a are these students describing?

1 I really like cutting the grass in the garden with it – it's a sort of machine but I don't know what it's called in English. _____

2 When I was a kid, I loved to throw the two – you know, they're like little wooden boxes. I got really excited if I got two sixes. _____

3 I used to spend all my time sticking pieces of wood together with ... a liquid like toothpaste. _____

4 Every weekend I put on my – what's it called? – it's like a short coat – it stops you getting cold and wet – and go with friends to the airport. _____

5 My father bought me a – you know, a big round glass which makes things bigger – and I looked at everything through it. _____

6 On my birthday I was given a – I don't know what the word is – you use it for looking at things which are far away – you use both eyes like this. _____

Phrasal verbs and expressions

4 Choose the correct answers.

Do you want an exciting new hobby?

Do you **(1)** *spend / pay* a lot of time watching TV in the evenings? When you need to wind **(2)** *up / down* at the end of a hard day, do you put your **(3)** *feet / legs* up in front of 'the box'? It's not very creative, is it?

Why not take **(4)** *up / out* a new and exciting hobby? The ancient Japanese art of origami – folding paper to make attractive objects – is a fascinating way of **(5)** *passing / occupying* the time. All you need are some coloured paper squares, a pair of scissors and our easy-to-follow, step-by-step guide.

If you are keen **(6)** *at / on* making things with your hands, then origami is for you! Groups of enthusiasts are springing **(7)** *up / over* everywhere. Reach for the telephone and **(8)** *make / give* us a call now!

☎ 0118 4960009

Expressing ability: *can, could, be able to*

1 Complete the article with the correct form of *can, could* or *be able to*. More than one answer may be possible.

My new passion: scuba diving

I **(1)** _____ swim since I was a teenager and scuba diving is something I've always wanted to do. So last summer I went on a four-day Ocean Frontiers training course in the Cayman Islands. I had a fantastic time! I'd encourage anyone who is interested in **(2)** _____ dive to go on this course.

On the first day, we met our diving instructor, Neil, who showed us a video and gave us a test. I **(3)** _____ answer all the questions because I'd carefully studied the training manual they'd sent me beforehand.

After lunch, we went to the swimming pool so that we **(4)** _____ start to put the theory into practice. Neil showed us all the equipment and told us to breathe normally under the water. At first, I panicked and **(5)** _____ breathe at all but it soon became much easier.

In the pool, we learnt several skills. One of the most difficult was achieving 'buoyancy'. It's very important for divers **(6)** _____ float in the water, so we spent a lot of time learning how to do this.

In the days that followed, we went diving in the sea. It was truly amazing. We soon found that we **(7)** _____ move around easily in the sea, gazing at the colourful sea life around us.

'In the future, you **(8)** _____ dive anywhere in the world you want,' Neil told us at the end of the course. 'Time has been short, so I **(9)** _____ show you how to take photos underwater or how to dive in a wreck. But those are things you **(10)** _____ learn whenever you want. You are now certified divers. Congratulations!'

Other ways of expressing ability

2 Complete the sentences using the correct form of the verbs in brackets and the verbs in the box. Add any other words that are necessary.

beat   climb   light   play   ~~ride~~   speak   use   win

1 I'd love to cycle around Europe but I _don't know how to ride_ a bike. (not know)
2 Although it was very windy on the beach, we _____ a fire. (manage)
3 Although his opponent was a better chess player, Jason _____ him in the first game. (succeed)
4 Can I come with you to Paris? I'll be useful because I _____ French. (know)
5 Dave is an inexperienced mountaineer. I don't think he _____ the South Face next month. (manage)
6 Sue was an excellent dancer and _____ all the prizes at the competition. (succeed)
7 Gill had a bad cold but she still _____ the violin beautifully on Saturday evening. (manage)
8 I wanted to make a cake yesterday but I _____ my mother's new food mixer. (not know)

Key word transformations

3 Complete the second sentence so that it has a similar meaning to the first sentence, using the word given. Do not change the word given. Use between two and five words, including the word given.

1 Can you take part in the show next week?
ABLE
Will _____ part in the show next week?
2 Eve is a strong swimmer but she can't swim across that lake.
CAPABLE
Although Eve is a strong swimmer, she _____ across that lake.
3 Amanda is not a very good pianist.
KNOW
Amanda doesn't _____ the piano very well.
4 My sister was the best singer in the choir.
COULD
Nobody in the choir _____ than my sister.
5 How were you able to make such a tiny model train?
MANAGE
How _____ such a tiny model train?
6 My brother managed to pass his driving test first time.
SUCCEEDED
My brother _____ his driving test first time.
7 I couldn't take any photos at the party because my camera was broken.
ABLE
Since my camera was broken, I _____ any photos at the party.
8 Despite the wind and rain, the climbers were able to put up their tent.
MANAGED
Despite the wind and rain, the climbers _____ their tent.

Exam practice: Open cloze
(Paper 1 Part 2)

4 Do the task.

*For questions **1–8**, read the text below and think of the word which best fits each gap. Use only **one** word in each gap. There is an example at the beginning (0).*

Collecting things

These days everyone seems to be (0) __*a*__ collector. A new book describes collectors (1) _____ the archaeologists of the present and contains some fascinating stories. (2) _____ instance, there's the man (3) _____ has 50,000 items of food packaging stored in his home and the teenager willing to spend all her savings on the rare *Star Wars* toy that would complete her collection.

In past centuries only wealthy people (4) _____ afford to travel and most collectors started out with just a(n) (5) _____ strange objects bought on trips abroad. In the days before photography and television, this was the only (6) _____ people could see objects from other cultures. Gradually, museums were established so that ordinary people would be (7) _____ to see these treasures too.

In explaining why we collect things, however, the book sees no difference (8) _____ great art collectors and teenagers collecting items related to their favourite pop stars. The social and psychological explanations for collecting are much the same.

EXPERT STRATEGY

Remember to read the whole text through before answering the questions.

➤ **HELP**
2 The missing word is a preposition.
7 The word you need expresses the idea of possibility.

EXPERT LANGUAGE

Find three examples of modal verbs in the text.

EXPERT WORD CHECK

archaeologists   food packaging   savings   treasures

Reading (Paper 1 Part 7)

Before you read 1 Read the title and subheadings of the article and answer the questions.

1 What job does each person do?
2 What kind of hobby do you think each person has?

Skimming 2 Skim the text to check your ideas in Exercise 1.

Multiple matching 3a Look at question 1 in the reading task. Mark the part of section D that tells you this is the answer.

b Do the task. Follow these steps.
- Read the question carefully and mark the key words so that you know what you are looking for.
- Scan the texts quickly to find the section which deals with the idea in the question. Look for parallel phrases and parts of sentences.
- When you have found the relevant part, read it carefully to make sure it has exactly the same meaning as the question. (The same topics and vocabulary may appear in more than one text, so be careful that the meaning matches the question exactly.)
- When you find the answer, mark it and write the question number on the text so that you can check it later.
- When you have answered all the questions, you can look again at the parts of the texts where you haven't found answers.

EXPERT STRATEGY

If you can't find the information immediately, put a question mark next to the question and go back to it later.

> **HELP**

2 Which hobby is likely to involve *regulations*? Look for another word with the same meaning. Remember that the text will not use the same words as the question.

5 A *commitment* is something you have to do, which stops you doing something else. Which section mentions this?

EXPERT WORD CHECK

beggars reservoirs upbringing vintage cars windsurfing

You are going to read an article about four people and their hobbies. For questions **1–10**, choose from the people (**A–D**). The people may be chosen more than once.

Which person says that their hobby:

is too expensive to do in some places?	1	D
must conform to certain fixed regulations?	2	
used to be associated with a particular type of person?	3	
involves learning by watching experts in the activity?	4	
fits in well with other commitments?	5	
has become easier thanks to recent improvements in the equipment?	6	
is associated with a certain type of clothing?	7	
sometimes provokes negative reactions in people?	8	
has advantages over another similar hobby?	9	
requires the clever combination of certain materials?	10	

Me and my passion

Four people talk about their hobbies

A Katie Holleran: accountant

When you mention windsurfing to people, they generally imagine
5 suntanned 20-year-olds. But the sport has matured since it started in the 1960s and so have its participants. Any
10 reasonably fit person can do it, and age isn't a barrier. Beginners need enough strength in their arms to pull themselves back up onto the board after falling off.

In the early days, sails and boards were made of heavy materials like polyethylene, and the sport was very physical. But improved
15 technology has changed all that. And you don't have to live by the sea – 50 percent of windsurfing takes place on inland lakes and reservoirs. I used to have a boat but with that you always need other people to help you. And you're not allowed to take a boat on some lakes, whereas you can windsurf anywhere.

B Kevin Shaw: builder
20

It's become a tradition in our household that I make an Indian curry every Monday evening.
25 I wanted to learn how to make my dishes more authentic, so I signed up for a cookery course at a top Indian restaurant in London. Every time I go, I learn something
30 new and I'm now building up quite a repertoire of curry recipes.

Andy, the head chef, is also a qualified teacher, which is a big advantage of the course. He explains how the herbs, spices, oils and rice used in Indian cooking are combined to get subtle variations in flavour. After all the theory, we go down to the
35 kitchen to observe Andy and his team of highly-qualified chefs in action and then, of course, we get to sample the dishes we've learned to cook.

C Karen Hallstrom: salesperson

When I tell people I race
40 vintage cars from the 1920s and 1930s, one question they're sure to ask is: 'Do you wear 1920s outfits, too?' 'No,'
45 is the polite version of my answer. I have to wear fireproof overalls and a helmet in order to meet modern safety laws, I'm afraid. Things have changed in other ways since the old days, too. To be allowed to race my cars, I had to pass both written
50 and practical tests. That wasn't difficult, but then vintage cars aren't a novelty to me: they were part of my upbringing. I used to spend hours, bored stiff, with my fingers stuck in my ears while my father watched races at the local motor-racing track. I said it was the last thing I'd ever do. But when I was a bit older, I too fell in love with
55 cars, first driving a vintage model at age 17.

D Joe Campilos: office worker

I'm lucky because, within reason, I can choose what hours I do
60 at the office and this means I have time to combine work with my real passion, which is jazz music. Every weekend, and sometimes on Fridays as well,
65 we play on the street. Not in the main square, as you need to buy a licence for that and it's a bit pricey, but in various places around the city where there are no regulations.

People sometimes complain because they think we're beggars but that's not fair. Although we do accept money, because it's
70 the accepted custom, that's not why we're there. It's really a kind of advertisement – if somebody likes what they hear, then they can hire us. We get to do weddings, parties, that sort of thing, which gives us a bit of extra pocket money.

9 The consumer society

9A A matter of conscience?

Vocabulary development 1

> **COURSEBOOK** pages 120–121

Phrasal verbs

1 Match the sentence halves. Then choose the correct particle in each phrasal verb.

1 Don't expect her to make a donation! She's saving *up / on* for

2 Charity organisations, like other businesses, need to keep *off / up* with

3 I'll soon be able to pay *up / back*

4 We've recently set *up / off*

5 The Oxfam shop in our town is so busy it needs to take *up / on*

6 He went to the bank to take *out / off*

7 They are so well off they were able to pay *for / off*

8 She took out her pen and wrote *down / out*

a the money I borrowed from you.
b some new members of staff.
c some money for his business trip.
d new developments in technology.
e a luxury cruise to the Bahamas.
f a business which employs only homeless people.
g a cheque for £5,000.
h their new car in cash.

Money

2 Put the letters in brackets in the correct order to complete the words.

1 I had to with_____ (wrad) £500 from my current ac_____ (tnouc) to pay for my computer.

2 When Bob in_____ (tedireh) money from his uncle, he decided to in_____ (stev) half of it in property and don_____ (eat) the rest to a charity.

3 Some friends of mine made a lot of money on the stock ma_____ (trek) recently. I took their advice and bought some sh_____ (ears) myself.

4 A man who had a painting he thought was worth_____ (sels) sold it at an au_____ (ticon) yesterday for £20,000.

5 My uncle runs a small business but the company's annual turn_____ (rove) has gone down. He's afraid that if the economy doesn't improve, he'll go bank_____ (trup).

6 The cost of li_____ (ngiv) has gone up slightly. The government says that the rate of in_____ (iaftlon) is now three percent.

Charity work

3a Complete the table.

Verb	Noun
donate	1 _____
distribute	2 _____
3 _____	suffering
be poor	4 live in _____
5 _____	a volunteer (= person)
6 _____	information
support	7 _____
collect	8 _____
9 _____	funds/funding
10 _____	a contribution

b Match the verbs (1–8) with the nouns (a–h) to make common collocations.

1 take
2 raise
3 set up
4 collect
5 distribute
6 make
7 relieve
8 receive

a a donation (from)
b a charity/an organisation
c a contribution (to)
d measures/action
e poverty/suffering
f funds (for)
g money (in the street)
h leaflets/food/medicines

c Complete the text with the correct form of words from Exercises 3a and 3b.

We are looking for (1) _____ to help us (2) _____ funds for a new Golden Age home for the elderly and homeless. We can't offer you money but we can offer you the chance to (3) _____ the suffering of many unfortunate older people. By giving us a little of your time each week, you will be (4) _____ a valuable contribution to society.

The first Golden Age home was (5) _____ in Cambridge in 1960. It was the idea of a group of students who wanted to help elderly people living in real (6) _____ . They were not content just to talk about the problem – they were determined to (7) _____ action. Since then the organisation has received thousands of pounds in (8) _____ from the public and runs three homes in different cities. We need you to go into the streets to (9) _____ more money for us. We also need you to (10) _____ leaflets which both inform people of the work we are doing and explain the need for their help.

Exam practice: Multiple-choice cloze

(Paper 1 Part 1)

4   Do the task.

*For questions **1–8**, read the text below and decide which answer (**A**, **B**, **C** or **D**) best fits each gap. There is an example at the beginning (**0**).*

The Rough Guide story

When Mark Ellingham went to Greece in the late 1970s, he couldn't find a guidebook he liked. There was nothing available which (**0**) __A__ Greece as a 20th-century, living culture and which didn't (**1**) _____ you feel inadequate for not having a lot of money. So Mark and his friends set out to write their own. *The Rough Guide to Greece*, published in 1982, was a (**2**) _____ success and the publisher asked this small (**3**) _____ of recent college graduates to repeat the formula for Spain and Portugal. Today there are over 200 *Rough Guide* titles (**4**) _____ the market.

Nowadays, the *Rough Guides* no longer seem (**5**) _____ 'rough' and are no longer solely aimed at readers on a budget because the books (**6**) _____ to a much wider (**7**) _____ of readers than was originally anticipated. Today, therefore, they (**8**) _____ information about upmarket hotels and restaurants as well as cheap ones.

0	A treated	B dealt	C handled	D faced
1	A cause	B result	C make	D lead
2	A bright	B great	C strong	D loud
3	A team	B crew	C gang	D committee
4	A to	B on	C at	D in
5	A absolutely	B particularly	C specifically	D definitely
6	A attracted	B influenced	C appealed	D affected
7	A range	B collection	C set	D number
8	A take	B compose	C put	D include

EXPERT STRATEGY

If you can't answer a question, go on to the next one and come back to it later.

➤ HELP

1 Read after the gap and choose the word that goes with the verb *feel*.
5 The word you need has the meaning *especially*.
7 Which words collocates with *range*?

EXPERT LANGUAGE

Find a word with a negative prefix and a word with a positive prefix in the text.

EXPERT WORD CHECK

formula   guidebook   publisher   rough   upmarket

Language development 1

➤ **COURSEBOOK** pages 122–123, **EXPERT GRAMMAR** pages 194–195

Zero, first and second conditionals

1a   Choose the correct answers.

1 If Stella *opens / will open* her shop in the high street, she'll make lots of money.
2 If the economy doesn't improve, lots of businesses *will close / would close* down.
3 If you were sensible, you *will put / would put* that money in the bank.
4 Sue is so generous she always gives money if someone *asks / will ask* her.
5 George may go to prison unless he *pays / will pay* his taxes.
6 The organisation *was / would be* more effective if it was sponsored by the government.
7 If the employees of a company *are / were* happy, they work harder.
8 We might sell our business if it *makes / would make* another loss this year.
9 If you *were / would be* in John's position, what would you do?
10 If the public *don't give / didn't give* money to homeless people, they would face great hardship.

b   Look at each sentence again and decide if the condition is:
   a always true.
   b possible or likely.
   c unlikely or imaginary.

Conjunctions

2   Complete the sentences with the conjunctions in the box. More than one answer may be possible, but use each conjunction once only.

as long as   even if   if   provided that   unless

1 I think I'll be able to stay in business _____ the bank lends me the money I need.
2 You can ask your boss for a rise but you won't get one. _____ you beg him, he won't give you one!
3 We'll make a nice profit this year _____ people continue to buy our books.
4 Amanda's well qualified but _____ she makes more effort she'll end up unemployed.
5 Rick will pass his driving test easily _____ he keeps a cool head.

Third conditional

3 Complete the third conditional sentences with the correct form of the verbs in brackets.

1 If I _____ (invest) money in that company last year, I _____ (make) a considerable profit.

2 If people _____ (support) small local businesses more, so many of them _____ (not close down).

3 If my brother _____ (not sell) those shares last month, he _____ (lose) £5,000.

4 Keith _____ (not set up) his own business if he _____ (listen) to his friends.

5 If Julia _____ (not leave) her purse at home, she _____ (give) some money to the busker.

6 Colin _____ (give) you some valuable financial advice if you _____ (ask) him.

7 Oliver _____ (not be able) to buy all the equipment he needed if he _____ (not borrow) £200 from his father.

8 I _____ (buy) a ticket for the concert if I _____ (know) that all the money was for famine relief.

Mixed conditionals

4 Write mixed conditional sentences using the information given.

1 Sheila went to Peru on holiday. She owns a language school in Lima today.
   If Sheila hadn't gone to Peru on holiday, she wouldn't own a language school in Lima today.

2 I didn't go into business with my best friend. I'm not rich and successful today.
   If _____
   _____ .

3 Friends supported me when I lost my home and job. I'm not a beggar on the street today.
   If _____
   _____ .

4 My brother didn't take the advice of his teachers. He has apartments in New York and London today.
   If _____
   _____ .

5 Julia is a really good journalist. She won the *Journalist of the Year* award recently.
   If _____
   _____ .

6 Large numbers of people are homeless today. The government didn't help the survivors of the earthquake.
   If _____
   _____ .

Key word transformations

5 Complete the second sentence so that it has a similar meaning to the first sentence, using the word given. Do not change the word given. Use between two and five words, including the word given.

1 I didn't know about her birthday, so I didn't send her any flowers.
   SOME
   If I had known about her birthday, I _____ flowers.

2 He is very rich today because he bought shares in an oil company.
   BE
   If he hadn't bought shares in an oil company, he _____ today.

3 If you obey the rules, you won't have any problems.
   LONG
   You won't have any problems _____ the rules.

4 You don't get good marks because you don't study hard.
   HARDER
   If you studied _____ better marks.

5 Listen carefully or you won't know what to do.
   IF
   You won't know what to do _____ carefully.

6 Anna speaks such good German because she lived in Hamburg for ten years.
   SO
   If Anna hadn't lived in Hamburg for ten years, she _____ well.

7 Unless you make some serious mistakes, I'm sure you'll do well in the interview.
   PROVIDED
   I'm sure you'll do well in the interview _____ make any serious mistakes.

8 You feel so tired every day because you go to bed late.
   EARLIER
   If you went to bed _____ so tired every day.

9 No matter how hard you work, you'll never earn as much money as a lawyer.
   EVEN
   You'll never earn as much money as a lawyer, _____ really hard.

10 Without a law degree, you won't get that job in Paris that you want.
   UNLESS
   You won't get that job in Paris that you want _____ a law degree.

Writing (Paper 2 Part 2: Article)

➤ COURSEBOOK pages 124–125, EXPERT WRITING page 201

Understand and plan the task

> **EXPERT STRATEGY**
> In Paper 2, writing, remember to make a paragraph plan before you write so your ideas are presented clearly.

1a Read the writing task and mark the points you have to include in your article.

b Make a paragraph plan for your article.
Paragraph 1: _____
Paragraph 2: _____
Paragraph 3: _____
Paragraph 4: _____

You have seen this announcement in a money magazine for students.

Articles wanted!

BEST BUY

- **What is the best thing you have ever bought?**
- **Why did you buy it?**
- **Why do you like it so much?**

Write us an article answering these questions. We will publish the best articles in the magazine.

*Write your **article** in **140–190** words in an appropriate style.*

Check and improve a sample answer

2a Read a student's answer and tick the points you marked in the task as they are mentioned. Does the article include all the information?

b How many paragraphs does the article have? Compare the organisation with your plan.

c Complete the article with the words/phrases in the box. There are two extra words/phrases which you do not need to use.

> *apart from   because of this   finally   one reason to my mind   way I see it*

Best buy

I have bought __a large quantity of__ things in my life but **(1)** _____ the best thing of all is my phone.

<u>Initially</u>, I bought my phone so that I could <u>communicate</u> with my friends and family. I knew also that I could use it to go online and to take photos. And **(2)** _____ that, I'll admit that I wanted the latest phone because all my friends <u>possessed</u> one!

I totally love my phone because, thanks to all the apps I've downloaded, it is so much more useful than I expected it to be. I use my phone to keep track of how much exercise I <u>perform</u>, its alarm clock wakes me up in the morning and **(3)** _____ , the money app helps me look after my money.

I'm much more organised now that I have my phone. The **(4)** _____ , it has changed my life. I couldn't live without it!

d The underlined words/phrases in the article are too formal. Replace them with the more appropriate informal ones below (a–f). There is one extra word/phrase which you do not need to use.
a do
b had
c in the beginning
d keep in touch
e lastly
f many

e Rewrite the article to include the improvements you made.

Listening (Paper 3 Part 4)

Before you listen

1 Read the listening task. Mark the key words and think about what you will hear. What do you think Mandy did with the money she won?

Multiple choice

2a 🎧 13 Listen once and choose the best answer (A, B or C). (The questions follow the order of the text.)

b 🎧 13 Listen again and check your answers. Make sure the options you did not choose are not possible.

c Was your prediction in Exercise 1 correct?

EXPERT STRATEGY

Remember that you hear each recording twice. Use the second time to check your answers.

➤ HELP

1 Listen to what Mandy says about her friend Louise.
2 Listen for how Mandy's father looked – the answer comes soon afterwards.
3 When Mandy says, 'If I'd known ...,' what is she referring to?

EXPERT LANGUAGE

Find two examples of the past perfect simple in the listening task.

EXPERT WORD CHECK

begging letters   lottery   publicised resenting   wisely

You will hear a radio interview with a woman who won a lot of money in a lottery. For questions 1–7, choose the best answer (A, B or C).

1 What does Mandy say about her winning lottery ticket?
   A It was the first one she'd ever bought.
   B She had a feeling it was going to win.
   C She was persuaded to buy it by a friend.

2 How did Mandy's father react to the news that she'd won?
   A He was too shocked to speak.
   B He became rather over-excited.
   C He rushed to tell her the news.

3 Mandy now feels that she made a mistake when
   A she allowed her win to be publicised.
   B she trusted the people at the TV station.
   C she told her story to a newspaper reporter.

4 How did Mandy feel about the way certain people reacted to her win?
   A disappointed with close friends
   B unsure of strangers
   C annoyed by her family

5 What does Mandy say about her friend Louise?
   A She refused to accept the gift Mandy bought her.
   B She became rude and unfriendly towards Mandy.
   C She couldn't help resenting Mandy's good fortune.

6 How did the begging letters affect Mandy?
   A She wished she'd never won the lottery at all.
   B She became angry with the people who sent them.
   C She realised that it wasn't right to have so much money.

7 What does Mandy feel about the money now?
   A glad that she's given it all away
   B content with the lifestyle it's given her
   C sorry that she didn't use it more wisely

Vocabulary development 2

➤ **COURSEBOOK** pages 126–127

Ways of shopping

1a Look at the pictures (A–D). Which method of shopping do the statements (1–12) refer to? Match the pictures with the statements.

1 There are big trolleys to put your shopping in. _____

2 You can find all the shops you need in one place. _____

3 The fruit and vegetables you buy are often very dirty. _____

4 You don't have to leave your living room to shop. _____

5 There is usually a place where people can sit and relax, with a fountain or some exotic plants. _____

6 Before you can buy anything, you have to send the company your credit card number. _____

7 There are usually several checkouts where you can pay, so you don't have to queue for long. _____

8 If it's raining, you can go from shop to shop without getting wet. _____

9 Sometimes they don't let you pick the fruit or vegetables you want yourself. _____

10 You have a lot of choice. If you want coffee, for example, there may be 20 different types of coffee on the shelf. _____

11 What they send you may be different from what you ordered. _____

12 The produce is always from local farms and tastes wonderful. _____

b Look at the statements in Exercise 1a and decide whether it is an advantage (✔) or a disadvantage (✗) or it doesn't matter (–).

Commonly confused words

2 Complete the sentences with the most appropriate word or phrase A, B, C or D.

1 I asked the assistant for a bottle of herbal shampoo but she said they were _____ .
   A in stock   C on sale
   B out of stock   D for sale

2 The assistant said that she couldn't give me a refund without a _____ .
   A receipt   C prescription
   B recipe   D ticket

3 In the sale I paid £20 instead of £50 for my new camera, so it was an absolute _____ .
   A reduction   C opportunity
   B discount   D bargain

4 How much is this shampoo? I can't see the _____ anywhere.
   A price   C cost
   B fee   D payment

5 Small shops usually treat their regular _____ better than supermarkets do.
   A patients   C customers
   B clients   D shoppers

6 What _____ of washing-up liquid do you normally buy?
   A mark   C brand
   B make   D label

7 In our local street market, there's a _____ which sells delicious hot potatoes.
   A counter   C table
   B stall   D store

8 If you buy clothes from a mail-order company, you choose what you want from a _____ .
   A prospectus   C directory
   B brochure   D catalogue

9 You can pay for your new computer in monthly _____ if you wish.
   A doses   C instalments
   B parts   D cheques

10 I wanted to buy a small radio, so I went to a shop which sells electrical _____ .
   A produce   C purchases
   B goods   D exports

Language development 2

➤ **COURSEBOOK** page 130

Subject–verb agreement: Singular and plural verbs

1a Decide if the underlined words need a singular or plural verb. Then choose the correct answers.

1 I think that 120 euros *is / are* a lot of <u>money</u> to pay for a shirt.
2 Some <u>people</u> only *buys / buy* clothes with a designer label.
3 The <u>furniture</u> we bought at that shop *was / were* not very well made.
4 <u>Economics</u> *is / are* my favourite subject at college.
5 <u>The police</u> *thinks / think* that Tom stole that camera from a shop.
6 <u>Everybody</u> in my village *has / have* to go shopping in the nearby town.
7 <u>The majority of</u> my friends *spends / spend* more than £30 a week on clothes.
8 Local <u>politics</u> *doesn't / don't* interest me at all, I'm afraid.
9 My father moved his shop to another building because the old <u>premises</u> *was / were* unsuitable.
10 These new <u>trousers</u> *is / are* far too tight for me.
11 <u>A number of</u> new shops *has / have* opened in town recently.
12 <u>The United States</u> *has / have* just passed a new law about advertising.

b Write the underlined words from Exercise 1a in the correct column.

Noun + singular verb	Noun + plural verb

c Complete the shop notice with the correct form of *be* or *have*.

The police **(1)** _____ suggested that we introduce closed-circuit television on the premises of this store. As most staff **(2)** _____ aware, a total of £3,000 worth of stock **(3)** _____ stolen last month as a result of shoplifting. Although a group of teenagers **(4)** _____ been arrested in connection with this theft, the problem continues. Whilst recognising that 90 percent of our customers **(5)** _____ honest people, we feel that urgent measures need to be taken. More than one shop in this neighbourhood **(6)** _____ had to close as a result of such losses. The police authorities **(7)** _____ advised us that the installation of cameras in the shop will have immediate results. Each member of staff **(8)** _____ asked to support us in this matter.

all, both, neither, none and one

2a Read the information about three celebrities who love shopping and spending money.

Victoria Beckham

Birth name: Victoria Caroline Adams
Date of birth: 17 April 17 1974
Place of birth: Essex, UK
Occupation(s): singer, songwriter, fashion designer, businesswoman
Marital status: married David Beckham, the football player (1999)
Family details: has three sons (Brooklyn, Romeo and Cruz) and a daughter (Harper)
Other information: David Beckham once bought her an entire Versace collection of clothes. Their wedding reception probably cost more than £500,000.

Taylor Swift

Birth name: Taylor Alison Swift
Date of birth: 13 December 1989
Place of birth: Wyomissing, Pennsylvania, USA
Occupation(s): singer-songwriter
Marital status: unmarried
Family details: father was a financial advisor, mother was a marketing executive
Other information: is a supporter of arts education; in 2012 pledged $4 million to fund the building of a new education centre in Nashville, Tennessee

Georg Clooney

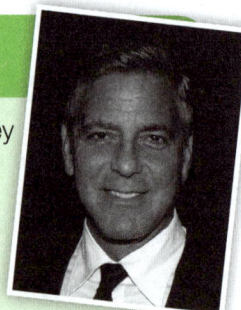

Birth name: George Timothy Clooney
Date of birth: 6 May 1961
Place of birth: Lexington, Kentucky, USA
Occupation(s): actor and film-maker
Marital status: married Amal Alamuddin in 2014
Family details: father was a game show host on TV, mother was a beauty pageant queen
Other information: has a house on the banks of the River Thames near London which is said to be worth £10 million

b Write sentences comparing the three celebrities. Use the information in Exercise 2a and the prompts below. Put the verbs in the correct tense. Begin your sentences with one of the phrases in the box.

All of them …   Both X and Y …   Neither X nor Y …
None of them …   One of them …
---

1 be / rich
   All of them are rich.
2 Taylor Swift / George Clooney / be / born / USA
3 be born / the 60s
4 have / parents / in show business
5 come from / Canada
6 Victoria Beckham / George Clooney / be / married
7 Victoria Beckham / Taylor Swift / be / songwriter
8 have / a child
9 Taylor Swift / George Clooney / have / a daughter
10 be / TV presenter
11 got married / 2014
12 Victoria Beckham / Taylor Swift / be / singers

c Write more sentences of your own using the information in Exercise 2a.

it / there

3 Find and correct the mistakes with the use of *it* and *there* in some of the sentences. Tick the correct ones.

1 I was late for a doctor's appointment yesterday because it was a lot of traffic.
2 I don't want to watch this programme anymore. It's really boring.
3 'I need to buy some stamps. Is it a post office near here?' 'Yes, it's a post office in George Street.'
4 It's a good idea to shop around before you buy a computer.
5 It used to be a second-hand bookshop in this street, but it's not here now.
6 Where's my mobile phone? Is it in the kitchen?
7 Did you know there's my birthday today? I'm 16.
8 I think we should go home now. There's nearly two in the morning.
9 Excuse me, how far is there to the airport from here?

Key word transformations

4 Complete the second sentence so that it has a similar meaning to the first sentence, using the word given. Do not change the word given. You must use between two and five words, including the word given.

1 I can hear you perfectly so you don't need to shout.
   NO
   I can hear you perfectly, so _____ to shout.
2 As Jack usually arrived on time, I began to feel rather worried.
   UNUSUAL
   As _____ to be late, I began to feel rather worried.
3 How long was your flight from London to Bucharest?
   TAKE
   How long _____ fly from London to Bucharest?
4 Don't worry if you can't find Mexcafé because most brands of coffee are similar.
   MATTER
   Most brands of coffee are similar, so _____ if you can't find Mexcafé.
5 Why are the supermarket shelves empty?
   NOTHING
   Why _____ the supermarket shelves?
6 Do you think this radio is faulty?
   PROBLEM
   Do you think _____ this radio?
7 For the time being, planes can't land as it's too foggy at the airport.
   FOG
   For the time being, planes can't land as _____ at the airport.
8 I enjoyed seeing Angela again, didn't you?
   LOVELY
   Wasn't _____ Angela again?
9 Will many people be waiting outside the cinema, do you think?
   QUEUE
   Will _____ outside the cinema, do you think?
10 It rained heavily last night and all the rivers have flooded.
   STORM
   All the rivers have flooded because _____ last night.

Reading (Paper 1 Part 6)

Before you read

1a Read the instructions for the reading task and the title of the article and answer the question.

What does *shy away from* mean?
a avoid using
b feel happy about

b Think of some possible answers to the question in the title.
The postage can be expensive.

Skimming

2 Skim the article. What answers does it give to the question in the title? Mark those parts of the text and compare with your own ideas in Exercise 1b.

Gapped text

3a Read paragraphs 1 and 2 and sentence D. Mark the words in sentence D that link to the highlighted words in the text.

b Read the rest of the article carefully and do the task. Follow these steps.

- Re-read the paragraph before and after each gap and think about what information is missing.
- Choose the sentence that fits in terms of topic and language links.
- Read the whole text again, with your answers, to check that it makes sense.

EXPERT STRATEGY

Remember that there is one option which you do not need to use. When you've answered all the questions, check to be sure that this option doesn't fit anywhere.

➤ HELP

B Look for what *this category* refers to in the text.
F Look for what *such people* refers to in the text.
G Look for a *finding* in the text on page 91.

EXPERT LANGUAGE

Find the following in sentences A–G:

1 two linking words that express contrast.
2 one linking phrase that is used to add information.

EXPERT WORD CHECK

hardware   mindset   navigate
outlets   postage   reluctant
to safeguard

You are going to read an article about shopping on the internet. Six sentences have been removed from the article. Choose from the sentences (A–G) the one that fits each gap (1–6). There is one extra sentence which you do not need to use.

A What's more, it's not just older people who find it hard to navigate e-commerce sites; younger people also say that the sites are dull to look at and that items aren't laid out logically.

B Indeed, a large proportion of online shoppers fall into this category, no doubt reflecting their interest in things like books and games rather than clothes and food.

C The more interesting question, however, is how sellers are likely to respond to this change and find new ways of offering a mix of online and offline outlets.

D But underlying these stated reasons, there's also a fundamental difference between conventional shopping and online services, and this has a part to play.

E Attitudes towards the available hardware are another factor in this domestic mindset, with many families continuing to regard their online presence as part of an entertainment set-up, or else as a tool for study, work or social relations.

F The concerns for such people tend to be broader social issues, such as privacy and the possible effects of the internet on the way we live.

G It is a finding that leads one to wonder what it would take to get the rest of the population e-shopping as their default option.

Vocabulary

4 Read the text again. Choose five useful expressions or collocations connected with shopping on the internet to add to your vocabulary notebook.

e-commerce site (= a website where you can buy goods or services)
purchase (something) online

Why do some shoppers still shy away from the net ?

Shopping on the internet should be easy and stress-free: no queues, no rude assistants, lots of choice and your purchases delivered to your door. Yet, *according to researchers, some people are still surprisingly reluctant to buy from e-commerce sites*, often limiting
5 their online purchases to things like books, games and travel tickets.

The main explanations given for this reluctance to go e-shopping are fears about the security of payments, the added costs of postage, concerns about the
10 practicalities of delivery and the possible need to return products that don't live up to expectations. [1] [D] Both the pleasure of unplanned purchases and the ability to examine products are missing online and for many, the experience of shopping – especially
15 for clothes – is just as important as the products themselves.

People recognise the convenience of e-commerce in principle – especially for food shopping – but even the regular supermarket visit is a complex activity where
20 personal and luxury items can be bought on impulse or with a specific occasion, person or meal in mind. It's hard to reproduce the pleasure of this experience using an unfriendly list-based choice on a computer screen. [2] [ ]

25 There appear to be three main groups of people who do not shop online. The first has little experience of internet shopping but is potentially interested. The second group tends to be older, less educated people who may never give it a try. Members of the third group
30 are relatively wealthy and computer literate but have other reasons for not shopping on the web. [3] [ ] Surprisingly, however, these reservations don't stop them using the web for other reasons.

And even amongst those who do shop online, most
35 continue to view it as an alternative, thinking more of the integration of e-commerce services into their current household routine, rather than taking the opportunity to rethink how they organise their home lives. [4] [ ]

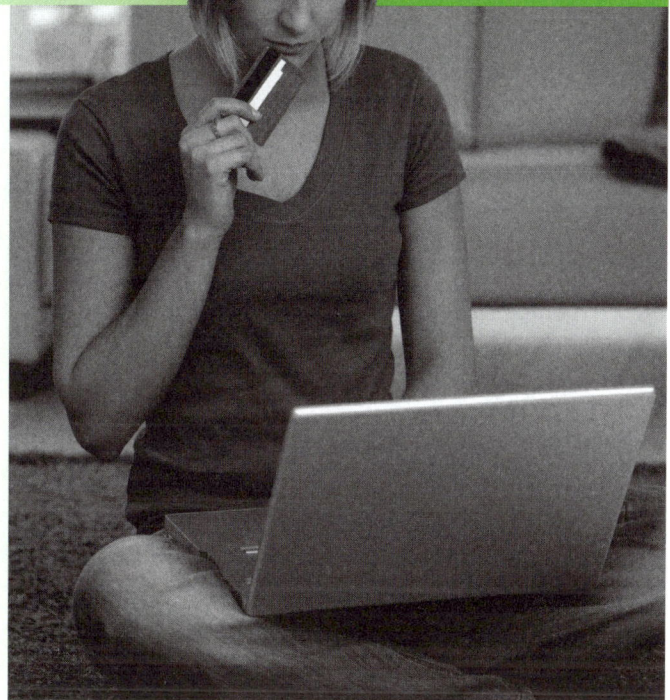

40 This could be a drawback, however, because often the hardware isn't always integrated into the places in the household where decisions about family shopping are made. Perhaps this is why single young men remain the greatest fans of e-commerce.
45 [5] [ ]

Researchers have concluded, therefore, that those who are most positive about e-commerce are focusing on the convenience and the price advantage for particular products and not on the shopping
50 experience itself. [6] [ ] There seems to be some doubt about this. More of us may be encouraged to shop online as manufacturers overcome bad web design and learn to safeguard our privacy but will internet shopping ever seriously replace the stress and
55 thrill of the real thing?

Vocabulary development 1

➤ **COURSEBOOK** pages 134–135

> **EXPERT STRATEGY**
>
> In Paper 4, Speaking, Part 1, you may be asked how you usually spend your holidays. In Part 2, photographs of different types of travel or holiday are quite common. You could be asked to compare them and to say why people chose to go on holidays like these. Make sure you know the necessary vocabulary to do this.

Different kinds of holiday

1a What type of holiday is each speaker describing? Match the holidays in the box with the comments. Mark the words which help you decide.

adventure holiday   camping holiday   city break
package holiday   safari   skiing holiday

1 'I love this kind of holiday. You do so many exciting things. Last year, our group went to a remote part of Spain. We had a fantastic time – white-water rafting, rock climbing, canoeing and even hang-gliding.' _____

2 'I go with my friends every year. We rent a chalet in the village and spend every day on the slopes. In the evenings, we just warm ourselves in front of the fire.' _____

3 'I know it's not as exciting as travelling on your own but it's not as stressful. Basically, everything is organised for you – flights, accommodation, meals – everything. The tour company may even organise excursions to different places of interest.' _____

4 'It can get a bit tiring sometimes, especially if you spend a long time going somewhere by jeep. It's incredible, though, when you see lions or elephants in the wild for the first time.' _____

5 'Every year I go with my parents to the same place. We even put up our tent under the same tree each time. There are lots of facilities on the site – there's even a games room!' _____

6 'I don't have much time for holidays. Occasionally, I take a couple of days off work and go to somewhere like Vienna or Prague. I stay in a luxury hotel and do as much sightseeing as I can. When I get home, I feel like a different person.' _____

b Write a short paragraph about your favourite kind of holiday.

Things you need on holiday

2 Match the items below with the types of holiday in the box and write them in your notebook. Some items may go in more than one category. Can you add any more words?

beach holiday   camping holiday   safari
skiing holiday   trekking holiday

- an airbed
- antiseptic cream
- a camera with telephoto lens
- a family tent
- insect repellent
- a mask and snorkel
- a one-man tent
- a pair of strong walking boots
- plasters

- a rucksack
- skis and ski boots
- a sleeping bag
- sunglasses
- suntan lotion
- a swimming costume
- a thermos flask
- a walking stick
- a warm anorak and bobble hat
- a wide-brimmed hat

Verb + noun collocations

3a Complete the sentences the words/phrases in the box.

credit cards   currency   flight   inoculations
insurance   passport   reservation   work permit

1 When you've decided where you want to go, you need to <u>book</u> a _____ . You can do this with an online travel company.
2 It may be advisable to make a hotel _____ . The city gets very busy in the summer months.
3 Don't forget to apply for a _____ in good time if you don't already have one. Without this, you won't be able to go anywhere!
4 For some tropical countries, it's important to have _____ for diseases like cholera before you set off.
5 Make sure you take out suitable _____ . This will cover you if you are ill or lose your belongings.
6 If you intend to work in a particular country, find out if you need to apply for a _____ beforehand.
7 Take some cash with you as _____ are not always accepted. Go to a bank and change some money into the _____ of the country you are going to.

b Look at the sentences in 3a again. Mark the verb which collocates with the noun you wrote in each gap. The first one has been done for you.

Exam practice: Multiple-choice cloze (Paper 1 Part 1)

4 Do the task.

*For questions **1–8**, read the text below and decide which answer (**A**, **B**, **C** or **D**) best fits each gap. There is an example at the beginning (**0**).*

A famous traveller

Wilfred Thesiger's work is a constant (0) _A_ of inspiration for other travel writers. Wilfred was born and (1) _____ up in East Africa. In the late 1940s, he travelled to the Arabian peninsula to (2) _____ information for a locust control project. There, he first (3) _____ across the Bedu people, the traditional nomadic inhabitants of the desert, who would accompany him on two historic crossings of an absolutely (4) _____ area known as the Empty Quarter and introduce him to their harsh way of life.

Travel and exploration gave meaning to Thesiger's life. (5) _____ he was travelling, he lived as a nomad, visiting remote (6) _____ of the world, often on (7) _____ , living simply among the local people and writing about his experiences. His books, more than any others, have caught our imagination and led us to (8) _____ the beauty and solitude of the great desert expanses.

0	A source	B spring	C reason	D origin
1	A brought	B raised	C fetched	D reared
2	A gather	B learn	C listen	D search
3	A met	B encountered	C came	D got
4	A vast	B big	C large	D extensive
5	A While	B Throughout	C During	D Alongside
6	A sides	B edges	C corners	D surfaces
7	A horse	B foot	C camel	D bicycle
8	A fascinate	B appreciate	C delight	D amuse

> **EXPERT STRATEGY**
>
> Keep reading the words before and after the gap when choosing your answer.

> **HELP**
>
> 2 The option you need means 'to collect'.
> 4 The answer is the only word that collocates with *absolutely*.
> 7 Only one of these words can follow the preposition *on*.

Language development 1

> ➤ **COURSEBOOK** pages 136–137, **EXPERT GRAMMAR** pages 195–196

Active and passive

1 Choose the correct answers.

1 A lot of people *suffer / are suffered* from travel sickness.
2 An excellent guidebook to France *has just / has just been* published.
3 The number of visitors to the UK *was decreased / decreased* last year.
4 A new holiday resort *is being built / is building* on the south coast.
5 The hotel *will finish / will be finished* next year.
6 Anyone wishing to visit China must *apply / be applied* for a visa.

Passive forms

2 Rewrite the sentences in the passive to make them appropriate for a leaflet giving information to airline passengers. Be careful with word order.

> ### Important information for passengers:
>
> 1 We kindly request passengers to keep their seat belts fastened during take-off.
> Passengers _____ .
> 2 We have banned smoking on all flights, in accordance with recent regulations.
> Smoking _____ .
> 3 You must put hand luggage under your seat or in the compartment above the seat.
> Hand _____ .
> 4 You can obtain information about the flight from the personnel on board.
> Information _____ .
> 5 We have trained all our flight assistants to deal with emergency situations.
> All _____ .
> 6 We will make every effort to ensure that passengers have a pleasant trip.
> Every _____ .

> **EXPERT LANGUAGE**
>
> Find two phrasal verbs in the text.

> **EXPERT WORD CHECK**
>
> *crossings   expanses   harsh   locust   nomad*

Verbs with two objects

3   Rewrite the sentences, making the words in *italics* the subject. Omit the agent (*by* …) if it is not necessary.

1 The travel agency posted us *the tickets*.
The tickets were posted to us by the travel agency.

2 The bank gave *me* a loan of £2,000.
_____

3 The hotel management offers every guest *a complimentary bowl of fruit*.
_____

4 Airlines have promised *travellers* cheaper flights for years.
_____

5 One of our guides will show *you* the city's main attractions.
_____

6 The judges awarded Peter *the first prize in the competition*.
_____

Passive report structures

4a   Rewrite each sentence in two ways.

1 People say that Prague is one of the most beautiful cities in the world.
a Prague is said to _____ .
b It is said that _____ .

2 Newspapers report that airport workers are going on strike next week.
a Airport workers are reported _____ .
b It is reported _____ .

3 People expect the government to introduce new measures to boost tourism.
a The government _____ .
b It is expected _____ .

4 People think the missing tourist has been abducted.
a The missing tourist _____ .
b It _____ .

b   Complete the text with the correct form of the verbs in brackets.

Hollywood star Rod Osbourne is believed **(1)** _____ (be) in hospital in a small village in Switzerland. It **(2)** _____ (not know) exactly what happened but it **(3)** _____ (think) that the Oscar-award-winning actor **(4)** _____ (involve) in an accident while skiing in the Alps last week. Sources at the hospital confirm that Osbourne's injuries are not serious. He is said **(5)** _____ (make) good progress since the accident and is expected **(6)** _____ (leave) the hospital in a few days. At the moment his wife, top model Lucy Evans, is believed **(7)** _____ (stay) in a hotel near the hospital. She is reported **(8)** _____ (fly) to the village as soon as she heard the news.

Key word transformations

5   Complete the second sentence so that it has a similar meaning to the first sentence, using the word given. Do not change the word given. You must use between two and five words, including the word given.

1 One of the local people gave us directions.
GIVEN
We _____ one of the local people.

2 The price of the ticket included refreshments.
INCLUDED
Refreshments _____ the price of the ticket.

3 The guide made us take our shoes off before entering the museum.
MADE
We _____ take our shoes off before entering the museum.

4 They are going to publish a new series of guidebooks soon.
PUBLISHED
A new series of guidebooks _____ soon.

5 They say that the Puppet Theatre is worth visiting.
SAID
The Puppet Theatre _____ worth visiting.

6 The shop has not developed our photographs yet.
HAVE
Our photographs _____ yet.

7 It is believed that they cancelled their trip at the last moment.
BELIEVED
They _____ their trip at the last moment.

8 The flight attendant offers the passengers sweets before take-off.
GIVEN
Sweets _____ before take-off.

9 They don't let you use electronic equipment during take-off and landing.
ALLOWED
You _____ electronic equipment during take-off and landing.

10 The tour leader welcomed us when we arrived at the hotel.
WELCOMED
On arrival at the hotel, _____ the tour leader.

Writing (Paper 2 Part 2: Semi-formal email)

➤ **COURSEBOOK** pages 138–139, **EXPERT WRITING** page 203

EXPERT STRATEGY
When writing an email, make sure you write for the reader specified in the task and answer all the parts of the question. Choose the right style – for example, formal or informal – and use it consistently. Remember to check your spelling, punctuation and the word count.

Understand the task

1 Read the writing task and answer the questions.
   1 What does Marta want you to do?
   2 What style will you use in your reply?
   3 How many parts are there to the question? Mark the parts of the task that tell you what to include in your email.

You have received this email from your English-speaking friend Marta.

From: Marta
Subject: Accommodation

Hi,

My cousin is visiting your area later this year with her husband and two small children. Can you suggest some places they can stay? They don't mind if it's a hotel or self-catering – the most important thing is that it's family-friendly.

I don't know what their budget is, so could you suggest three places: expensive, reasonable and cheap!

Thanks!
Marta

*Write your **email** in 140–190 words in an appropriate style.*

Check and improve a sample answer

2a Read a student's email. Does it include all the information required? Tick the parts of the task you marked.

b The student's email is short because not enough 'supporting details' are provided. Read the supporting details in the notes below and decide where you would add them.

c The underlined expressions in the email are too formal. Rewrite them in a more appropriate way.

d Rewrite the email, including the improvements you made.

@ [Home] [Previous] [Next]   [Search]

To: Marta

From: _____

Subject: Accommodation

Dear Madam,

Great to hear from you! I'd like to apologise for not replying sooner but I was away for the weekend.

Some research has been done and I think these three might suit your cousin.

The five-star Victoria Hotel is in the centre of town and has some family rooms. It's the most expensive but it's in a good location and has the best reviews online. (supporting details (1) _____)

Green Court Self-Catering Apartments is the least expensive but it looks satisfactory. The accommodation is basic but it's clean and not too far from town. (supporting details (2) _____)

There's a mid-price Travellers' Home Hotel near the motorway. It's about five miles from the centre but has a swimming pool and a children's play area. (supporting details (3) _____)

I trust this helps!

Supporting details

a   Obviously, they'd need to buy their own food but there's a supermarket next door and a couple of pizza places on the same road.

b   Although it's the least convenient, it's perhaps the most family-friendly. It only has a café but there are three restaurants in the same area.

c   The family rooms have a double bed and a sofa that converts into another one. The restaurant is expensive but breakfast is included in the price.

Listening (Paper 3 Part 2)

Before you listen

1 Read the listening task. Think about the topic and try to predict the kind of information that is missing.

Sentence completion

2a 🎧 14 Listen once and do the task.

b 🎧 14 Listen again and check your answers.

EXPERT STRATEGY

In a good talk or presentation, the speaker explains what the talk will be about and introduces each main point clearly before going into the details. Listen out for these signals as they tell you when you have to listen for specific information.

➤ **HELP**

1 You're listening for the name of the booklet.
4 This is the third point in a list. Listen for the word *thirdly*.
9 Listen to the information about colours.

EXPERT LANGUAGE

Underline the modal verbs in the task. Which of them express:
1 obligation?
2 possibility?

EXPERT WORD CHECK

*allocations   deposit   golden rules
porter   wake-up call*

You will hear part of a staff training meeting in a hotel. For questions 1–10, complete the sentences with a word or short phrase.

Clipstone Hotel: staff training

The trainer refers the staff to a booklet entitled (1) _____ .

Receptionists should always use the guests' (2) _____ .

Receptionists should always (3) _____ guests and apologise for any delays.

Receptionists mustn't forget to (4) _____ at all times.

Rooms ready for guests checking in are marked by a(n) (5) _____ on the screen.

Staff should check whether a(n) (6) _____ room has been requested or not.

Staff should ask whether guests have a(n) (7) _____ with them.

Staff should check whether guests want a(n) (8) _____ in the morning.

When guests check out, a(n) (9) _____ on the screen means that extras need to be paid for.

When checking out, guests may need information or a(n) (10) _____ .

Structuring a talk

3 In these extracts from the recording, the speaker introduces each main point of her talk. Number them in order.

☐ **a** The company regards the reception desk as one of the most important places in the hotel. … So, first and foremost, remember the three golden rules: …

☐ **b** So, the purpose of this meeting is just to quickly run through some of the training points that can get forgotten in busy periods.

☐ **c** So, that's check-in. Although there are busy periods for this, it's not as bad as checking out.

☐ **d** Now, most guests have two main points of contact with the reception desk. When they check in and when they leave. So, I'll go through those two procedures in detail. When guests first arrive, …

☐ **e** First of all, I'd like to talk about the reception desk.

Vocabulary development 2

> **COURSEBOOK** pages 140–141

Transport questionnaire

1   Do the quiz. Choose the correct answer (A, B, C or D). Then add up your score and find out what kind of traveller you are! (A = 1 point, B = 2 points, C = 3 points)

What kind of traveller are you?

1   When you go to work/college in the morning, you:
   A   use your car or get a lift in a friend's car.
   B   use public transport, even though you own a car.
   C   walk or cycle.

2   When you want to go to the local supermarket, you:
   A   get into your car and drive there.
   B   walk to the nearest bus stop and hop on a bus.
   C   walk or jump on your bike.

3   If you have to catch a train and there is a delay of more than half an hour, you:
   A   lose your temper and start to shout at those around you.
   B   pace impatiently up and down the platform.
   C   sit on a bench, listen to your MP3 player and whistle to yourself.

4   When a bus or underground train is very crowded, you:
   A   squeeze on board but promise yourself that you will never travel by public transport again.
   B   get on and try to make yourself comfortable.
   C   wait for the next one to arrive.

5   When the government talks about building a new underground line, you:
   A   grumble about the amount of money it will cost.
   B   say that it'll probably never happen.
   C   congratulate politicians on their attempts to solve the traffic problems of the city.

6   You don't want to drive after a party, so you:
   A   take a taxi, though you know the fare will be outrageous.
   B   cadge a lift with someone going in the same direction.
   C   go to the nearest bus stop and wait an hour for the bus.

7   When you go on holiday abroad, you usually:
   A   book a flight through your travel agent or over the internet.
   B   travel by car or train, even though this takes a long time.
   C   avoid flying at all costs because you worry about the damage jets cause to the environment.

8   Your idea of luxury is:
   A   jumping on a plane and staying in a five-star Manhattan hotel for the weekend.
   B   sunbathing on the deck of a luxury cruise ship.
   C   going on a walking holiday and relaxing in a hot bath at the end of each day.

9   While on holiday, you like to:
   A   see the sights in style from a horse-drawn carriage.
   B   take a sightseeing bus for tourists.
   C   stroll around with a guidebook in your hand.

10   Your idea of having a good time is:
   A   travelling at high speed in a powerful sports car.
   B   feeling the wind in your hair on the back of a motorbike.
   C   peering at a map in the rain on the top of a mountain.

What kind of traveller are you?

Score: 10–16
You like to be comfortable when you travel. This is more important to you than how much you pay for the journey. You also think that it's important to arrive at your destination quickly, with a minimum amount of fuss. However, you like to spoil yourself when you're on holiday and will sometimes spend a lot of money in order to travel in style.

Score: 17–23
You are a fan of fast, clean and efficient public transport and often grumble to your friends about the traffic and the pollution caused by too many cars. You like to arrive at your destination on time but are not prepared to pay high taxi fares in order to do so. Finally, you are a bit of a romantic and would jump at the opportunity to travel on the Orient Express – but only if someone offered you some free tickets!

Score: 24 –30
You would probably have been much happier living 100 years ago, walking everywhere or riding a horse! You don't like the way cities have changed in recent years and often complain about traffic jams, car exhaust fumes and noise pollution. Finally, you like to keep fit and have a number of pastimes which keep your body in shape.

Word formation: Negative prefixes and suffixes

2a Make the adjectives and verbs in the box negative and write them in the correct column.

> *acceptable agreeable approve attractive*
> *avoidable behave believable careful*
> *damaged harmful honest hopeful interpret*
> *like limited popular satisfied suitable*
> *thoughtful understand useful*

un-	dis-	mis-	-less

b Use the word given at the end of the sentences to form a word that fits in the gap.

1 There is a lot of _____ among local people about government plans to build a new airport nearby.
   SATISFY

2 Many people feel that they have been _____ and treated unfairly.
   UNDERSTAND

3 Not surprisingly, plans to build the airport near a conservation area are _____ with environmentalists.
   POPULAR

4 People say that a planned hotel complex will be extremely _____ and ruin the whole area.
   ATTRACT

5 Wildlife experts claim that the new airport will be _____ noisy and destructive to the local ecosystem.
   BELIEVE

6 The local MP has voiced his _____ of the plans in parliament.
   APPROVE

7 The _____ of the government in the way they presented the scheme to the local community shocked a lot of people.
   HONEST

8 Government officials say their remarks have been _____ by community leaders.
   INTERPRET

9 Government assurances about the levels of noise and pollution are considered to be _____ inadequate.
   HOPE

10 'A certain amount of noise will be _____ when planes land and take off,' said one spokesperson.
   AVOID

Key word transformations

3 Complete the second sentence so that it has a similar meaning to the first sentence, using the word given. Do not change the word given. You must use between two and five words, including the word given.

1 We enjoyed ourselves at the party last night.
   TIME
   We had _____ at the party last night.

2 Is there a party at John's house tonight?
   HAVING
   Is _____ at his house tonight?

3 George read the newspaper quickly before going out.
   LOOK
   George had _____ the newspaper before going out.

4 I've just thought of something really good!
   HAD
   I've just _____ idea!

5 Shall we go for a meal at that new restaurant?
   EAT
   Shall we have _____ at that new restaurant?

6 I can't go out tonight because I am very busy.
   WORK
   I can't go out tonight because I have a _____ do.

Language development 2

> COURSEBOOK page 143, EXPERT GRAMMAR page 196

wish + past simple/past perfect/*would*/*could*

1a Choose the correct answers.
1 I wish there *are / were / would be* more cycle lanes in this town but there aren't.
2 I wish I *can / am able to / could* ride a motorbike but I can't.
3 They say the party yesterday was fantastic. I wish I *went / had gone / would go* but I didn't.
4 What's the matter now? I wish you *stop / stopped / would stop* complaining!
5 There's a great film on TV tomorrow. I wish I *saw / could see / would see* it.
6 Mark is in a really bad mood. I wish he *would / will / had* cheer up but he probably won't.

b Complete the sentences with the correct form of the verbs in brackets.
1 I wish they _____ (tell) us yesterday that taxi drivers were going on strike today.
2 I wish I _____ (can) borrow my father's car but he won't let me.
3 There's nowhere to park in this town! I wish they _____ (build) an underground car park in the centre!
4 I wish I _____ (not be) so rude to Kate yesterday. I feel terrible.
5 You're always talking about your new girlfriend! I wish you _____ (talk) about something else!
6 Tom said that the film on TV last night was fantastic. I wish I _____ (see) it.

I wish / if only

2 What would you say in these situations? Complete the sentences using the words in brackets.

1 You are staying with a family in Milan but you don't know any Italian.
I wish ___I could speak Italian___ . (speak)

2 It's late at night and your neighbour is playing his music really loud.
I wish _____ . (turn down)

3 You feel terrible because you went to bed at three o'clock in the morning.
If only _____ . (earlier)

4 You failed an important exam because you didn't study very hard.
If only _____ . (harder)

5 You feel depressed because it's been raining all day.
If only _____ . (stop)

6 There is a rock concert on Monday but you can't go.
I wish _____ . (go)

7 Your sister lives a long way away from you.
I wish _____ . (so far away)

Other expressions for hypothetical situations

3 Choose the correct answers.

1 I think it's time we *say* / *said* goodbye now. I'll see you in the morning.

2 I have a bad cold, so I'd rather you *wouldn't open* / *didn't open* the window.

3 Don't look at me as if I *were* / *had been* mad! I like walking in the rain!

4 What do you mean you can't ride a bicycle? It's high time you *learnt* / *have learnt!*

5 Why did you tell my parents about last night? I'd rather you *didn't say* / *hadn't said* anything.

6 It's been over a week since your argument with Jen. Don't you think it's time you *phone* / *phoned* her?

Key word transformations

4 Complete the second sentence so that it has a similar meaning to the first sentence, using the word given. Do not change the word given. You must use between two and five words, including the word given.

1 I think we ought to call a taxi to take us home.
TIME
I think it _____ a taxi to take us home.

2 I'd prefer you not to use my car.
RATHER
I _____ use my car.

3 I regret telling Julie about my plans for the future.
WISH
I _____ Julie about my plans for the future.

4 It's a shame your friend can't go with you on holiday.
ONLY
If _____ with you on holiday.

5 Mary, please stop playing that horrible music!
WISH
Mary, I _____ playing that horrible music!

6 Don't you think we should set off for home now?
TIME
Isn't it about _____ for home?

7 I regret not being able to go on that walking holiday.
COULD
I wish _____ on that walking holiday.

8 I sometimes feel like a stranger in my own home.
IF
I sometimes feel _____ a stranger in my own home.

9 Shouldn't you stop lying to her?
TIME
Don't you think it _____ her the truth?

10 You should have asked me before borrowing my car.
RATHER
I _____ me before borrowing my car.

Exam practice: Open cloze
(Paper 1 Part 2)

5 Do the task.

For questions **1–8**, read the text below and think of the word which best fits each gap. Use only **one** word in each gap. There is an example at the beginning (**0**).

School for DJs

I go out clubbing a lot and Ocelot is (**0**) ___my___ favourite club. They've got some really good DJs (**1**) _____ play a good range of music, including hip hop, funk and boogie. But there is more to the club (**2**) _____ just Saturday nights. During the week, they run DJ classes for people (**3**) _____ me, who dream of becoming DJs themselves one day. I've already done the introductory course and learnt the basics. Next week I start a master class, where one of the country's top DJs shows you (**4**) _____ to put together a really great set of music. Apparently, they (**5**) _____ you take along your own music if you want, but you don't (**6**) _____ to because everything is supplied within the price. You get two hours' one-to-one tuition and then, from nine o'clock (**7**) _____ eleven, as people begin to arrive for a night out, you (**8**) _____ the chance to perform as if you were a real DJ, but under expert supervision.

EXPERT WORD CHECK

clubbing   introductory course   master class
set of music   under supervision

Reading (Paper 1 Part 7)

Before you read 1 Read the title of the article and answer the questions.

1 What makes 'a good day out' for you?
2 What kind of things do you like to do?
3 What kind of places do you like to visit?

Skimming 2 Skim and scan the text. In which section are these kinds of attraction mentioned?

1 places of natural beauty __A__
2 homes of writers, artists, etc. _____
3 museums _____
4 different kinds of buildings, e.g. religious buildings _____
5 factories _____

Multiple matching 3a Look at question 1 in the reading task. Follow these steps.

- Mark the key words in the question.
- Scan the text to find the section(s) which may contain the answer.
- Read this section carefully and mark the place where you find the answer.
- Check that the text you have found exactly matches the question.

b Now continue with questions 2–10.

El Greco's house in Toledo

You are going to read an extract from a book about tourist attractions. For questions 1–10, choose from the sections (A–D). The sections may be chosen more than once.

Which section mentions:

attractions where the design of the building itself is of great interest to visitors?	1 □
the possibility that visitors might spoil the places they visit?	2 □
attempts to make exhibits at some attractions seem more realistic?	3 □
the need for each attraction to have its own individual features?	4 □
attractions which do not have particularly impressive venues?	5 □
attractions where visitors can watch a process in action?	6 □
a type of attraction that combines leisure with an educational purpose?	7 □
an attraction where consumer goods are on sale?	8 □
attractions associated with celebrated individuals?	9 □
the fact that attractions need to keep up-to-date with what visitors expect?	10 □

Beamish, the North of England 'living museum'

EXPERT LANGUAGE

Find four examples of the passive voice in section A.

EXPERT WORD CHECK

*beauty spots   conjure up   decanters
dual function   goblets*

A good DAY OUT

A For some people, leisure means relaxing and getting away from it all, for example, by visiting natural beauty spots in the country or places for outdoor recreation. Of course, such natural
5 attractions are affected by the people who visit them but the things that make them attractive tend not to alter greatly through time. Built attractions, however, are designed to appeal to people for whom relaxation means going somewhere and engaging in some kind
10 of specifically organised leisure activity. These attractions do, therefore, tend to change over time, in line with public taste and fashion. With each new attraction that is built, the competition to attract visitors increases, so great imagination and creativity
15 is required of designers and managers in order to make their particular place stand out.

B Over the past 30 years, there has been a marked trend in the leisure industry towards more exciting and sophisticated attractions of all
20 kinds. Many museums, for example, have seen quite dramatic changes, becoming more interesting and entertaining places to visit, while still maintaining their role of informing visitors about the past. Some have been converted into 'living museums' where actors
25 and actresses in costumes meet the public and play the roles of characters from the past, in attempts to make the exhibits come alive for visitors. In others, history is made vivid and exciting through the use of sounds, and even smells, to
30 conjure up a sense of the past. In a number of museums, audiovisual innovations have allowed very popular interactive displays to be developed.

C Another trend which is emerging is for
35 more places to be opened to the public as attractions, although the original purpose for which they were built had nothing to do with leisure. Some of the earliest examples of this trend are religious buildings which attract tourists thanks to
40 their great architectural value. These have come to serve a dual purpose, as places of worship and as attractions for visitors. This trend, however, has now extended to various types of fascinating buildings for a variety of reasons. Visitors often have an interest in
45 exploring the homes of famous writers and artists from the past, however humble the buildings themselves may be. Not far from Madrid, in the town of Toledo, tourists flock to the tiny house of the famous painter El Greco, who lived there 400 years
50 ago. Similarly, the parsonage which was the home of the Brontë sisters, whose 19th-century novels include Jane Eyre and Wuthering Heights, brings many thousands of tourists each year to Haworth in northern England.

55 **D** More recently, especially in the UK, there has been a growing interest in the type of attraction where visitors can see a familiar object being manufactured. One example of this is the Edinburgh Crystal factory, which regularly opens its
60 doors to the visiting public. Visitors are shown around the factory by a guide and they see the famous Edinburgh Crystal glassware being manufactured in traditional red-hot ovens. After the tour, they have the opportunity to buy crystal decanters and goblets
65 similar to those they have seen being made. The visitors do not interfere with the glassmaking itself, so the factory serves a dual function of being both a real workplace and an attraction.

Vocabulary development 1

➤ **COURSEBOOK** pages 148–149

Types of personality

1a Write the character adjectives in the box in the correct column.

> ambitious arrogant ~~creative~~ easy-going
> generous impulsive intellectual irritable mean
> moody open-minded pessimistic punctual
> sensible sensitive sociable suspicious vain witty

Positive	Negative	It depends
creative		

b Read the descriptions and choose three adjectives from Exercise 1a for each person. Use each adjective once only. You do not need to use all the adjectives.

1 Keith is very well educated and likes discussing serious subjects with his friends. He's a junior lecturer in philosophy at the university but he's determined to become a full professor by the time he's 35. Unfortunately, he thinks he's more intelligent and important than anyone else. _____ , _____ , _____

2 Joanna is very good at art. She has lots of original ideas and paints the most amazing pictures. She understands other people's problems and feelings very easily. When she talks, she says a lot of clever and amusing things, which make people laugh. _____ , _____ , _____

3 You have to be careful what you say to David because he gets angry and annoyed very easily. He never believes that anything good is going to happen, so it usually doesn't! Although he's quite well-off, he hates spending money. _____ , _____ , _____

4 Everyone loves Martin. He never seems to worry about anything or get upset or annoyed. He's ready to listen to other people's ideas and opinions, even if they are very different from his own. On top of that, he's always giving people money or presents. _____ , _____ , _____

5 Marilyn is an actress. She's very proud of her beauty. She can be a difficult person sometimes and there are days when she is depressed or annoyed for no good reason. Marilyn finds it difficult to trust people and seems to think that everyone is doing something bad behind her back. _____ , _____ , _____

c Write a short character description of someone you know.

Verb/Noun/Adjective + preposition

2 Read this reference from a university tutor and complete it with prepositions.

> I've been very satisfied **(1)** _____ Sebastian's performance over the past few years. I was a little concerned **(2)** _____ him when he first arrived at this college but he has improved greatly since that time.
>
> Sebastian is an extremely happy and cheerful student. He participates **(3)** _____ a large number of different activities and gets very enthusiastic **(4)** _____ everything he does. Sebastian belongs **(5)** _____ both the college football team and the basketball team and is also involved **(6)** _____ the drama group and the environmental society. It is obvious that he has felt the benefit **(7)** _____ cooperating **(8)** _____ other students in these teams and groups. As regards his membership of the environmental society, I am glad that Sebastian has found something he believes **(9)** _____ and finds personally fulfilling.
>
> While taking his final exams, Sebastian was both sensible and hard-working, finding a balance **(10)** _____ his studies and these other activities. This has resulted **(11)** _____ his obtaining an excellent degree from this university. I have every confidence **(12)** _____ his ability to do well in the future and recommend him to you without reservation.

Pronunciation

3a 🎧 15 Listen and mark the stress on the words. The first one has been done for you.
1 pessim<u>i</u>stic, enthusiastic, artistic, historic
2 cheer, cheerful; delight, delightful; wonder, wonderful; beauty, beautiful; disgrace, disgraceful
3 amaze, amazing; confuse, confusing; frustrate, frustrating; satisfy, satisfying; embarrass, embarrassing

b Choose the correct answer (A, B or C) to complete the pronunciation rules.
1 When a word ends in –ic, we stress
   A the suffix.
   B the second syllable.
   C the syllable before the suffix.
2 When we add the suffix -ful or -ing to a word, we
   A stress the suffix.
   B stress the syllable before the suffix.
   C do not change the stress of the word.

Exam practice: Word formation

(Paper 1 Part 3)

4 Do the task.

*For questions **1–8**, read the text below. Use the word given in capitals at the end of some of the lines to form a word that fits in the gap **in the same line**. There is an example at the beginning (0).*

Can hypnosis reduce stress?

When we think of hypnosis, we
(0) __usually__ think of those television   USUAL
shows where (1) _____ members   FORTUNE
of the audience are encouraged
to do foolish things while they are
under hypnosis. In such shows, the
hypnotist is an (2) _____ , almost   ENTERTAIN
like a magician, whose main aim
is to keep the audience happy. But
hypnosis deserves to be taken more
(3) _____ . If it is used properly,   SERIOUS
it can help people who suffer from
(4) _____ related to stress.   ILL

We use the word *stress* to describe
quite a large (5) _____ of   VARY
different feelings, especially those
connected with (6) _____ about   ANXIOUS
our jobs. Hypnosis can help people
to believe in their (7) _____   ABLE
to do their jobs well. It also helps
them to feel more relaxed about
their work, which gives them greater
(8) _____ to deal with any   CONFIDENT
problems they may be facing in
their daily lives.

EXPERT STRATEGY

Remember that you may need to make more than one change to the word.

➤ HELP

1 Add both a prefix and a suffix to this word.
2 You need a noun that describes the person.
6 What is the noun made from this adjective?

EXPERT LANGUAGE

Find an example of the passive in the text.

EXPERT WORD CHECK

audience   deserves   foolish   hypnotist   magician

Language development 1

➤ **COURSEBOOK** pages 150–151, **EXPERT GRAMMAR** page 197

Clauses of reason, purpose and contrast

1 Decide if the clause in each sentence expresses *Reason* (R), *Purpose* (P) or *Contrast* (C). Then choose the correct answers.

1 Recently I felt run-down *because / owing to* I was studying so hard for my exams. _____
2 *Even though / Despite* I took vitamin pills, I still seemed to have no energy. _____
3 I decided to take up jogging *in order that / in order to* do some exercise. _____
4 I went to the doctor yesterday *because of / as* I didn't feel very well. _____
5 The doctor said that my ill health was *due to / since* stress and overwork. _____
6 I decided to take up yoga *in order that / so as to* learn how to relax properly. _____
7 I now feel fitter and happier *despite / although* the fact that I am still very busy. _____
8 I even want to go to India *so that / in order to* I can learn more about yoga! _____

2 Read part of an interview with a successful runner and complete it with linking words or phrases from Exercise 1. More than one answer may be possible.

A: (1) _____ giving an amazing performance in the 10,000 metres today, you didn't win a medal. How do you feel about that?
B: Well, it's true that three runners overtook me at the finish, (2) _____ I had led the way for 24 laps. It was obviously a disappointment (3) _____ I was sure I would win. But there's always another race to look forward to.
A: Has that always been your philosophy?
B: Yes. (4) _____ the fact that I was a top runner from the age of 12, I didn't win my first national championship until I was 17. There was no pressure on me. In fact, my coaches trained me carefully (5) _____ I wouldn't suffer from 'burnout' at an early age.
A: You often say that your greatest triumph was winning the Junior Cross Country Championships as a teenager.
B: Definitely. (6) _____ many great moments in my career since then, my victory in that race remains a cherished memory.
A: Many people have commented on the red ribbon you wear when you run. Is it true that you wear it (7) _____ focus attention on the problem of drugs in athletics?
B: That's right. I wear a red ribbon (8) _____ people can see my willingness to give a blood sample to the authorities. I'm very concerned about drug-taking among athletes.

Sentence combining

3 Read the statements by the runner in Exercise 2. Join each pair of sentences using the words/phrases in the box. Use each word only once and make any changes necessary. More than one answer may be possible.

because   because of   due to   even though
in order to   since   so as to   so that

1 A lot of male athletes at university wouldn't train with me. I was too fast for them.
_____
_____

2 I'm successful in athletics. I receive tremendous support from my husband and family.
_____
_____

3 I often discuss my diet with my dietician. I love eating out and trying new dishes.
_____
_____

4 Every year I go to a camp in Albuquerque in the USA. I train there.
_____
_____

5 I want to spend some time in the USA. I will be able to run on the road circuit.
_____
_____

6 I love running on roads and mountain trails. I feel a sense of freedom.
_____
_____

7 I live a fulfilled life. I'm not concerned about my athletics career ending.
_____
_____

8 After athletics, I'd do something else. I could continue to channel my energy and ambitions.
_____
_____

Exam practice: Open cloze
(Paper 1 Part 2)

4 Do the task.

*For questions **1–8**, read the text below and think of the word which best fits each gap. Use only **one** word in each gap. There is an example at the beginning (0).*

Thrill of a lifetime

According (0) __to__ recent research, visiting a theme park in childhood can give people particularly happy memories. One thousand people aged between 18 and 22 took (1) _____ in a survey which was designed to find (2) _____ which happy childhood memories were most important to them. David Lewis is the child psychologist who led the research. He says that people remembered trips to theme parks much (3) _____ fondly than trips to the beach or to other leisure attractions (4) _____ as zoos. What is more, they remembered the most dangerous and exciting theme park rides best of (5) _____ .

Dr Lewis says that both adults and children go through various emotions (6) _____ a result of the 'white-knuckle' rides – the ones that provide the greatest thrills. These feelings include apprehension before the ride, fear during it and relief (7) _____ it is all over. He has also noticed how often children want to repeat the experience immediately after getting off a ride (8) _____ that they can prolong the feeling of achievement and satisfaction it gives them.

EXPERT STRATEGY
Remember to check your spelling.

> **HELP**
2 Add a preposition to create a phrasal verb.
3 The word you need creates a comparison.
6 Which word completes the clause of reason?

EXPERT LANGUAGE
Find three irregular past forms in the text.

EXPERT WORD CHECK
apprehension   fondly   prolong   survey
white-knuckle rides

Writing (Paper 2 Part 1: Essay)

➤ COURSEBOOK pages 152–153, EXPERT WRITING pages 199–200

EXPERT STRATEGY
Remember to use paragraphs to structure your essay
(e.g. introduction, point 1, point 2, point 3, conclusion).

Understand the task

1 Read the writing task and answer the questions.
   1 Are you being asked for both sides of an argument or your own opinion?
   2 What style should you use?
   3 How many points do you need to make?

In your English class, you have been talking about money and happiness. Now your English teacher has asked you to write an essay.

Write an essay using all the notes and give reasons for your point of view.

> In order to be happy, you need to have lots of possessions and a well-paid job. Do you agree?
>
> Notes
>
> Write about:
>
> 1 relationships
> 2 health
> 3 _____ (your own idea)

*Write your **essay** in **140–190** words in an appropriate style.*

Check and improve a sample answer

2 Match the comments (1–3) with three introductions to the essay (A–C) written by different students.
   1 Inappropriate – it does not focus on the topic of the essay.
   2 Inappropriate – the style is too informal.
   3 Appropriate – the style is formal, the topic of the essay is stated and the writer's opinion is clear.

A
In order to get a well-paid job, you need qualifications and many years of experience in your career.

B
Many people believe that they can only be successful if they earn a lot of money and own lots of luxury goods. Clearly, this is not true.

C
It's not money that's going to make you happy. Think about your friends and stuff like that.

3 Read the rest of the essay written by Student B from Exercise 2. Find and underline the topic sentences.

Obviously, we need some money to pay for things like rent and food but other things are more important when it comes to hapiness. (1) _____ , a strong network of friends and a good relationship with our family members is vital if you want to be happy.

(2) _____ , being fit and healthy is definately much more important than being surrounded by wealth. If you're ill, you can't enjoy your wealth anyway, so you won't be happy.

Finally, you are more likely to feel happy if you choose a job or a course of study you enjoy. (3) _____ you should chose the highest-paid careers but surely, the happiest people do something they love rather than something that is well paid.

(4) _____ , lots of posessions and a well-paid job may make your life comfortable but they do not make you happy.

4 Find and correct four spelling mistakes in the essay in Exercise 3.
   Paragraph 1 _____ .
   Paragraph 2 _____ .
   Paragraph 3 _____ .
   Paragraph 4 _____ .

5 Complete the essay in Exercise 3 with the words/phrases in the box. There is one extra word/phrase which you do not need to use.

according to   for example   furthermore
in my opinion   some people argue that

6 Write your own essay.

Listening (Paper 3 Part 1)

Before you listen

1 Read the listening task. For questions 1–8, read the sentence that gives the context of the extract, the question and the three options (A–C). Think about the situation: who will be talking and what will they be talking about? Mark the key words in each question.

Multiple choice

2a 🎧 16 Do the task.

b 🎧 16 Listen again and check your answers. Make sure the options you did not choose are not possible.

EXPERT STRATEGY

First you hear the context question and then you have time to read the question and the options. Think about who you will hear talking and the topic. Mark the key words in the question stem and options so that you're ready to listen for the answer.

➤ HELP

2 Listen for the words *mad* and *cross*, which mean 'angry'.
3 Listen for the name of the psychologist – the answer comes soon afterwards.
4 Listen for why the woman wants to hear music.
8 Betsy is the name of the car – what does the woman say about it?

EXPERT LANGUAGE

Which questions in the listening task are asking about:
1 a reason?
2 a feeling?
3 an opinion?

EXPERT WORD CHECK

*dissatisfaction doorway feedback
inconvenient irresistible life coach
optimist purr speechless tactful
temper triggers uplifting*

You will hear people talking in eight different situations. For questions 1–8, choose the best answer (A, B or C).

1 You hear part of a radio programme about working conditions. What is the speaker doing?
   A suggesting how a problem should be approached
   B recommending a particular course of study
   C advising against conflicts with employers

2 You hear a woman talking about a hotel. At what point did she start to feel angry?
   A when her letter went unanswered
   B when the service was not good during her stay
   C when she phoned the hotel and spoke to somebody

3 You hear the beginning of a radio programme on the subject of human behaviour. What question is the presenter going to ask the psychologist?
   A why children are sometimes embarrassing
   B how people learn to be tactful with others
   C whether adults should try to be more honest

4 In a radio play, you hear two people talking. Why doesn't the woman want to eat in the restaurant?
   A Nobody else is eating there.
   B A noisier place would be better.
   C She doesn't like the music there.

5 On a visit to a college, you overhear part of a lecture. What is the lecturer explaining?
   A why laughter is important to us
   B why laughter has been so widely studied
   C why laughter is sometimes misunderstood

6 You hear a woman talking about a book she bought. What is her opinion of the book?
   A It fulfilled all her expectations.
   B It surprised her how entertaining it was.
   C It turned out to be more useful than she thought.

7 You hear a professional footballer talking about his retirement. How does he feel?
   A open to whatever new opportunities arise
   B unsure whether he'll enjoy his new lifestyle
   C determined to remain in touch with the sport

8 You hear a woman talking about her car. Why did she decide to buy it?
   A A friend suggested it.
   B She liked the look of it.
   C She needed to replace her old one.

Vocabulary development 2

> **COURSEBOOK** pages 154–155

EXPERT STRATEGY

In Paper 2, Writing, you may have to describe different ways of keeping fit and healthy. You may also be asked to talk about this subject in Paper 4, Speaking. Record useful vocabulary in your vocabulary notebook.

Commonly confused words

1   Read the texts and choose the correct answers.

The importance of diet

Nowadays, it is more and more common to hear that someone is a **(1)** *vegetation / vegetarian*. Many people have realised that eating vegetables, particularly lightly cooked or **(2)** *raw / crude* vegetables, is good for you. Frequent colds, headaches and other **(3)** *illnesses / diseases* are often symptoms of an unhealthy diet and a **(4)** *stressed / stressful* lifestyle. Eating more **(5)** *nutritious / edible* types of food and, if possible, living and working somewhere where the **(6)** *speed / pace* of life is slower will result in a healthier body and mind.

HEALTHCARE TODAY

In the past 80 years, healthcare has changed a lot. You still often have to wait a long time for the doctor to see you in his **(7)** *office / surgery* but many other things are different. Hospital **(8)** *wards / dormitories* are smaller and brighter, and doctors and nurses can **(9)** *treat / cure* you more effectively. If you are **(10)** *wounded / injured* in an accident, or have to **(11)** *make / have* an operation, you are much more likely to survive today than you were in the past. Then it was extremely common for wounds to become **(12)** *infected / polluted* and for complications to develop.

Collocations

2a   Match the verbs in the box with the words they collocate with. Each verb must collocate with all the words in a set.

break   catch   feel   give   have   make   sprain   take

1   _____ a headache/an earache/a sore throat/a high temperature/an accident/an operation/an injection

2   _____ ill/dizzy/sick/depressed/fit and healthy

3   _____ a quick recovery/an appointment with the doctor

4   _____ a cold/flu/a virus from someone

5   _____ your leg/your arm/your wrist/one of your ribs

6   _____ your ankle/your wrist

7   _____ your temperature/an X-ray/some medicine/an aspirin/a rest/some exercise/your blood pressure

8   _____ you an injection/you a thorough examination

b   Complete the sentences with collocations from Exercise 2a. You may need to change the form of the verb.

1   What does the thermometer say? If I see that you <u>have a temperature</u> , I'm going to call the doctor!

2   The doctor said that if I had appendicitis, I would need to go into hospital to _____ .

3   My sister had an ear infection last month but she _____ when the doctor prescribed antibiotics.

4   Put your coat on when you go out! You'll _____ if you don't wrap up!

5   The dentist asked me if I wanted to _____ before he drilled my tooth.

6   Don't worry, you've only _____ – you haven't broken any bones! You'll be able to walk again in a few days.

7   'I think you may have fractured your skull. We'll have to _____ of the back of your head to check,' said Dr Benn.

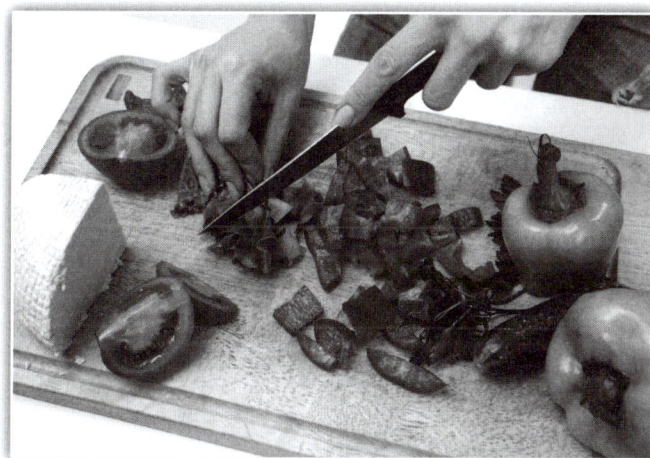

Comparing photos

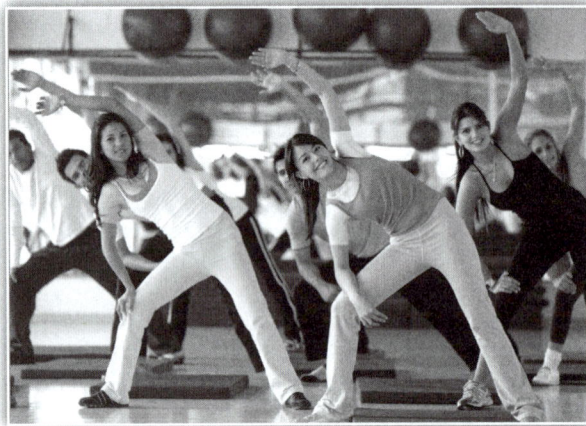

3a Look at the two photos of people doing exercise and read how a student answered the question in the box. Ignore the gaps at this stage.

Compare the two photographs and say which form of exercise looks more fun.

Both photographs **(1)** _____ people taking exercise. In the first photograph, I can see a man cycling in the country, **(2)** _____ in the second photograph **(3)** _____ a lot of people in a room doing aerobics.

The man in this picture is on his own and he's cycling along a path. He's wearing a … er, a **(4)** _____ helmet on his head, so it **(5)** _____ rather dangerous. The aerobics class, **(6)** _____ , is safe and organised. The people are wearing … er, they're wearing those things people wear for doing aerobics – a bit **(7)** _____ tights.

(8) _____ , I think both ways of exercising are fun. In an aerobics class you're with a lot of other people, doing exercises to music, and when you're cycling in the mountains, you're surrounded by beautiful countryside.

(9) _____ , if I had to choose, I **(10)** _____ this one – cycling. It's hard work when you have to cycle up a hill but it's really enjoyable and healthy.

b Complete the student's answer with the words/phrases in the box.

*could be   however   kind of   like   on the other hand
personally   show   there are   while   would choose*

Language development 2

➤ **COURSEBOOK** page 157

so / such

1a Put the words in the correct order to make sentences.

1 such / we / have / a / view / from / beautiful / our window
   _____

2 such / is / a / to / day / that / I / swimming / nice / want / go / it
   _____

3 such / have / never / I / delicious / eaten / food / before
   _____

4 why / it / so / to / important / exercise / take / is / ?
   _____

5 this / so / boring / think / documentary / is / that / I / will / asleep / I / fall
   _____

6 he / wants / has / so / much / can / buy / money / that / he / anything / he
   _____

7 weather / we / another / such / good / on / holiday / had / that / stayed / week / we
   _____

8 many / you / not / eat / so / hamburgers / should
   _____

b Choose the correct answers.

1 His diet contains *such a / a such* lot of cholesterol that I'm worried he'll develop heart disease in later life.
2 It was *such a / a so* good feeling when the doctor told me that I wasn't suffering from a food allergy.
3 There are *so few / so little* calories in lettuce that you can eat as much as you like.
4 Some processed food contains *so / such* many preservatives that it might damage your health.
5 It was *such / such an* awful food that we agreed never to go again to that restaurant.
6 My boyfriend eats *so / such* quickly that he always has indigestion after a meal.
7 I had so *much / many* to eat last night that I felt quite ill.
8 Rice is *so / so much* rich in carbohydrates that many parts of Asia have developed 'rice cultures'.

too / enough / very

2 Complete the sentences with *too, enough* or *very*.

1 Those exercises are much _____ difficult for me to do.
2 I don't think there is _____ vitamin C in my diet.
3 Our gym instructor is rather serious but _____ nice.
4 This tracksuit is not big _____ for me, I'm afraid.
5 I think you put _____ much sugar in your coffee.
6 My father thinks he is _____ old to take up a sport.
7 Sheila doesn't spend _____ time exercising every day.
8 Everyone knows that fresh fruit is _____ good for you.

so, such, too, enough and very

3 Complete the email with *so, such, too, enough* or *very*.

@ Home 🏠 Previous ◀ Next ▶ Search 🔍

Hi Stephen,

My exams are over at last! They were **(1)** _____ difficult that I didn't think I'd pass. I did though, and now I'm a doctor! I hope you're coming to my party on Saturday. It should be **(2)** _____ good. I can't believe that **(3)** _____ many of my friends are coming. In fact, Tony thinks that there'll be **(4)** _____ many people and that we won't have **(5)** _____ food and drink for everybody. I don't think that'll happen. I've prepared **(6)** _____ a lot of food that I have **(7)** _____ to feed an army! I was thinking of having the party in the garden but Tony says it'll be much **(8)** _____ cold outside. I suppose he's right. The weather changes **(9)** _____ quickly that it could even rain, couldn't it? By the way, Stephen, could you lend me some glasses? I don't have **(10)** _____ at home, I'm afraid.

Please give me a call as soon as you can.

Love,

Anna

---

as, like and such as

4 Complete the sentences with *as, like* or *such as*.

1 Dr Jones is regarded _____ one of the greatest heart surgeons alive.
2 Many students work _____ tourist guides during their summer holidays.
3 Famous people _____ Bill Clinton and Madonna have visited this restaurant.
4 I'm 18 but my parents treat me _____ a child.
5 I wish I could skate _____ you! You're really good at it.
6 Vegetables _____ red peppers, broccoli and Brussels sprouts contain a lot of vitamin C.
7 Teachers described Luke _____ a clever, hard-working student.
8 Cherie is really _____ her sister, isn't she?

Key word transformations

5 Complete the second sentence so that it has a similar meaning to the first sentence, using the word given. Do not change the word given. You must use between two and five words, including the word given.

1 You don't have the strength to lift those weights.
   STRONG
   You _____ to lift those weights.
2 Kate plays the piano so well even though she is only 16.
   SUCH
   Kate is _____ even though she is only 16.
3 My father is a hospital doctor.
   WORKS
   My father _____ a hospital.
4 The music at the party was too loud for us to be able to talk to each other.
   SO
   The music at the party _____ couldn't talk to each other.
5 We had such a good time that we didn't want to leave.
   ENJOYED
   We _____ we didn't want to leave.
6 You are not fit enough to take part in the competition.
   UNFIT
   You _____ take part in the competition
7 I left the party early because it was so crowded.
   PEOPLE
   There _____ the party that I left early.
8 Dr Simmons treats his older patients like children.
   IF
   Dr Simmons treats his older patients _____ children.
9 It looks like rain, doesn't it?
   AS
   It looks _____ to rain, doesn't it?
10 Why can't you give up eating chocolate?
   SO
   Why is it _____ give up eating chocolate?

Reading (Paper 1 Part 5)

Before you read

1 Read the instructions for the reading task, and the heading and subheading of the article. Try to answer these questions.

1 What do you think a personal trainer does?
2 What kind of people does Matt Roberts train?
3 Why do you think he took up this career?
4 What does Matt offer which makes him 'more than just a fitness trainer'?

Skimming

2 Skim the text and check your ideas in Exercise 1. Write the numbers of the paragraphs in which you found the information and correct your answers if necessary.

Question 1: paragraph _____
Question 2: paragraph _____
Question 3: paragraph _____
Question 4: paragraph _____

Multiple choice

3 Do the task. Remember to follow these steps.

• First, read the questions and mark the key words.
• Find the place in the text where the information is.
• Find your own answer to the question and mark the relevant piece of text.
• Now read the options and choose the one closest to your answer.
• Read the text again to check that your answer is right and that the other options are definitely wrong.

Vocabulary: Expressions

4 Complete the second sentence so that it has a similar meaning to the first sentence, using the word given. Do not change the word given.

1 Matt's father played professional football and it looked as if Matt would do the same.
   SET
   Matt's father played professional football and Matt _____ do the same.
2 Being unable to exercise showed Matt what it's like to be out of condition.
   TASTE
   Being unable to exercise _____ what it's like to be out of condition.
3 He arrived in the USA at a time when personal trainers were becoming fashionable.
   WITH
   His arrival in the USA _____ the rise in the fashion for personal trainers.
4 It isn't surprising that Matt had lots of clients.
   COMES
   It _____ that Matt had lots of clients.

You are going to read a newspaper article about a personal trainer. For questions 1–6, choose the answer (A, B, C or D) which you think fits best according to the text.

1 Why did Matt decide not to follow a career in football?
  A He realised it was a dangerous sport.
  B He was advised against it for medical reasons.
  C He discovered he was better suited to athletics.
  D He didn't want to do the same thing as his father.

2 The expression *set his sights* on in line 17 refers to
  A a place Matt had seen.
  B a job Matt had tried.
  C something Matt had learnt to do.
  D something Matt hoped to achieve.

3 According to the article, when Matt went to the USA,
  A he was able to take advantage of a new trend.
  B he was the first trainer to attract celebrity clients.
  C he was sure of finding work as a personal trainer.
  D he made good contacts amongst fashionable trainers.

4 In the writer's view, what did Matt's early clients appreciate most?
  A He wasn't well known himself.
  B He respected their need for privacy.
  C He was recommended by their friends.
  D He provided a personal training package.

5 In London, Matt trained his clients in their homes at first because
  A that was what they preferred.
  B his gym was not in a fashionable area.
  C he couldn't afford to set up his own gym.
  D they were able to provide their own equipment.

6 What approach to training does Matt adopt?
  A He seeks to change people's attitudes.
  B He tries to teach people the best methods.
  C He works with people to achieve results.
  D He expects people to follow his example.

EXPERT LANGUAGE

Which paragraph begins with a participle clause?

EXPERT WORD CHECK

chain   couch potato   discus   inner athlete   lease overweight   premises   ruled out   sprinting word-of-mouth

FIT FOR FAME

He's the man who keeps the stars in good shape. But Matt Roberts is more than just a fitness trainer.

Matt Roberts is one of the UK's leading personal trainers. His clients have included the rich and the famous: people like supermodel Naomi Campbell and well-known pop singers. He has written 12 books about fitness and has his own range of health and fitness products.

Unlike many of his clients, Matt has always been sporty. His father, John Roberts, played professional football for top London club Arsenal in the early seventies and Matt looked set to follow in his footsteps. Then, during an athletics match at school, his plans suddenly changed when he was knocked on the head by a stray discus. Doctors ruled out team sports from then on and for a few months, he got no exercise at all. This gave Matt a brief taste of what it's like to be out of condition. After that, he decided to focus on another activity he had always excelled at: sprinting.

Matt trained hard and once even represented England, but already by the age of 16, he had set his sights on becoming a fitness trainer with his own gym. He recalls: 'When my injury meant I wasn't getting any exercise, I just wasn't myself. It's the same for people who are overweight or unfit – they aren't themselves.' For Matt remains convinced that fitness is the basis of a full and happy life.

After leaving school, Matt went to the USA. This was a lucky move because his arrival coincided with the rise in the fashion for personal trainers amongst celebrities and he became one of the pioneers in the field. His first big break came when a rock star who was preparing for a world tour employed him full-time. 'It was a great experience,' Matt recalls, 'coming up with the entire health package for somebody. But intense.' He's careful, however, even now, not to give away his employer's identity. And it is this acceptance of the confidential nature of their relationship that his clients value highly, perhaps even more than the training itself. So it comes as no surprise that news of his skills spread through word-of-mouth recommendations.

After six months Matt moved back to London, where he built up a base of clients whom he trained in their homes, before spotting the premises he was looking for in the city's fashionable Mayfair district. As he was only 22, the banks wouldn't lend Matt the start-up money he needed and suppliers wouldn't lease equipment. But Matt worked hard to save the capital and moved into what would be the first of his chain of gyms.

'It's great to see results in clients,' Matt says. 'I see myself more as a training partner. I don't think the pupil–teacher thing works with most people.' He's probably right there but it's clear to me that the best trainers are also psychologists of a kind, achieving the kind of mental transformation that changes a couch potato into a gymnast, helping us find the inner athlete just waiting to burst free.

Vocabulary development 1

> **COURSEBOOK** pages 162–163

Crime

1a Label the picture with the words in the box.

*defence lawyer   defendant   judge   jury
~~lawyer~~   police officer   reporters   witness*

> **EXPERT STRATEGY**
>
> Crime is an interesting topic area, especially if you're interested in following the news in English reading crime fiction, and talking about current events in your writing and speaking exams. Crime often has its own particular vocabulary, for example, *prosecution*, *defence*, so make sure that you're familiar with it.

1 _____
2 _____
3 _____
4 _____
5 _____
6 _____
7 *lawyer* _____
8 _____

b Two journalists are discussing a trial. Match the questions (1–8) with the answers (a–h).

1 What crime did the defendant commit?
2 What did he do exactly?
3 How did the police manage to catch him?
4 Apart from the witness, is there any other evidence?
5 He'll need a good lawyer, won't he?
6 How do you think he will plead?
7 I wonder what verdict the jury will reach.
8 What kind of sentence is the judge likely to pass?

a Guilty, probably. I don't think it'll take them very long to decide.
b He certainly will. The lawyer for the prosecution is said to win almost all his cases.
c He's on trial for murder. He has a long record of burglary and other minor offences though.
d Oh yes. The police have found his fingerprints everywhere. They've also managed to get a DNA sample from some of his hair, which they found at the scene of the crime.

e Apparently, he had broken into a house and was stealing some jewellery when the owner appeared. There was a fight and …
f Almost certainly, the judge will sentence him to several years in prison. He may even give him life imprisonment.
g There was a witness who saw him leaving the house. She gave a description to the police and they arrested him the next day.
h I'm sure he'll plead innocent. He'll claim that he was attacked by the owner of the house and that he acted in self-defence.

c Read the sentences in Exercise 1b again and find as many verb + noun collocations as you can. Add them to your vocabulary notebook. Then make a note of any other useful expressions related to crime.

commit a crime

Exam practice: Multiple-choice cloze

(Paper 1 Part 1)

2 Do the task.

*For questions **1–8**, read the text below and decide which answer (**A**, **B**, **C** or **D**) best fits each gap. There is an example at the beginning (0).*

An opportunity too good to miss

It was something that might have (0) __C__ even the most honest teenager: the discovery of £3,000 in used banknotes in an envelope left next to an ATM machine. That was what two British teenagers, aged 14 and 17, (1) _____ across when they were hanging (2) _____ near a bank one Friday evening in January with (3) _____ much to do.

After a short discussion, they (4) _____ the banknotes and ran away. Unfortunately for them, however, the (5) _____ was being (6) _____ by security cameras.

The money was reported missing on the following Monday morning and the teenagers were (7) _____ for the crime within the week. Although neither of them would be (8) _____ upon as a 'master criminal', they both, nevertheless, ended up with criminal records.

0	A persuaded	B urged	C tempted	D provoked
1	A came	B met	C chanced	D found
2	A over	B out	C off	D up
3	A hardly	B something	C little	D nothing
4	A grabbed	B swept	C held	D picked
5	A burglary	B fraud	C theft	D forgery
6	A registered	B recorded	C recalled	D received
7	A charged	B sentenced	C arrested	D convicted
8	A looked	B regarded	C viewed	D considered

EXPERT STRATEGY

Remember to read through the whole text once you've finished.

➤ HELP

3 The word you need expresses a negative idea.
7 The word for the first stage in the conviction of a criminal.

EXPERT LANGUAGE

Find three phrasal verbs amongst your answers.

EXPERT WORD CHECK

ATM machine   criminal records   security cameras   used banknotes

Language development 1

➤ **COURSEBOOK** pages 164–165,
EXPERT GRAMMAR page 197

EXPERT STRATEGY

Remember to use a variety of linking expressions and structures to link ideas in your writing. But be careful: don't overuse the same structure. Also vary the length of your sentences: don't just use long sentences; use some short ones as well.

Connecting ideas

1 Complete the sentences with the words/phrases in the box. There are two extra words/phrases which you do not need to use.

*after   and   because   before
but   however   if   in order to
such   which   while   who*

1 I read a lot of novels by Agatha Christie _____ improve my English.
2 Agatha Christie is _____ a good writer that I could read her novels all day.
3 Every night, I read a chapter of *Murder on the Orient Express* _____ going to sleep.
4 _____ I was reading last night, I heard a sound outside the window.
5 It was late _____ obviously I felt a bit scared.
6 _____ , I got up from my chair and walked to the window.
7 I couldn't see anything _____ it was so dark outside.
8 I would have phoned the police _____ I had a phone nearby.
9 _____ thinking about it for a minute, I suddenly realised what the sound was.
10 There was a cat in the garden _____ wanted to come inside!

Participle clauses

2 Rewrite or join the sentences using the words given.

1 Simon spent all his time reading books because he was out of work.
Being _____ , Simon _____ .

2 He heard the telephone ring. He put down his book. He got up to answer it.
Hearing _____ , he_____ and_____ .

3 He felt annoyed at the interruption. He picked up the telephone. He shouted 'yes' as loud as he could.
Feeling _____ , he picked_____ and
_____ .

4 He put the receiver down again because he realised that the caller had hung up.
Realising _____ , he _____ .

5 He got ready to go for a walk because he hadn't been out all day.
Not having _____ , he got _____ .

6 He reached the door. He heard the telephone ring again.
On reaching _____ , he _____ .

7 He ran to the phone. He picked up the receiver. He heard the voice of his girlfriend, who asked what the matter was.
Running _____ , he picked_____ and
_____ .

8 Despite the fact that he felt rather guilty, he couldn't help smiling.
Despite feeling _____ , he couldn't_____ .

Combining sentences

3 Improve the following story by combining the groups of sentences using the words in brackets. Make any changes necessary. Do not change the order of the sentences.

1 Peter arrived at his brother's house. He realised something was wrong. (as soon as)

2 It was a hot day. All the doors and windows were closed. (even though)

3 Peter was sure Tom was at home. He had phoned him an hour before. (as)

4 He opened the front door. He went inside. He looked in all the rooms. (opening, and)

5 Tom had gone out. He would have left a note. (if)

6 His brother was a sensible man. He always told others what his plans were. (who)

7 Peter was climbing the stairs. The doorbell rang. (as)

8 He rushed down the stairs very quickly. He almost fell. (so … that)

9 He saw his brother on the doorstep. He gave a cry of relief. (seeing)

10 Tom laughed. He told Peter that the police had arrested him in the afternoon. They had mistaken him for an escaped bank robber! (and, because)

Exam practice: Open cloze
(Paper 1 Part 2)

4 Do the task.

*For questions 1–8, read the text below and think of the word which best fits each gap. Use only **one** word in each gap. There is an example at the beginning (0).*

Agatha Christie, crime writer

Agatha Christie is probably the (0) __most__ widely-known crime writer in the world. Although her writing now seems rather old-fashioned, her novels of mystery and suspense continue to sell very well.

Agatha Christie was born in 1890 and began her working life as a nurse, responsible for dispensing medicines. The knowledge of poisons which she gained during this time came (1) _____ useful when she wrote her books.

Her first novel, *The Mysterious Affair at Styles,* (2) _____ published in 1920. The main character in the novel, Hercule Poirot, became (3) _____ popular that she used the detective in 40 further books. In (4) _____ to her novels, Agatha Christie wrote a number of plays. *The Mousetrap* was (5) _____ a success that it ran in London for more than 50 years.

Agatha Christie's personal life was sometimes (6) _____ exciting as the plots of her novels. She caused a sensation in 1926 (7) _____ she disappeared for ten days, possibly suffering (8) _____ amnesia.

EXPERT STRATEGY
Remember to write only one word in each gap.

➤ **HELP**
1 You need a preposition here.
8 Which preposition is used after 'suffer'?

EXPERT LANGUAGE
Find an example of a compound adjective in the text.

EXPERT WORD CHECK
amnesia   dispensing   plots   poisons   suspense

Writing (Paper 2 Part 2: Review)

➤ **COURSEBOOK** pages 166–167, **EXPERT WRITING** page 205

EXPERT STRATEGY

Review questions are an opportunity for you to give your opinion of something you have experienced – for example, a concert or a film. The purpose of your writing is to give the reader a clear idea of your impressions of the experience and to tell them whether or not you would recommend it.

Understand the task

1 Read the writing task and answer the questions.

    1 Who are you writing for: someone you know or someone you don't know?

    2 What style should you use: formal or informal?

    3 What should you include in your review? Mark the parts of the task that tell you.

You have seen this announcement on a website.

Children's classic fiction

As part of International Reading Week, the college library is putting reviews of classic children's fiction on its website.

Write a review of your favourite childhood book, including why you loved it, a brief summary of the plot and why you think it is relevant to children now.

The best reviews will be published on the library's website.

*Write your **review** in **140–190** words in an appropriate style.*

Check and improve a sample answer

2a Read a student's answer and mark (/) the paragraph breaks.

  b Choose the correct attitude phrases (1–3).

  c Correct the spelling of the highlighted words.

My favourite childhood book was *The Secret Garden* by Frances Hodgson Burnett. I loved it because it took me into a world that was completely different from my own. I was a 21st-century boy **livving** in a city-centre flat, while the book is about a girl living in the countryside 100 years ago. *The Secret Garden's* main character is ten-year-old Mary, who is sent to live with an uncle when her **parants** die. Living in a remote house with only his servants, the uncle is a miserable man. He leaves Mary to look after herself, so **(1)** *as far as I know / not surprisingly*, she is lonely and unhappy. **Gradualy**, she explores the area around the house and she finds the secret garden of the title. Over the course of the book, she makes friends, learns how to care for other people and becomes a **happyer**, healthier child. Although it was written a long time ago, **(2)** *as far as I know / as far as I'm concerned*, today's children will still find the story engaging. There is an element of **mistery** which keeps you reading, and the themes of the need for parental love and the importance of friendship are, **(3)** *without doubt / in doubt*, always **relevent**.

3 Read the review again and answer the questions.

    1 Is it the correct length?

    2 Is the style appropriate?

    3 Has the student covered all the points listed in the question?

4 Write your own review.

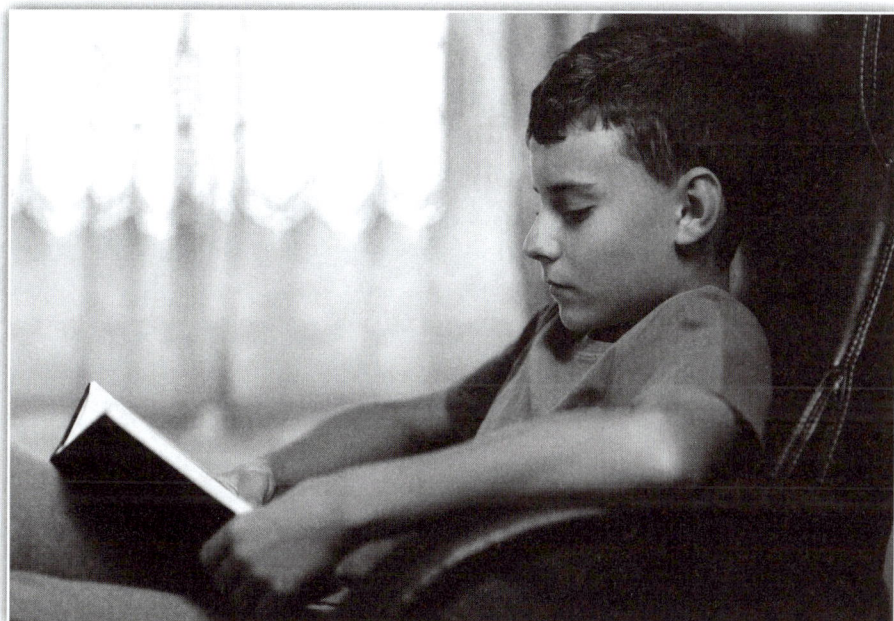

Listening (Paper 3 Part 2)

Before you listen

1 Read the listening task. Try and predict what kind of information is missing. Remember to look at the words before and after the gap. Answer the questions.

1 Which answer do you think will contain a number?
2 Which answers do you think will be adjectives?

Sentence completion

2a 🎧 17 Listen to the recording and complete the sentences.

b 🎧 17 Listen again to check and complete your answers.

EXPERT STRATEGY

Remember to check your spelling.

➤ **HELP**

1 Be careful. Two subjects are mentioned – which one did Laura choose?
3 Listen for the word *satisfying* – you hear the adjective you need soon afterwards.
7 Listen for what Laura did when she did research for her historical thriller.

EXPERT LANGUAGE

Which two sentences in the task begin with a time clause?

EXPERT WORD CHECK

*astronomy   detective novel
murder mystery   time-consuming*

You will hear a novelist talking about her life and work. For questions 1–10, complete the sentences with a word or short phrase.

Interview with a novelist

Laura explains that she studied (1) _____ at university.

Laura followed a career as a(n) (2) _____ for many years.

Laura says she found her job both satisfying and (3) _____ .

The first type of book which Laura attempted to write was a(n) (4) _____ novel.

Laura noticed that novels dealing with the (5) _____ were doing well.

Laura's novel is about a man who believed he'd discovered a(n) (6) _____ .

Laura gives the example of (7) _____ as a historical detail she needed to research.

In Laura's novel, most of the (8) _____ are invented.

When planning a novel, Laura concentrates on the (9) _____ first.

When she's working on a book, Laura usually writes about (10) _____ per day.

Vocabulary development 2

➤ **COURSEBOOK** pages 168–169

The media

1a Write the words/phrases in the box in the correct column. Some words may go in more than one category.

*article   circulation   commercials   documentary
download   editor   gossip column   log on
newscaster   presenter   reporter   server   small ads
surf   tabloid   viewers   weather forecast   web page*

Television	Newspapers	The internet

b Complete the sentences with words/phrases from Exercise 1a.

1 I worked on a local paper once. It was a weekly paper and had a(n) _____ of about 10,000.
2 I read a really interesting _____ the other day about teenagers and crime.
3 Sometimes I _____ the internet for hours, looking for something interesting.
4 My father is a bit snobbish. He says that _____ newspapers are no better than comics.
5 According to the _____ on TV last night, today is going to be a lovely day!
6 If it's a big video file, it can take ages to _____ , so I usually go and make a cup of coffee.
7 The worst thing about TV is the number of _____ . They interrupt the programmes every 20 minutes on this channel.
8 Look in the _____ of the local newspaper if you want to find some cheap second-hand furniture.
9 It's the _____ of a newspaper who decides what news is reported every day.
10 I really like the _____ on the *News Tonight* programme. She's quite humorous sometimes when she reads the news.

c Write the words/phrases in your vocabulary notebook. Add more as you come across them in your reading.

Phrasal verbs

2a Read the texts and choose the correct answers.

Journalism has changed a lot in recent years. In the past, journalists were taken **(1)** *up / on* by a newspaper without any training at all. They had to pick **(2)** *up / on* their skills on the job. For example, the editor would tell them to go and hang **(3)** *by / around* the police so that they could find out what was going **(4)** *on / through*. Nowadays, a lot of journalists sit in front of their computers all day. They hardly get out **(5)** *of / from* their offices at all.

I'm going to study photography at university next year. My father is a sports photographer and he talked me **(6)** *up / into* becoming a photographer myself. It sounds like a really interesting job. A couple of years ago I wanted to go in **(7)** *for / at* law but I think being a photojournalist or sports photographer will be more exciting.

What makes someone want to take **(8)** *on / up* a job in the media? I'm sure some people set **(9)** *out / off* to change the way people think and behave. But I think that most people who work in the media see it as an exciting job which puts them at the centre of events. I'd love to be a presenter on TV. To do that well, you need to get **(10)** *on / across* well with people – and be able to express yourself clearly, of course.

b Replace the words in bold with the correct form of phrasal verbs from Exercise 2a.

1 I **acquired a knowledge of** Japanese while I was working there as a journalist. I didn't have any lessons. _____
2 Have you ever thought of **choosing** sports writing as a career? _____
3 My best friend **persuaded me to do** media studies at university. _____
4 I **have a good relationship** with my tutor at university. _____
5 A good reporter needs to know what is **happening** in the world. _____
6 That new newspaper is doing really well. It recently **employed** another 20 journalists. _____
7 If you **go everywhere with** Jim, you'll learn everything you need to know. _____
8 Tourists are being warned to **leave** town as quickly as possible – things are getting dangerous! _____

Exam practice: Multiple-choice cloze
(Paper 1 Part 1)

3 Do the task.

For questions 1–8, read the text below and decide which answer (A, B, C or D) best fits each gap. There is an example at the beginning (0).

The history of journalism

Journalism as we know it today probably (0) _A_ from the 18th century, with the (1) _____ of daily newspapers that were written to spread the views of particular parties or social groups. There is a great variety of journalism on (2) _____ in the UK, ranging from the scandals of the tabloid newspapers to the high-quality reporting of the more serious publications.

Changes in journalism in the 20th century (3) _____ place as a result of technological (4) _____ : the teletypewriter, the radio and then television. While the (5) _____ of the newspaper journalist may have (6) _____ in recent years, many radio and television journalists became (7) _____ names as they reported events while they were actually happening. News broadcaster Walter Cronkite, for instance, will be remembered by millions of television (8) _____ for his coverage of events such as the landing of the first man on the moon.

	A	B	C	D
0	A dates	B lasts	C result	D times
1	A appearance	B receipt	C release	D attendance
2	A choice	B market	C stock	D offer
3	A gave	B stood	C took	D held
4	A advances	B revisions	C amendments	D promotions
5	A mark	B influence	C command	D position
6	A reduced	B declined	C retired	D departed
7	A familiar	B known	C usual	D accustomed
8	A spectators	B passers-by	C observers	D viewers

EXPERT STRATEGY

Remember to read through the whole text before you start answering the questions.

➤ HELP
3 The word you need collocates with *place*.
8 Choose the correct term for 'people who watch TV'.

EXPERT LANGUAGE

Find two expressions in the text that are used to introduce an example.

EXPERT WORD CHECK

coverage   high-quality   scandals   tabloid

Language development 2

➤ **COURSEBOOK** page 172

need + -ing / to be done

1a Choose the correct answers.

1 We've run out of milk. We need *to buy / buying* some more today.
2 The battery in my camera needs *to replace / replacing*.
3 I've lost touch with Tania. I need *to write / writing* to her.
4 All my computer files are very old and need *to update / to be updated*.
5 My father is rather overweight. He needs *to go / going* on a diet.
6 This television is faulty. The shop needs *to give / giving* you a new one.
7 Yesterday my mother said that my hair needed *to cut / cutting*.
8 This letter is not very good. It needs *to rewrite / to be rewritten*.

b Complete the sentences with the correct form of the verbs in brackets. More than one answer may be possible.

1 My car is due for a service – I need _____ (take) it to the garage.
2 Your dog looks very hungry. Perhaps he needs _____ (feed) more often.
3 I'm going to the optician tomorrow. My eyes need _____ (test).
4 The radio is not working very well. Do you think it'll need _____ (replace)?
5 Did you need _____ (go) to the doctor when you were ill?
6 That old pullover of yours really needed _____ (wash). It was filthy!
7 When you fix the roof tomorrow, will someone need _____ (help) you?
8 Our oven is really dirty. In fact, it's needed _____ (clean) for ages.

have / get something done

2a Complete the text. Use only one word in each gap.

A couple of months ago I bought an old house in the country and I'm (1) _____ it done up. Most of the windows are broken, so I'll have (2) _____ replaced when I can. A lot of the roof tiles are missing as well, and I (3) _____ probably need to (4) _____ the whole roof retiled.

Inside, I'm going to (5) _____ central heating put in, which will be another big job. Fortunately, the wiring of the house is fine, so I don't need to have (6) _____ rewired. That'll save some money. But the first thing I want to do is (7) _____ the wall between the dining room and living room knocked down to make one big room.

I'm going to redecorate the house myself rather than have it (8) _____ by professionals, because I love painting and I want to do it myself. The only problem is that I (9) _____ all my paints and brushes stolen a few days ago. I suppose it was fortunate my car (10) _____ not stolen as well!

b Complete the responses using the word(s) in brackets and the correct form of *have / get something (done)*.

1 A: Why is your hair such a strange colour?
   B: Well, I _had it dyed_ (dye) yesterday.
2 A: I've been having a lot of headaches recently. Why do you think that is?
   B: Maybe you should _____ (eyes/test) tomorrow.
3 A: Why is your car always breaking down?
   B: I really don't know. I _____ (service) every six months.
4 A: You look as if you're in pain. Do you have toothache?
   B: Yes. I haven't _____ (teeth/check) for ages.
5 A: Why are there so many workmen in your garden?
   B: Well, we're going to _____ (swimming pool/build) there.
6 A: Why is there so much smoke coming from your log fire?
   B: I don't know. We probably need to _____ (chimney/clean).

Key word transformations

3 Complete the second sentence so that it has a similar meaning to the first sentence, using the word given. Do not change the word given. You must use between two and five words, including the word given.

1 Someone broke into Jane's house yesterday.
   BROKEN
   Jane had _____ yesterday.
2 Have they taken your photograph yet?
   HAD
   Have you _____ taken yet?

3 I think we ought to get the house painted.
   NEEDS
   I think the _____ painted.
4 I can't email you because they are repairing my computer at the moment.
   REPAIRED
   I can't email you because I'm _____ at the moment.
5 Peter wants them to put in central heating soon.
   HAVE
   Peter wants to _____ soon.
6 You need to get someone to knock down that garden wall.
   KNOCKING
   That garden wall _____ down.
7 I haven't been to the car wash for ages.
   WASHED
   I haven't had my _____ for ages.
8 You should get some sleep now because it's late.
   NEED
   You _____ to bed now because it's late.
9 Someone has just stolen my new watch!
   HAD
   I have _____ stolen!
10 They are delivering Sue's new fridge today.
   DELIVERED
   Sue is _____ today.

Exam practice: Open cloze

(Paper 1 Part 2)

4 Do the task.

*For questions 1–8, read the text below and think of the word which best fits each gap. Use only **one** word in each gap. There is an example at the beginning (0).*

Product placement

If you're a fan of James Bond films, you (0) _will_ have seen him driving the latest sports car in a number of key scenes. The car, (1) _____ , isn't only important in terms of the plot. It's the result of an agreement (2) _____ the car manufacturers and the film studio, aimed at promoting the luxury model on screen. This is an example of (3) _____ is called 'product placement'. In other words, the products and logos that you see in films are (4) _____ because of advertising deals. For some products, (5) _____ as mobile phones and fast food, companies may compete (6) _____ each other to get on screen, pushing the price up even further. But if you're there just to enjoy the movie, aren't the advertisements getting in the (7) _____ of the story? Fortunately, advertisers do realise that advertisements (8) _____ annoy film-goers will do more harm than good, so there's probably a limit to how many we see.

Reading (Paper 1 Part 6)

Before you read 1 Read the instructions for the reading task and the title of the article. Answer the questions.

1 What do you think are the advantages and disadvantages of television?
2 Is the influence of television generally good or bad?

Skimming 2 Skim the text and answer the questions.

1 What main points does the writer make about television?
2 How does the writer answer question 2 in Exercise 1?

Gapped text 3 Do the task. Remember to follow these steps.

- Read the whole of the text carefully.
- For each question, read the text before and after the gap and think about the type of information which is missing.
- Look for a sentence in the box which talks about this topic area.
- Choose the correct answer by checking the grammatical and lexical links between the base text and the key sentence. Look out for pronouns, synonyms, etc.
- Read the text again with your answers, to check that it makes sense.

EXPERT STRATEGY

Choose the best option for each gap. If you're not sure about a gap, go on to the next question and return to it later.

➤ HELP

2 The sentence you need starts with *but* and provides contrasting information.
3 The text after the gap is about shopping – which sentence talks about this topic?
4 You are looking for a sentence that talks about something that is particular to television.

EXPERT LANGUAGE

Which of the sentences (A–G) start with a clause of contrast?

EXPERT WORD CHECK

*broadcaster   glued to
light entertainment   nasty   stock up*

You are going to read an article about television. Six sentences have been removed from the article. Choose from the sentences (A–G) the one that fits each gap (1–6). There is one extra sentence which you do not need to use.

A Despite this, the influence of television continues to grow.

B There is, however, a particular aspect of television which makes it unlike almost all other influences on our lives.

C It involves what happens to us during that time.

D But equally, they can appeal to the worst sides of our nature or turn everything into light entertainment.

E But most of the time, we turn it on to watch, and we give it our full attention.

F But the reality we get from television is not like that because we don't participate in it; we just watch it.

G Similarly, if a book comes out based on one of these programmes, then bookshops stock up for the extra sales that will surely follow.

Vocabulary: Expressions 4 Choose the correct answer (A, B, C or D).

1 The writer _____ a talk to a group of school-leavers.
  A made   B gave   C had   D led
2 Most of them wanted to _____ into television.
  A work   B be   C go   D watch
3 In the UK, people _____ up to four hours per day watching television.
  A pass   B take   C sit   D spend
4 Most of us rely _____ TV as a source of information about the world.
  A at   B on   C in   D to
5 If a politician _____ a fool of himself/herself on TV, his/her career is over.
  A makes   B looks   C does   D behaves
6 TV has a very big influence _____ our lives.
  A to   B with   C on   D through
7 That's why it's very important _____ the programme makers show us.
  A that   B why   C if   D what

THE INFLUENCE OF TELEVISION

When I first became a broadcaster many years ago, I didn't know, and neither did most other people, that I was entering what was going to become the greatest growth industry of the next half century: the media. We didn't use that rather
5 nasty word then, of course: we had newspapers, radio and television. We've only started to talk about 'the media' relatively recently, but nowadays everybody seems to want to be part of it. When I gave a talk to a group of school-leavers recently, I asked how many thought they might eventually
10 look for a career in politics, medicine, the law. A few dozen of the 2,000 raised their hands for each. Then I asked who wanted a career in the media. Half the hands in the hall went up and most of them wanted to go into television.

Apart from sleeping, watching television is what people do
15 most of in the UK, each person spending, on average, just under four hours per day in front of the box. But the influence of television goes further and cannot be measured just by the number of hours people have their television sets on.
[1]

20 Some people certainly treat it as background while they carry on having a meal, reading the paper or even listening to music. [2] As anybody with small children knows, we quickly become deeply involved in what's happening on the screen and the language we use reflects this – we talk about
25 being 'glued' to the television.

What's more, most of us rely on television as the main source of information for what is happening out there in the world – and I'm not just talking about the news or documentaries. We gain our impressions of what Australia or the USA are
30 like from their soap operas. [3] And even without the commercials, television can determine what we buy, what we talk about and what children play with. As for the grown-ups, if a popular series is set in a specific area of the countryside, that is where the tourists will go. If a politician
35 makes a serious fool of himself/herself on television, his/her career is over.

Television has become, for most of us, as much a part of our lives as the electricity that comes into our homes or the air we breathe. It is now a central part of what makes us
40 who we are. [4] It is not yet truly interactive. It speaks to us but we do not speak back, except on a few phone-in programmes. This is an interesting feature of something that has such a big influence on our lives.

When I was a child, a whole host of things and people
45 influenced me but the one thing they all had in common was the fact that you got a reaction from them. That was how you learnt what real life was all about and how you fitted into it. [5] In other words, we don't have to do any thinking for ourselves. We just get reality given to us by
50 those who make the programmes. That's why it matters so much what they decide to show us.

The television networks can present us with a picture of the world as it really is – complicated and interesting and full of variety – and they can make us think about it and
55 about ourselves as a result. [6] If they do that, then that's how we will start to respond to the world, too. My concern is that the trend is clearly in the wrong direction.

Practice exam

Part 1

For questions **1–8**, read the text below and decide which answer (**A**, **B**, **C** or **D**) best fits each gap. There is an example at the beginning (**0**).

Mark your answers **on the separate answer sheet**.

Example:

0 A leads   **B** keeps   **C** passes   **D** follows

| 0 | A | B | C | D |

The life of a country vet

Don Strange, who works as a vet in northern England, **(0)** _____ a busy life. As well as having to **(1)** _____ pets which are unwell, he often visits farms where problems of various kinds await him. He has lost **(2)** _____ of the number of times he has been called out at midnight to give **(3)** _____ to a farmer with sick sheep or cows.

Recently, a television company chose Don as the **(4)** _____ of a documentary programme it was making about the life of a country vet. The programme showed the difficult situations Don **(5)** _____ every day, such as helping a cow to give birth or winning the trust of an aggressive dog which needs an injection. Not all of Don's patients are domestic animals, **(6)** _____ , and in the programme people saw him helping an owl which had a damaged wing. It also showed Don **(7)** _____ a meeting with villagers concerned about the damage a new road might do to their **(8)** _____ environment.

1	**A** deal	**B** fix	**C** treat	**D** solve
2	**A** memory	**B** count	**C** score	**D** patience
3	**A** suggestion	**B** warning	**C** advice	**D** recommendation
4	**A** feature	**B** subject	**C** case	**D** character
5	**A** faces	**B** greets	**C** copes	**D** stands
6	**A** although	**B** therefore	**C** yet	**D** however
7	**A** keeping	**B** holding	**C** carrying	**D** taking
8	**A** nearby	**B** area	**C** local	**D** close

Part 2

For questions **9–16**, read the text below and think of the word which best fits each gap. Use only **one** word in each gap. There is an example at the beginning (**0**).

Write your answers **IN CAPITAL LETTERS on the separate answer sheet**.

Example: | 0 | F | O | R | | | | | | | | | | | | |

Nicer than chocolate

Sales of chocolate in the UK have fallen **(0)** _____ the first time in 50 years. According to researchers, this is largely **(9)** _____ children prefer to spend their pocket money on mobile phones. Schoolchildren who **(10)** _____ to visit their local shop to buy sweets are now buying top-up cards for their mobiles instead, **(11)** _____ that they can send their friends text messages. Sociologists see this move away **(12)** _____ sweets towards the use of mobile telephones as an example of **(13)** _____ teenage life is changing as a result **(14)** _____ new technology.

Fourteen-year-old Susannah Hedgely, **(15)** _____ has run up a bill of nearly £300 on her mobile phone in the past two months, most of it on texting, is typical of the trend. Susannah was originally given a mobile so she could **(16)** _____ her parents know when she was going to be late home from school but she now sends up to 60 text messages per day.

Part 3

For questions **17–24**, read the text below. Use the word given in capitals at the end of some of the lines to form a word that fits in the gap **in the same line**. There is an example at the beginning (**0**).

Write your answers **IN CAPITAL LETTERS on the separate answer sheet**.

Example: | 0 | P | O | P | U | L | A | R | I | T | Y | | | | | | | | | | |

Jogging in the park

Despite the increasing (**0**) _____ of physical exercise in recent years, only ten percent of British people have taken out (**17**) _____ of a gym. According to researchers, one reason for this is that gyms may have a negative psychological effect on people. In tests, natural environments were found to be far more (**18**) _____ than the artificial surroundings of a gym.

Maybe this provides an (**19**) _____ for why there has been a steady (**20**) _____ in the number of people to be seen jogging in and around city parks in recent years. (**21**) _____ the gym, where people are limited to a certain range of machines, or (**22**) _____ classes, outdoor activity has no boundaries and parks are (**23**) _____ becoming places of adult, as well as child, recreation, (**24**) _____ in the warmer weather.

POPULAR
MEMBER

BENEFIT

EXPLAIN
GROW
LIKE
FIT
INCREASE
SPECIAL

Part 4

For questions **25–30**, complete the second sentence so that it has a similar meaning to the first sentence, using the word given. **Do not change the word given.** You must use between **two** and **five** words, including the word given. Here is an example (**0**).

Example:

0 You must do exactly what the manager tells you.

CARRY

You must _____ instructions exactly.

The gap can be filled by the words *carry out the manager's*, so you write:

Example: | 0 | CARRY OUT THE MANAGER'S

Write **only** the missing words **IN CAPITAL LETTERS on the separate answer sheet**.

---

25 I have never been as excited as I was during that football match.

HAVE

That football match was the _____ ever seen.

26 People say that the pop star has given a lot of money to charity.

SAID

The pop star _____ a lot of money to charity.

27 Simon decided to accept the salesperson's offer of a 20 percent discount.

ADVANTAGE

Simon decided he would _____ the salesperson's offer of a 20 percent discount.

28 The heavy rainfall made it impossible for them to complete the walk.

PREVENTED

They _____ the walk by the heavy rainfall.

29 A local garage always services my motorbike.

GET

I always _____ at a local garage.

30 Tony regrets not being able to speak to his girlfriend last night.

COULD

Tony wishes that _____ to his girlfriend last night.

Part 5

You are going to read a newspaper article about Hollywood. For questions **31–36**, choose the answer (**A**, **B**, **C** or **D**) which you think fits best according to the text.

Mark your answers **on the separate answer sheet**.

I'm not a waitress, I'm an actress!

For every Kate Winslet or Catherine Zeta Jones, there are thousands of British 'wannabe' actresses who never make it in Hollywood. 'It is disheartening,' admits 28-year-old Rachael Nortance. 'I've been to so many auditions for film parts where I walk in and there's a room full of equally talented people, and I ask myself: "Why am I here?" But ironically, what Rachael finds hardest to accept is how nice people are to her at auditions. 'The organisers tell you they love your work and for the first month or so I believed them, but eventually, I realised it's totally fake because mostly you never hear from them again.'

During her four years in the USA, Rachael has been to more auditions than she can remember, has sent out thousands of photos of herself and been to every celebrity party that she's been invited to. For all that, the closest she has come to a camera is the one she takes snaps with to email home to her family in England. She has yet to land any film or TV work and is currently working at a children's talent agency to make ends meet. 'Basically, I do my best to keep happy and focused on the industry,' she says. 'I was very realistic when I came to Hollywood – I presumed I would have to be a waitress, so I can't complain about a job that not only pays the bills but which also gives me a lot of satisfaction.'

Rachael is just one of an estimated 1,000 hopefuls who arrive in Los Angeles every week, chasing dreams of stardom. Many are British, and almost all are unprepared for the intensity of the competition for acting jobs, and end up taking menial jobs because they have to support themselves. 'British actresses think Los Angeles is the land of opportunity,' she explains. 'They see icons like Kate Winslet and think it's possible to be successful here. But for every one that makes it, there are thousands who end up doing dead-end jobs. Many get stuck here because they don't want to go home again, not so much because they can't afford it but because that would be admitting defeat – they'd risk losing face.'

In spite of the constant rejection, Rachael keeps going. 'I'm passionate about acting and I think I've reached a standard where I can prove I'm a good actress,' she explains. 'But I do get down sometimes. That's when I cry on the phone to Mum, who talks me out of packing my bags and makes me realise I need to strive harder. There isn't a day that goes by when I don't wonder if I made the right decision to come here, but then a big audition comes up or someone introduces me to a useful contact and I realise how lucky I am.'

After four years, even though she has yet to secure an acting role, she still feels she is doing the right thing. 'I know it takes time to make it here. At this stage it's all about contacts. A week ago I had a meeting with a production company, and they've asked me to audition for a part in a possible film in two years' time. It's a long way off but this could be where the ball starts rolling. It's like any goal you set yourself – you get so far and you can't give up.'

31 What does Rachael find disheartening about auditions?

    A Too many actors are invited.

    B The wrong type of actors are invited.

    C The organisers are insincere in their comments.

    D The organisers refuse to give feedback on her performance.

32 What does Rachael say about her job at the talent agency?

    A She's not really suited to it.

    B She finds it relatively rewarding.

    C It's not as well paid as waitressing.

    D It's something she just does for the money.

33 What are 'menial jobs' (line 34)?

    A jobs with low status

    B jobs with good salaries

    C jobs which provide useful contacts

    D jobs for which there's lots of competition

34 According to Rachael, why do unsuccessful actresses stay in Los Angeles?

    A They get used to the lifestyle.

    B They are too proud to admit defeat.

    C They lack the money to go back home.

    D The have found alternative careers there.

35 On the phone, Rachael's mother often

    A encourages her to keep on trying.

    B tries to persuade her to return home.

    C questions decisions that Rachael has made.

    D makes useful suggestions about Rachael's career.

36 How does Rachael feel about her latest audition?

    A unsure whether it's worth attending

    B encouraged by the timing of the project

    C doubtful about the people she's already met

    D optimistic about her chances of succeeding

Part 6

You are going to read a magazine article written by a wildlife cameraman. Six sentences have been removed from the article. Choose from the sentences **A–G** the one which fits each gap (37–42). There is one extra sentence which you do not need to use.

Mark your answers **on the separate answer sheet**.

The Chair Bear

When filming in Sri Lanka, wildlife cameraman Gordon Buchanan got the fright of his life.

When I was asked to spend a year in Sri Lanka, filming the local leopards, I jumped at the chance. The leopard is a shy animal which even the best trackers only see on rare occasions. There was, however, only one way to discover if it was possible to film them and that was to try. It was the idea of life in the jungle that really attracted me, actually – sleeping under the stars and surviving on meals of wild fruits – but this wasn't quite how it turned out.

At first, I was put up in a four-star hotel. But what I gained in fresh towels and hot water, I lacked in leopards. Weeks passed with only glimpses of the animals. To have any chance of fulfilling my contract, I would have to locate signs of recent leopard activity in the jungle, and then sit it out overnight in a portable wooden hide. **37**

We set up the hide near the spot he'd indicated and I settled down to wait with my night-filming equipment, in the hope that the animal would come back to finish its meal. Soon after sunset, I was thrilled to see a mother leopard and cub silently appear on my infrared monitor and begin to feed. **38**

I knew exactly what was making it, though this knowledge only alarmed me further. It was a sloth bear – a beast that is responsible for the most horrific attacks on humans. **39**

If you're wondering what makes these creatures so dangerous, it's said that they have the temper of a wasp and the jaws of a lion. I swung the infrared camera around to get the animal in frame but he was too close – something I only realised when a huge black nose appeared through a gap in the corner of the hide. **40**

I went back to my camera in time to see the bear sit down in front of the hissing mother leopard. I got ready to film the leopard as she fled. But just as the bear was about to grab the meat, she leapt at it, lashing out with her claws. **41** Within minutes the bear was back, this time with a friend. One fed as the other went around the back of the hide. Feeling exceptionally unsafe, I radioed for someone to come and get me.

Making our way back to the scene in daylight, I spotted something odd in the track. It was the folding seat I use when filming. Looking down, I saw a set of bear tracks coming from the direction of the hide, while the teeth marks on the metal object confirmed that the bear had claimed it as its own. **42**

The front of that hide now had an oddly shaped hole in it which looked as though it had been made by a bear leaving with a chair in its mouth – which must be exactly what had happened.

A But my pleasure turned almost instantly to barely controlled terror when, from behind the hide, there came an unearthly sound – a combined roar, growl, wail, scream and snarl, all at maximum volume.

B I grabbed my spotlight and flashed it in the animal's face, at which point it fortunately chose to move off.

C It was difficult to make out exactly how far away the animal was but after a few minutes I heard the clatter of its claws on the rocks as it moved closer.

D I was sure I'd fastened the door shut, with all my gear inside, so, cautiously, we went to investigate – wary of what might be awaiting us.

E It wasn't long before KG, my right-hand man, found a deer which had recently been killed by a leopard, and so, armed with this evidence, we headed into the forest.

F I was totally stunned – not only was this a completely unexpected reaction but I had also captured the behaviour on film, including the cub continuing to feed with its mother until they both walked off.

G Nothing prepared me for what was to happen next, however, which was an experience I shall remember for the rest of my days.

Part 7

You are going to read a magazine article about working in the music industry. For questions **43–52**, choose from the people (**A–D**). The people may be chosen more than once.

Mark your answers **on the separate answer sheet**.

Which person:

has fulfilled a childhood ambition to work in this industry?	43
chose to live in an area at the centre of the music industry?	44
wishes that his/her job was not so desk-bound?	45
has no regrets about turning down an alternative career opportunity?	46
mentions meeting some famous people?	47
once lost a job in the music industry?	48
took professional advice before finding a job?	49
has to stand in for colleagues in their absence?	50
has to balance work and family commitments?	51
feels that qualifications are the key to getting a job in the industry?	52

Jobs in the music industry

We talk to four people who work behind the scenes at a recording company.

A Dan Welney, financial planning assistant

Dan worked for a merchant bank during university holidays to save up for a year out travelling. 'They offered me a permanent job,' he says. 'But I decided it wasn't for me. So I went to a firm of recruitment consultants who pointed me in the direction of the music industry and I started in January. I'm responsible for things like employees' expenses when they go on foreign trips, so there's quite a bit of paperwork. But we're also the ones who say, 'You haven't got enough money to sign that band,' or 'You'll have to cut the video budget,' which is the interesting part. I don't get out of the office a great deal, which can be a drawback, but there are compensations – free concerts and CDs were certainly one attraction of the job. Although the celebrities tend to bypass my office, this certainly beats working for a bank, even if it's not as well paid.'

B Gemma Ortolano, office manager

Although Gemma studied music at university, she chose courses that prepared her for the music business rather than the creative side. 'We learnt about music law, tour management, all that side of it. Now I'm office manager in the marketing department here. It's a pretty varied job. I have to make sure everyone has what they need, I organise mailings to the press and I compile and send round reports so everyone in the organisation knows what's happening with the bands. I get to work across departments, so it's an interesting job and I've mixed with my fair share of celebrities. I didn't know anyone in the industry when I started out, though, obviously, that can help. I chose to do a specialised degree instead and walked into a job afterwards. I would recommend it as a way of getting into the industry.'

C Sam Tysler, music lawyer

Sam trained as a lawyer but admits to being a frustrated musician. 'I played in a band as a kid at school and always dreamt of getting involved in entertainment sooner or later. I joined this company in 1994 and I'm now the senior lawyer in the department. It's not all desk-based and the day doesn't end at 6:30 p.m. because you've got to be out there in the public eye – although since I got married, I have had to cut back a bit on the partying. The artists and songwriters I represent are worth £70 million in record sales. One has sold 30 million records, others just have their 15 minutes of fame – that's the nature of the business. I find working in the industry is a thrill in itself because, although I just draw up the contracts, I still enjoy the buzz and the thrill of the deal.'

D Valerie Picot, receptionist

As a French student doing International Business and English language, Valerie got to know the British music scene when she was over doing work experience as part of her course. 'After my degree, I returned and worked as an assistant at a recording studio,' she explains. 'Then last March I was made redundant and did temporary secretarial work before landing my present job. Music has always been a big part of my life so I came to where it all happens – London. I meet and greet visitors, and get to do cover across the departments if anyone is off sick. That means I've acted as PA to the Chairman, worked in international marketing – all good experience. I'm hoping it will lead to a more creative role.'

Part 1

You **must** answer this question. Write your answer in **140–190** words in an appropriate style.

1 In your English class, you have been talking about advertising. Now, your teacher has asked you to
write an essay.

Write an essay using **all** the notes and give reasons for your point of view.

Advertising has an important role to play in modern life.

Notes

Write about:

     1   why advertising is important

     2   some problems related to advertising

     3   _____ (your own idea)

Part 2

Write an answer to **one** of the questions **2–4** in this part. Write your answer in **140–190** words in an appropriate style.

2 You see the following notice in an international magazine.

Articles wanted!

Describe your ideal friend

What qualities do you look for in a friend and which are the most important?

The best article will be published in our magazine next month.

Write your **article**.

3 You recently spent a weekend in a large city hotel. You have received this message from the website you used to book the hotel.

Reviews wanted!

Did you enjoy your stay? Please write a review of your hotel for us to put on our website. In your review, say how satisfied you were with the hotel, if it was good value for money and whether you'd recommend it to other clients.

Write your **review**.

4 You have received this email from your English-speaking friend, Alex.

Hi there,

I need your help! I've got to do a research project about public holidays in different countries. Can you write back and tell me about your country? I'd like to know how many public holidays you have a year, what people usually do on public holidays and why you think there should be more or fewer of them.

Thank you!

Alex

Write your **email**.

Part 1

🎧 18 You will hear people talking in eight different situations. For questions **1–8**, choose the best answer (**A**, **B** or **C**).

1 You hear somebody talking about a recent holiday.
What disappointed her about the villa complex she stayed in?
A the way it was laid out
B the type of people it attracted
C the facilities provided for guests

2 You overhear a conversation about a missed appointment.
How does the woman feel now?
A embarrassed about the way she behaved
B angry that she didn't see the dentist
C satisfied that she made her point

3 You overhear two colleagues talking about something which happened at work.
What do they agree about?
A Communications within the company are poor.
B A mistake occurred as a result of human error.
C It's important not to miss meetings.

4 You hear an advertisement for sports clothes.
What aspect of the clothes is being emphasised?
A how practical they are
B how durable they are
C how attractive they are

5 On the radio, you hear a man talking about children and computers.
What is he doing when he speaks?
A disagreeing with recent research
B giving advice on how to approach something
C explaining how a particular problem can be overcome

6 You hear a programme in which a new book by a well-known novelist is being reviewed.
What does the speaker think about this novel?
A It is untypical of the writer's work.
B It is not as well written as she'd expected.
C It seems to be lacking in originality.

7 You hear part of a radio phone-in programme about problems at work.
What is the caller having difficulty with?
A attracting new members of staff to the company
B convincing her staff that the pay and conditions are fair
C encouraging members of staff to stay with the company

8 You hear a conversation in a radio play.
Where is the conversation taking place?
A at a theatre box office
B at a hotel reception desk
C in a restaurant

Part 2

🎧 19 You will hear a man called Peter Denison, who repairs clocks and watches, talking about his life and work. For questions **9–18**, complete the sentences with a word or short phrase.

Repairing clocks and watches

Peter's **(9)** _____ was the person who encouraged his early interest in mechanical things.

Peter says that for him, old clocks represent a link with **(10)** _____ .

In Peter's first job, he worked as an improver in a jeweller's in **(11)** _____ .

The building where Peter works now used to be a(n) **(12)** _____ .

As well as having good eyes, a watch repairer must be patient and have **(13)** _____ .

As a result of his work, Peter sometimes has health problems involving his **(14)** _____ .

The oldest clock Peter has repaired was made in the year **(15)** _____ .

Peter explains that people often have **(16)** _____ feelings about old clocks.

Peter says that few people realise the need to **(17)** _____ old clocks regularly.

In talking about his life and work, Peter describes himself as a(n) **(18)** _____ .

Part 3

🎧 20 You will hear five short extracts in which people are talking about living in blocks of flats. For questions **19–23**, choose from the list (**A–H**) the main reason each speaker gives for choosing the flat where they live now. Use the letters only once. There are three extra letters which you do not need to use.

A the low cost

B the proximity of local amenities

C good transport links

D the friendliness of the neighbours

E a feeling of security

F the level of maintenance

G the peaceful location

H the size of the rooms

Speaker 1	19	
Speaker 2	20	
Speaker 3	21	
Speaker 4	22	
Speaker 5	23	

Part 4

🎧 21 You will hear an interview with a man called Grant Sowerby, who is about to go on a trip into outer space. For questions **24–30**, choose the best answer (**A**, **B** or **C**).

24 What is Grant most looking forward to on his flight?

    A taking off from Earth

    B seeing the Earth from space

    C leaving the Earth's atmosphere

25 When asked if he is scared, Grant

    A denies this strongly.

    B insists that he's overcome his fear.

    C suggests that this is a normal thing to feel.

26 What will Grant be responsible for during the flight?

    A providing a commentary for the media

    B observing what the crew members do

    C operating some of the controls

27 What did Grant find most difficult about his training?

    A learning to deal with weightlessness

    B preparing for unexpected landings

    C improving his general level of fitness

28 Grant feels that the term 'space tourism'

    A gives people the wrong idea about what he's doing.

    B makes what he's doing sound attractive to people.

    C leads people to doubt whether he's really going.

29 Grant admits that many people wanting to do what he is doing

    A would find the training too challenging.

    B would get bored during the training.

    C would not have the necessary experience.

30 Grant thinks that in the future,

    A many people will be able to afford space flights.

    B more companies will be organising space trips.

    C most spaceflights will take paying passengers.

General questions
- What's your name?
- Where do you come from?
- Do you work or are you a full-time student? What do you do/study?

Now, answer one question from each section:

Home and family
- Do you have any brothers or sisters?
- Tell me about your favourite room at home.
- Do you like large family parties? Why/Why not?

Daily life and special occasions
- Do you like getting up early in the morning. Why/Why not?
- How do you travel to work/school/college?
- When is your birthday? How do you like to celebrate it?

Work/Education
- What's the most interesting thing you've ever studied?
- How important is English in your work/studies?
- What ambitions do you have for the future?

Health
- What sports did you enjoy when you were younger?
- What do you do to keep fit these days?
- Do you try to eat healthy foods? Why/Why not?

Interests
- Did you have a particular hobby as a child?
- Have your interests changed as you've got older?
- Is there something you'd like to learn to do in the future?

Holidays
- Tell me about your last holiday.
- Do you like to travel on holiday or stay in one place? Why?
- Where would you like to go on holiday in the future? Why?

Part 2 (A)   4 minutes. (6 minutes for groups of three)

Interlocutor: In this part of the test, I'm going to give each of you two photographs. I'd like you to talk about your photographs on your own for about a minute, and also to answer a question about your partner's photographs.

(Candidate A), it's your turn first. Here are your photographs. They show **people greeting each other**.

I'd like you to compare the photographs, and say **why you think the people are greeting each other in this way**.

All right?

Candidate A: [approximately 1 minute]

Interlocutor: Thank you.

(Candidate B), **how do you greet different types of people**?

Candidate B: [approximately 30 seconds]

Interlocutor: Thank you.

Part 2 (B)

Interlocutor:	Thank you.
	Now, *(Candidate B)*, here are your photographs. They show **people using technology**. I'd like you to compare the photographs, **and say how you think the people feel about the equipment they are using**. All right?
Candidate B:	*[Approximately 1 minute]*
Interlocutor:	Thank you.
	(Candidate A), **do you use a computer much**?
Candidate A:	*[Approximately 30 seconds]*
Interlocutor:	Thank you.

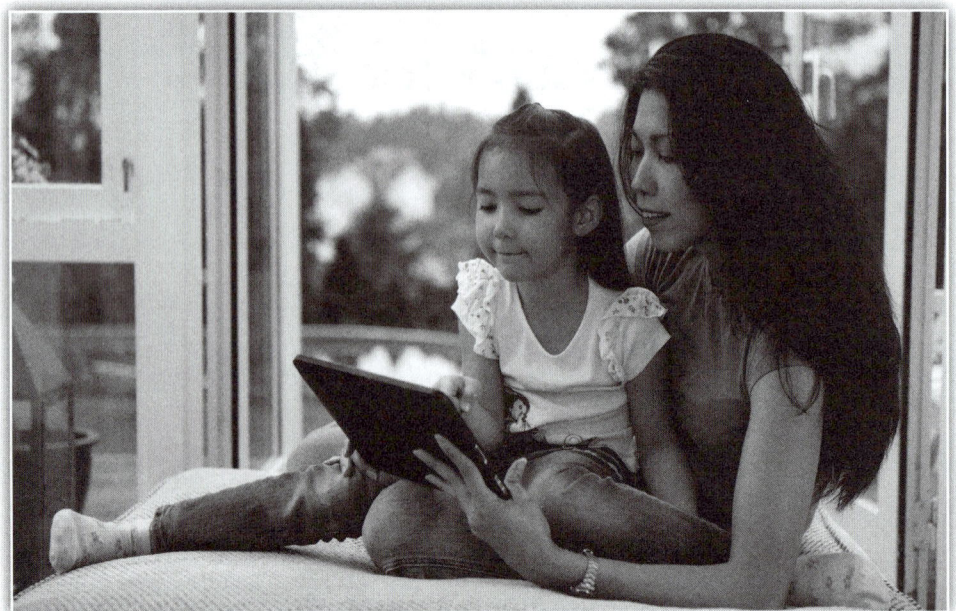

Part 3   4 minutes. (5 minutes for groups of three)

Interlocutor: Now, I'd like you to talk about something together for about two minutes.
(3 minutes for groups of three)

I'd like you to imagine that an open-air music festival is being organised in the countryside. It will last a whole weekend and the organisers need to provide facilities for the large number of people who will attend. Here are some of the facilities. First you have some time to look at the task.

[15 seconds]

Now, talk to each other about **why it's important to provide each of these facilities**.

Candidates: *[2 minutes (3 minutes for groups of three)]*

Interlocutor: Thank you.
Now you have a minute to decide **which of the facilities you think it is most important to provide**.

Candidates: *[1 minute for pairs and groups of three]*
Thank you.

a car park

a meeting point

an area for tents

'Why is it important to provide these facilities at an open-air music festival?'

fast-food stalls

some large screens

Part 4 — 4 minutes. (6 minutes for groups of three)

Interlocutor: Use the following questions, in order, as appropriate:

- Have you ever been to an open-air concert like the one you discussed in Part3?

- What are the advantages of big events like this for music fans?

- What problems do you think the organisers might face during the weekend?

- Do you prefer to listen to live music or recorded music? Why?

- What type of music is it best to listen to in the open air?

- Do you like being in a large crowd of people? Why/Why not?

Answer Sheet 1 (FCE R)

CAMBRIDGE ENGLISH
Language Assessment
Part of the University of Cambridge

Do not write in this box

SAMPLE

Candidate Name
If not already printed, write name in CAPITALS and complete the Candidate No. grid (in pencil).

Candidate Signature

Examination Title

Centre

Supervisor:
If the candidate is ABSENT or has WITHDRAWN shade here

Centre No.

Candidate No.

Examination Details

Candidate Answer Sheet

Instructions

Use a PENCIL (B or HB).

Rub out any answer you wish to change using an eraser.

Parts 1, 5, 6 and 7:
Mark ONE letter for each question.

For example, if you think **B** is the right answer to the question, mark your answer sheet like this:

0 A B C D

Parts 2, 3 and 4:
Write your answer clearly in CAPITAL LETTERS.

For Parts 2 and 3 write one letter in each box. For example:

0 EXAMPLE

Part 1

1	A	B	C	D
2	A	B	C	D
3	A	B	C	D
4	A	B	C	D
5	A	B	C	D
6	A	B	C	D
7	A	B	C	D
8	A	B	C	D

Part 2   Do not write below here

9
10
11
12
13
14
15
16

Continues over ➡

FCE R   DP602

Part 3   Do not write below here

17
18
19
20
21
22
23
24

Part 4   Do not write below here

25
26
27
28
29
30

Part 5

31	A	B	C	D
32	A	B	C	D
33	A	B	C	D
34	A	B	C	D
35	A	B	C	D
36	A	B	C	D

Part 6

37	A	B	C	D	E	F	G
38	A	B	C	D	E	F	G
39	A	B	C	D	E	F	G
40	A	B	C	D	E	F	G
41	A	B	C	D	E	F	G
42	A	B	C	D	E	F	G

Part 7

43	A	B	C	D	E	F
44	A	B	C	D	E	F
45	A	B	C	D	E	F
46	A	B	C	D	E	F
47	A	B	C	D	E	F
48	A	B	C	D	E	F
49	A	B	C	D	E	F
50	A	B	C	D	E	F
51	A	B	C	D	E	F
52	A	B	C	D	E	F

denote 0121 528 5100

Answer Sheet 2 (FCE L)

CAMBRIDGE ENGLISH
Language Assessment
Part of the University of Cambridge

Do not write in this box

SAMPLE

Candidate Name
If not already printed, write name in CAPITALS and complete the Candidate No. grid (in pencil).

Candidate Signature

Examination Title

Centre

Supervisor:
If the candidate is ABSENT or has WITHDRAWN shade here

Centre No.

Candidate No.

Examination Details

Candidate Answer Sheet

Instructions

Use a PENCIL (B or HB).
Rub out any answer you wish to change using an eraser.

Parts 1, 3 and 4:
Mark ONE letter for each question.

For example, if you think **B** is the right answer to the question, mark your answer sheet like this:

0 A B C

Part 2:
Write your answer clearly in CAPITAL LETTERS.

Write one letter or number in each box.
If the answer has more than one word, leave one box empty between words.

For example

0 AN EXAMPLE

Turn this sheet over to start.

FCE L   DP799

Part 1

1	A	B	C
2	A	B	C
3	A	B	C
4	A	B	C
5	A	B	C
6	A	B	C
7	A	B	C
8	A	B	C

Part 2 (Remember to write in CAPITAL LETTERS or numbers)   Do not write below here

9
10
11
12
13
14
15
16
17
18

Part 3

19	A	B	C	D	E	F	G	H
20	A	B	C	D	E	F	G	H
21	A	B	C	D	E	F	G	H
22	A	B	C	D	E	F	G	H
23	A	B	C	D	E	F	G	H

Part 4

24	A	B	C
25	A	B	C
26	A	B	C
27	A	B	C
28	A	B	C
29	A	B	C
30	A	B	C

denote 0121 528 5100

Exam countdown – top tips

Nine months before

- You've already built up a good knowledge of English and now you're starting on the final year of preparation for the *Cambridge English: First* examination. Work consistently, study conscientiously and above all, enjoy learning!
- Establish good habits from the outset.
- Keep vocabulary lists in your notebook that include derivations, opposites, useful phrases, etc.
- Note down any word formations that might present a problem.
- Read widely outside the classroom. Use the resources of the internet to help you (online newspapers, magazines, etc.) plus official Cambridge ESOL guidelines and advice.
- Make use of communication websites to listen to interesting talks in English in order to develop your listening skills further.

Six months before

- Start looking back at what you've learnt over the previous three months. Constant revision is essential to successful learning. It's no use leaving it all until the last minute! The more often you study a new word or phrase, the more likely it is to remain fixed in your memory.
- Go through your written work. Are you developing your use of language sufficiently? Make a conscious effort to use new language in your written work.

Three months before

- By now, you should have acquired a comprehensive understanding of the exam and its requirements and you should be completely familiar with all the exam tasks.
- Revise your vocabulary and word formation lists, highlighting any areas that you feel need special attention. Spend as much time as possible on your English.
- Start to practise the exam tasks under exam conditions: whenever you do an exam task, time yourself so that you can finish it within the time limit.

On the day

- Make sure you take your identification. It must have your photo on it and must be the original document, not a copy.
- You will also need a pen, an HB or B pencil and an eraser.
- You should feel confident, knowing that you have prepared as well as you can for the exam.
- There will be a clock in the exam room but wear a watch if possible and time each section of the exam very carefully. There won't be very much time to spare, so it's important that you know exactly how much time you have. Try not to run over your timing for each part.
- Answer all questions as you work through the paper since you might not have time to check your answers at the end. Ideally, however, you should plan to spend time at the end of each paper checking your answers so that you can change them if necessary.

The day before

- You should have a quick look through your most important notes, the highlighted points in your vocabulary and word formations, together with any other important areas. Do not try to cram in new material that you haven't managed to cover before.
- Know when to say, 'Enough is enough,' and get a good night's sleep. Your brain cannot work efficiently on five hours' sleep!

One month before

- Having done so much exam practice and preparation, you should by now feel confident in your knowledge of the language and your ability to cope successfully in the exam.
- You know that lexical chunks (verb phrases, prepositional phrases and so on) make up a large part of language learning. Revise all the phrases you have learnt, highlighting any particular ones that you find difficult to remember.
- Do a mock exam under exam conditions, whether through your school or on your own at home, if you are following a course of self-study. Check your performance according to timing, word count, etc.

Answer key

Module 1

Vocabulary development 1 p. 6

1 **1** b **2** c **3** a **4** f **5** g **6** e **7** d **8** h

2 **1** The phonemic transcription tells you how the word is pronounced and which syllable is stressed. In the word *inherit* you stress the middle syllable.

2 No. (The vowel in the middle of *inherit* is 'short *e*', as in *bed, men,* etc.)
Note: Look at the Pronunciation Table at the beginning of the dictionary. Try and learn these symbols by heart.

3 Yes. (In the dictionary, the symbol *[T]* means that a verb is transitive – it takes a direct object. Verbs which are intransitive *[I]* do not take a direct object, e.g. *go*.)

4 The stress is on the first syllable (*house*hold).

5 Yes. (See meaning 2.)

6 Countable (so you could say, e.g. *several households*).

7 No. (The grammatical information in square brackets tells you that the adjective *household* must come **before** the noun. So you can say *household items* but not *items which are household*.)

8 Yes (meaning she is *well known*).

Language development 1 p. 7

1 **1** after **3** after
2 before **4** before; after

2 **1** Adam always leaves for school at seven o'clock in the morning.
2 He goes to school by bus every day. / Every day he goes to school by bus.
3 In the past he never used to wait a long time for the bus.
4 The bus would sometimes be two or three minutes late.
5 Nowadays the bus is often late.
6 As a result, Adam frequently arrives late for school.
7 Fortunately, his teacher doesn't usually complain.
8 Adam regularly does his homework on the bus.

3 **1** a has; b am having **5** a appears; b is appearing
2 a see; b is seeing **6** a are you smelling;
3 a am tasting; b tastes   b smell
4 a are you thinking; b do **7** a looks; b are you looking
   you think **8** a expect; b am expecting

4 **3** We would ~~have spent~~ **spend** hours waiting for a fish to bite.
4 I used **to** love listening to him talk about nature.
5 Often we didn't ~~used~~ **use** to come home until after dark.
6 ✓

Listening p. 8

1a six extracts

2a **1** B **2** C **3** C **4** A **5** A **6** C

> **Expert language**
> **1** questions 1, 2, 3 **2** questions 5, 6 **3** question 4

Writing p. 9

1 **1** a
2 b
3 say when you're going; tell her about your friend; mention some activities you and your friend enjoy doing.

2a yes

2c Hi Pat,

Thank you for inviting me and my friend to stay with your family this summer. We would both love to come. Can we come for two weeks in August?

I know that you have never met my friend Angela but I'm sure you'll like her very much. She's a very easy-going person. She's two years younger than me and is studying to be a doctor.

Like me, Angela likes walking and horse-riding. She's also very good at tennis. There's only one thing that Angela isn't very keen on: swimming. It's rather strange because we used to go with our families to Lake Balaton every year when we were children. Her family even has a house there now.

I won't write any more, Pat, because I'm taking exams at the moment and I'm very busy. Thank you again for your invitation. I'm looking forward to seeing you and your family this summer. I've told Angela all about you! Please let me know if we can come in August, won't you?

Best wishes/Lots of love,
Anna

Vocabulary development 2 p. 10

1 **Photo A:** athletes, medals, olive leaves, sports events
Photo B: degree, graduate, shake someone's hand, university

2a **1** show **6** Like **10** while/
2 taken **7** and   whereas
3 athletes **8** between **11** graduate
4 medals **9** event **12** leaves
5 degree

2b **1** Both … (and); Like the people in the first photo, she also …
2 The main difference between … is …; these athletes have … , while/whereas the student …
3 I think I'd prefer …
4 some kind of …; a sort of …

Language development 2 p. 11

1a **1** F **2** F **3** T **4** F **5** T **6** T **7** F

1b **1** a far larger … than; by far the most; a lot more … than; not nearly as many … as; almost five times as many … as
2 slightly more … than; not quite as many … as

1c **2** The number of women who/that took part in the Beijing Olympics was a bit smaller than in the London Olympics.
3 Beijing organised slightly more events than Athens.
4 Athens didn't organise quite as many events as London.

5 UK athletes were not nearly as successful at the Beijing Olympics as at the London Olympics.

6 Chinese athletes did slightly worse at the Athens Olympics than at the London Olympics.

7 Greek athletes won exactly as many gold medals in Beijing as in London.

8 The Olympic Stadium in London was nowhere near as big as the Olympic stadium in Beijing.

9 The Olympic Stadium in Athens was a lot smaller than the Olympic Stadium in Beijing.

2 1 The food I ate at that restaurant in Beijing was ~~the most spiciest~~ **the spiciest** I have ever eaten.

2 The first event we saw was ~~far better one~~ **far better** than the others.

3 The opening ceremony in London was much more exciting ~~that~~ **than** the ceremonies in Beijing or Sydney.

4 ✓

5 He is a ~~more faster~~ **faster** sprinter than all the other athletes.

6 The people in the town were not nearly ~~as much friendly~~ **as friendly** as the villagers.

7 ✓

8 Unfortunately, we ~~didn't have~~ **had** nowhere/didn't have ~~nowhere~~ **anywhere** near as much time to spend shopping in London as in Beijing.

Reading pp. 12–13

1 a

2 1 Japan **2** Australia

3 1 C **2** A **3** D **4** B **5** C **6** A **7** B **8** D **9** C **10** B

Expert language
hospitality, generosity, necessity, informality

Audio script

1 Cars in general have never been a real passion for me. However, my own car is another matter. I have three children under six, their toys, buggies and bikes to ferry round, plus an enormous supermarket shop to load into the boot every week. I may wave my husband off on month-long overseas business trips without a second thought, but when my car goes into the garage for an afternoon, I'm lost.

2 I've always loved music but I wasn't sure what I wanted to do as a career, so I did a one-year course in music technology. At first, I still wasn't convinced it was for me but once I realised I would eventually be able to put my own music together, I really started loving it. The course is a part-time one, so once I'd mastered the basics of how to use the microphones and mixing desk, I was able to get casual work in a recording studio. That was really useful and I haven't looked back. I love doing what I do and I wouldn't swap it for anything.

3 Some people say that shopping is a mindless kind of activity. Well, I love shopping – not for the things I buy but just for the fun of it. So I was pleased to read that shopping is actually good for your brain. When scientists measured activity in the brains of shoppers, they found a lot of activity in the important back part of the brain in the two-and-a-half seconds that it took them to choose a product. In other words, it fires up the part of the brain used in making decisions. So it can't be mindless, can it?

4

A: Do you wish you could learn a language or take up a new hobby but it's too expensive, or there isn't a class nearby? A new trend known as 'talent swapping' could be the answer. On today's programme, two listeners reveal how it worked for them.

B: A neighbour told me she was having problems filling in her tax forms, so I offered to help. In return, she made me a lovely meal and now she's teaching me to cook.

C: A friend was helping children at a local school with their reading and encouraged me to go, too. I love it because I get a real buzz from seeing them improving.

5 I went to university with quite a few false ideas about how much living on my own and being a student in London would cost. Before I started, I gave myself a budget for food, rent, etc. and tried to stick to it but it didn't work out, I'm afraid. I realised that I'm quite fussy about things like having the right kind of shampoo and eating well and so it was difficult to economise. I ended up keeping a careful record of everything I spent, which made my friends laugh. You see, my mum's an accountant and I had always complained when she suggested doing that!

6 Travelling regularly in Europe and North America for my work means that I spend relatively little time at home. There's a lot of hard work involved but one of the compensations of my job is staying in five-star hotels, where the furnishings are cool and modern and the bathroom's out of this world. But you can get tired of all that. So when it came to my own place, I knew exactly what I wanted it to look like. I decided to try and create the opposite of 21st-century five-star hotel living.

Module 2

Vocabulary 1 pp. 14–15

1 Note: in Paper 4 (Speaking) Part 1, you and your partner may have to make a choice between a number of things. It is important that you discuss the options with your partner and justify the choices you make. In this exercise, for example, did you say **why** the factors you chose were more important than other factors?

2a 1 scientist **3** lawyer **5** architect
2 accountant **4** musician **6** journalist

2b 1 work on my own, creative **4** very creative, can take long holidays
2 really interesting **5** well paid, creative
3 salary is excellent, good career opportunities **6** interesting, rewarding

3 1 A (You **fail** an exam; you do not succeed in an exam.)
2 B
3 B (You go **for** an interview.)
4 C
5 B
6 A
7 A
8 B (You **strike** or **go on strike**.)
9 C (Your boss **gives** you **the sack** or **fires** you if he/she is not happy with your work.)
10 A (You graduate from a college or university when you get your degree.)

4a/b /t/: passed, worked
/d/: applied, gained, closed, offered
/ɪd/: wanted, attended, persuaded, promoted

Language development 1 pp. 15–16

1 1 took (last week)
2 haven't had (since then)
3 haven't learnt/learned (still)
4 organised (in January)
5 has complained (up to now)
6 haven't found (yet)
7 answered (the other day)
8 enjoyed (the other day)

2a 1 just **2** still **3** yet **4** already

2b 1 yet **2** just **3** still **4** already

3a 1 lived
2 been studying
3 missed
4 been working
5 phoned
6 been trying

3b 1 I've just written my application letter. Can you check it?
2 George has been working on his CV all day but he still hasn't finished it.
3 Joanna still hasn't arrived. Do you think she's got lost?
4 Although I've been learning English for over five years, I've never been to England.
5 Help! Someone's stolen the money from the safe!
6 I've been trying to phone Sue all afternoon but I haven't been able to get through yet.

4 1 still haven't been to
2 haven't seen Jenny for
3 has never forgotten
4 has been working
5 has just phoned
6 haven't met for

Listening p. 16

1 1 five speakers
2 They have all given up stressful jobs.

2/3
1 D **2** A **3** B **4** C **5** E

Writing p. 17

1 1 Peter Harlow
2 to apply for the job
3 formal
4 details of previous work experience, why you think you're the right person for the job

2a 1, 3, 5, 7, 9, 11

2b *Suggested answers*
Paragraph 1: point 5
Paragraph 2: points 1, 3, 7
Paragraph 3: point 11
Paragraph 4: point 9

3a *Suggested answers*
1 Dear Mr Harlow
2 to apply for the position/post of
3 At present/Currently
4 a good command of
5 I would be suitable
6 opportunity
7 consider my application
8 available to attend an interview/for interview
9 Yours sincerely

3c *Suggested answers;*
New paragraphs begin at:
I would like …
I am 23 years old …
I feel …
I hope you will …

Vocabulary development 2 p. 18

2 1 a teacher, b professor
2 a control, b check
3 a career, b course
4 a lesson, b subject
5 a train, b educate
6 a grade, b degree

3 1 you think so
2 What about
3 you're right
4 Don't you think
5 suppose so
6 couldn't agree
7 up to a point
8 quite true

Note: Make sure you write down these words and expressions in your notebook. Use them in Paper 4 Parts 3 and 4.

Language development 2 p. 19

1 1 the army, school
2 a degree, chemistry, the University
3 a week, a lecture, Professor
4 the cinema, the theatre
5 Poland, the European Union
6 a drink, the end-of-semester
7 a good, the River
8 The computer, the way
9 excellent, the school
10 the English, an English

2 1 My flatmate, Mark, wanted to do ~~anything~~ **something** special last night.
2 ✓
3 He phoned ~~any~~ **some** friends of his to ask them if they'd like to come as well.
4 ✓
5 ✓
6 ✓
7 Unfortunately, it was late and the owner said that he had hardly ~~some~~ **any** pizzas left.
8 'Give us ~~something~~ **anything** you have then. It doesn't matter what it is!' Mark told the owner in desperation.
9 The owner returned with two sad-looking pizzas and half a dozen sandwiches. Some **of** them looked distinctly stale.
10 'Next time we'll stay at home and make the food ourselves. ~~Something~~ **Anything**'s better than this!' Mark groaned.

3 3 hardly
4 ✓
5 the (~~the~~ education)
6 the
7 the
8 of (any ~~of~~ places)
9 ✓
10 a (~~a~~ work)

4 1 you got a computer at
2 on the train to
3 to be a bus driver
4 he play the piano
5 about Scotland on television/on Scotland on television
6 we go to the cinema
7 is telling the truth
8 has got a reputation
Note: In English there are a large number of prepositional phrases, e.g. *in prison, in hospital, by bus, at school.* Keep a record of them in your vocabulary notebook.

Reading pp. 20–21

1a 1 a magazine
2 an older woman
3 semi-formal
4 coping with studying again, different kinds of courses, study skills

2 2 B

4 1 D **2** B **3** A **4** C **5** B **6** D

Audio script

1 I worked as a city trader for 12 years and really enjoyed both the job and the lifestyle that went with it but in the last two years I started to wonder whether it was what I wanted to do for the rest of my life. Because I commuted a long way across London by train, I saw my baby son for only a few minutes at the end of each day if I was lucky and I'd spend all weekend sleeping. Fortunately, I'd always been a saver and that made the decision to leave much easier. I had a keen interest in interior design and decided to use my savings to set up my own business.

2 Last summer I resigned from my job as an insurance broker and started a year-long course to train as a wildlife artist. Learning a new skill was hugely satisfying. But I'll never forget the day I walked past a very expensive restaurant next to the college. I had dined there frequently with clients. Now I was a student in jeans and T-shirt, carrying a backpack. I felt odd. It wasn't that I missed it but I did wonder if I would be able to afford to eat somewhere like that ever again. I'm excited, although, obviously, a little apprehensive about the future. But I love being outdoors and travelling around the country and everybody says I'm far more relaxed.

3 The first three years were very isolating. But as my wife and I got used to the life, we became very interested in the countryside and grew to love it. I know nothing about gardening and growing things, so taught myself by reading books. I no longer have to waste time on commuting or long business lunches but my business only brings in about two-thirds of what I earned in my previous salary. But then we don't need so much money to live on. Our heaviest expenses are the two cars because we're so remote. I grow all our own fruit and vegetables and we rear chickens to eat. We're about 90 percent self-sufficient in summer.

4 The city had been my life. I worked for a public-relations company which specialised in art exhibitions and so my evenings were devoted to social events. Then, without warning, I was made redundant. That made me stop and reconsider my priorities. I realised I was ready for a simpler, more enjoyable life and decided that with computers, smart phones and email I could work from home and didn't even need to be near London. Now I've got two children I can't work full-time but I'm doing some market research for a local hotel. I've no regrets; it's a happier, healthier and better quality of life for the whole family.

5 I'd start work at 6.30 a.m. and often carry on until midnight if there was a big deal on. The pressure was incredible. There was no time for exercise or eating well and I found myself becoming a very tense and bad-tempered person. I was close to burning out in a totally unfulfilling lifestyle. By sheer chance I saw an article about how someone called a 'life coach' had changed someone's life. I got in touch and as a result of just one consultation, she helped me realise that I'd be much happier as a yoga teacher. I'm now running my own health club. It's quite demanding but at least I know why I'm doing it.

Module 3

Vocabulary development 1 p. 22

1a 2 gloomy factories
3 ugly Victorian buildings
4 run-down slums
5 riverside offices and housing
6 restored 18th-century warehouses
7 dilapidated building
8 prosperous mansions

1c 1 rewarding
2 industrial
3 present-day
4 thriving
5 live
6 wonderful
7 architectural
8 popular

2 1 strength
2 prosper
3 prosperity
4 optimism
5 threaten
6 threat
7 economic
8 achieve
9 cultural
10 architectural
11 decline
12 solution

3 1 residence
2 impressive
3 historical
4 significance
5 commercial
6 exploration
7 romantic
8 cultural

> **Expert language**
> 1 residence, significance, exploration
> 2 impressive, historical, commercial, romantic, cultural

Language development 1 pp. 23–24

1 1 a well, b good
2 a steady, b steadily
3 a lately, b late
4 a hardly, b hard
5 a wide, b widely
6 a direct, b directly

2a **Gradable:** decisive, fast, fragile, impressive, lively, powerful, romantic, well-known
Ungradable: fantastic, furious, marvellous, tremendous, unique

2b 1 absolutely
2 very/extremely
3 very/extremely
4 very/extremely
5 absolutely
6 very/extremely
7 absolutely
8 very/extremely
9 very/extremely
10 absolutely

3 1 snowed hard
2 have increased steadily
3 quite a big
4 a bit of an
5 hardly any
6 was absolutely amazed by
7 a direct flight
8 got extremely angry

4 1 been
2 out
3 what
4 as
5 which/that
6 has
7 since
8 than

Writing p. 25

1 1 a
2 a
3 Write about:
1 why some people think this
2 why touching the exhibits might be a good or bad idea
3 your own point of view/idea

2a 1 There is no information about why it might be a good idea (point 2).
2 The essay is less than 140 words long.

2c 1 would'nt (line 13), one's (line 16)
2 most (line 7), Science (line 17)
3 things, on (line 7), it it, (line 13)

2d *Suggested answer*

Some people think that museums are boring places where you're not allowed to touch anything. This is because they have only been to old-fashioned museums where everything is behind glass and you're supposed to stand and look at them. Most of the things on display are either very old or very valuable. If visitors were allowed to touch them, they could easily get damaged or stolen. Also, the exhibits are often very rare. Sometimes the thing you're looking at is the only one in existence and that's why it's in the museum. If everybody could touch it, it wouldn't stay in good condition for very long.

On the other hand, you can learn a lot from touching things. When you hold an old object in your hand, it makes a great impression on you. So maybe museums should allow people to touch the less valuable objects.

In my opinion, the best type of museums are the ones that have interactive displays, like science museums where you can press a button and see things actually happening. I think all museums should have a variety of activities, including some which are 'hands-on'.

[190 words]

Listening p. 26

2 Order of photographs:
- **1** D (immigrants arriving at Ellis Island by boat)
- **2** E (the Baggage Room)
- **3** C (the Registry Room)
- **4** B (Wall of Honor)
- **5** A (the Bunk Room)

3a 1 1 (dates) and 8 (time)
2 3, 5, 6, 7 and 9
3 2

3b 1 1897, 1924
2 ferry (boat)
3 Baggage
4 (an) interview(s)
5 Wall of Hono(u)r
6 Bunk
7 *Hope and Fears*
8 11:10 (a.m.)/eleven ten (a.m.)/ten past/after eleven (a.m.)
9 Oral History Library
10 ticket office

Expert language
1 2, 3, 5, 7, 8, 9, 10
2 1, 4, 6

Vocabulary development 2 p. 27

1a 1 C **2** A **3** B **4** E **5** D

1b 1 down
2 catastrophe
3 habitats
4 species
5 destroy
6 extinct
7 take
8 greenhouse
9 warming
10 solar
11 Poisonous
12 dump
13 Radioactive
14 effect
15 ban
16 out
17 recycle
18 fertilisers
19 modified
20 grow

2 1 C (hardly = negative)
2 D
3 C
4 B (part of a fixed phrase)
5 A
6 A
7 C (a single light bulb left on all year = not switched off)
8 D

Expert language
What's more, For example

Language development 2 p. 28–29

1 1 … an enormous whale ~~to swim~~ **swimming** in …
2 ✓
3 Onlookers enjoyed ~~to watch~~ **watching** the …
4 … appeared ~~being~~ **to be** lost …
5 ✓
6 … people refused ~~giving~~ **to give** up hope
7 … managed ~~lifting~~ **to lift** Willy …
8 ✓
9 … having problems ~~to breathe~~ **breathing** and …
10 ✓
11 … made millions of people ~~to feel~~ **feel** a sense of …

2 1 on
2 in
3 about
4 in
5 about
6 to
7 at
8 for
9 on
10 for
11 about
12 for

3 1 a killing (They no longer kill.); b to take (We were driving there, so we stopped the car.)
2 a to bring (I hope you didn't forget.); b putting (It is a clear memory.)
3 a taking (as an experiment); b to persuade (I attempted to do this.)
4 a to tell (I'm sorry to tell you this.); b paying (I wish I hadn't done it.)
5 a to mention (He didn't remember.); b seeing (I still have the memory of it.)
6 a to take (The government intends to take action.); b changing (It will require this.)

4 1 (really) can't stand travelling
2 was my decision
3 couldn't afford to go
4 spent ages getting
5 help smiling when I
6 can hear people laughing
7 threatened to go to
8 looking forward to visiting
9 was worth going to
10 keen on (the idea of)

5 2 for **3** be **4** taking **5** to

Reading pp. 30-31

3 2 C **3** E **4** B **5** F **6** D **7** A **8** E **9** B **10** A

Expert language
most intelligent, brainiest, cleverest

Audio script

Hello, everyone. First of all, a big welcome to New York from all of us here at the hotel. My name's Bob and I'm here to make sure you enjoy your stay in the city. I've organised some great guided tours for you and we start tomorrow with a trip to the Museum of Immigration, on Ellis Island. Now I'm going to give you a few background details that will help you get the most out of your visit.

As you know, millions of people came to the USA from Europe in the late 19th and early 20th centuries, especially during the period between 1897 and 1924 – that's the year when immigration controls were introduced – and Ellis Island was the place where they first landed. The buildings which immigrants had to pass through before they were allowed to come and live in the USA were used right up till 1954. Then they stood empty until they were restored as a museum, which opened in September 1990. And that's where we'll be going tomorrow.

Your tour of the museum begins when you step off the ferry, at the very point where the immigrants stepped off the ships that had brought them on their long journey all the way from Europe.

The first place they passed through is called the Baggage Room – that's where they picked up their bags and other possessions – and you'll be able to see a display of typical baggage from the period there as you pass through.

You then go into what's called the Registry Room – just as the immigrants did. This is where they had medical check-ups and interviews and then, if all went well, they were allowed to enter the USA. Imagine how it must have felt to be so close to your new home but still not be sure if you'd be accepted or put on the next ship home again.

But most people were accepted, and it's incredible but 100 million Americans can trace their family history in the USA to a man, woman or child who passed through this room. And 420,000 of them have their names written on what is known as the Wall of Honor, which you can see at the museum.

If things were real busy or if there was a problem, the newcomers might have to spend a few days on the island, and the next place you see on the guided tour is the sleeping area, known as the Bunk Room, and then after that what's called the Hearing Room – that's where people who'd been refused entry could have their case heard by a judge.

The museum also has three theatres. Theatre 1 is a movie theatre and I've reserved tickets for you to see the 30-minute movie called *Hope and Fears*. In the movie, you'll see immigrants telling their own stories of how they pulled up their roots in Europe and came to live in the USA. Next door, in Theatre 2, there'll be the chance to see the play called *Ellis Island Stories*, which also lasts 30 minutes. This play features two immigrants and one immigration officer and it's based on real-life interviews recorded at Ellis Island. We haven't made reservations for the play, but it begins at 11.10 a.m. and there'll be plenty of time to see it if you'd like to.

Or you might want to visit the Oral History Library. The Ellis Island Oral History Project has collected recordings of first-hand accounts of people's experiences at Ellis Island and you can listen to some of these on a computer system with 20 individual listening stations.

And if there's still time after that, why not visit the exhibition called *The Peopling of America*, which is located in the old ticket office, which was across the water from the old railroad station. This exhibition places Ellis Island in the context of 400 years of North American immigration history.

So, all in all, it looks like being a great tour …

Module 4

Vocabulary development 1 p. 32

1
1	was born	7	late teens	13	opportunity
2	orphan	8	got on	14	wealthy
3	childhood	9	earn	15	wedding
4	lonely	10	poverty	16	achieve
5	brought up	11	put by		
6	well-off	12	luxury		

2a
1	out	4	into	7	out
2	on	5	out	8	with
3	up	6	without		

2b
1	set out	4	put up with	7	giving up
2	ran into	5	worn me out	8	keep on
3	do without	6	ran out of water		

3
1	challenging	4	traditional	7	heat
2	preparation	5	inhospitable	8	endurance
3	fitness	6	competitors		

> **Expert language**
> If you've ever run a marathon … thing to do.
> If you're going to finish … level of fitness.

Language development 1 pp. 33–34

1 Correct story order and verb forms:
2	e, had lost	7	i, was raining
3	h, had looked	8	g , hadn't found
4	b, went	9	f, were having
5	d, had been crying	10	c, was lying
6	j, went out		

2a 1 e 2 d 3 f 4 a 5 b 6 c

2b
1 By the time we arrived at the party, everyone had gone home.
2 I was watching a horror film on television when the lights suddenly went out.
3 Once the air hostess had counted all the passengers, the plane took off.
4 I had never lived on my own before I went to university.
5 As soon as Peter (had) heard the good news, he telephoned his wife.
6 We had been waiting for an hour when the train eventually arrived.
7 After the customs officer had searched all our luggage, he allowed us to go.
8 While I was staying at my grandfather's house, I discovered an old photograph album.
9 Sarah didn't go back to work until she had recovered from the flu.
10 When my sister read her exam results, she burst out laughing.

3
1 had already started by
2 when they heard
3 had just taken
4 had not expected them to
5 as soon as I opened
6 was midday when we set
7 anything until he had read
8 while I was
9 she had never visited/been to
10 had been travelling for

Writing p. 35

1a 1 young people
2 the writer and his/her greatest ever challenge
3 why you did the challenge, preparation, feelings afterwards

2a (See paragraph breaks in improved article below.)

2b Paragraph 1: a   Paragraph 3: b
Paragraph 2: d   Paragraph 4: c

2c (Examples are underlined in the improved article below.)
1 past perfect   **2** past simple

2d 1 nervous/terrified   **5** confident
2 voluntary   **6** glad
3 reluctantly   **7** face up to
4 (PowerPoint) slides

Sample answer/Improved article
When I <u>stood</u> on the stage and <u>saw</u> all the faces in the audience, I <u>was</u> almost too nervous to speak. But I <u>knew</u> I <u>had</u> to do it.

My challenge <u>had started</u> three weeks before. I do voluntary work for a wildlife charity. When our leader <u>asked</u> for a volunteer to give a talk about our work at a national conference, I <u>said</u> 'no' at first. I <u>had never given</u> a speech in my life and the idea <u>terrified</u> me. Nobody else <u>was</u> free that day, however, so I reluctantly <u>agreed</u>. I <u>spent</u> the next three weeks preparing.

I <u>had done</u> class presentations at school, so I <u>looked</u> at my old notes and <u>started</u> to prepare PowerPoint slides. Once it <u>was</u> all ready, I <u>practised</u> giving my talk in front of the mirror, until I <u>felt</u> completely confident. Although I <u>was</u> nervous when I gave my talk, it <u>went</u> very well.

I'm glad I <u>agreed</u> to do the presentation. It <u>taught</u> me that you can do the things which seem impossible if you face up to the challenge.

Listening p. 36

1a 1 one speaker
2 training for different physical activities

1b 1 4   **2** 7, 9, 10   **3** 3

2 1 rower
2 (a) charity
3 sailing
4 100/one hundred/a hundred kilo(gramme)s/kg
5 motivation
6 challenge
7 disappointed
8 variety
9 short-term
10 lonely

Expert language
1 2, 5, 6, 7, 8, 9, 10
2 1, 3, 4

Vocabulary development 2 pp. 37–38

1a *Suggested answers*
Risk (extreme) sports: *climbing (I),* hang-gliding (I), parachute jumping (I)
Track and field events: high jump (I), running (I)
Water sports: scuba diving (I), water skiing (I), windsurfing (I)
Winter sports: ice hockey (T), snowboarding (I)
Martial arts: karate (I)
Ball games: basketball (T), golf (I), rugby (T), tennis (I, T)

1b 1 hang-gliding   **5** climbing
2 water skiing   **6** scuba diving
3 karate   **7** snowboarding
4 tennis   **8** ice hockey

2 1 B   **2** C   **3** C   **4** B   **5** B   **6** A   **7** D   **8** A   **9** D   **10** A

3 1 B   **2** A   **3** C   **4** B   **5** A   **6** A   **7** B   **8** A

Language development 2 pp. 38–39

1 1 **a** a; **b** –   **4** **a** a; **b** any
2 **a** –; **b** a   **5** **a** a; **b** –
3 **a** some/–; **b** a

2a 1 ✓
2 There is a large ~~number~~ **amount** of sports information on the internet.
3 There isn't ~~many~~ **much** news about David Beckham at the moment.
4 ✓
5 How ~~much~~ **many** players were injured during the game?
6 ✓
7 We don't have ~~many~~ **much** time to prepare for the championship.
8 ✓
9 They only have a small ~~amount~~ **number** of tickets left for the final game.
10 How ~~many~~ **much** money will the new tennis courts cost?

2b 1 little   **3** a little   **5** a few
2 a few   **4** little   **6** few

3 1 a great deal of   **4** lots of money
2 by very few   **5** no sports facilities at
3 much interest in   **6** a small amount of

4 1 few   **4** well   **7** nothing
2 up   **5** or   **8** of
3 up   **6** because/as

Expert language
2 (take up) and 3 (built up)

Reading pp. 40–41

2 a not mentioned   **c** paragraphs 1, 2
b paragraphs 2, 3, 6   **d** paragraphs 3, 4, 5, 6

3a 2 the sports equipment manufacturer, Slazenger
3 of free publicity

3b/c **2** D   **3** E   **4** C   **5** A   **6** F

Expert language
too much influence, many loyal local fans, much is demanded

Audio script

Hi. My name's Malcolm Price and today I'm going to be talking about activities which require strength and endurance, and the best way to go about preparing for those activities, whether you're a mountain climber, a cross-country skier or just want to play a mean game of tennis. Because I'm a champion rower, people often ask me what the secret is – they think it can't just be physical fitness.

Well, many people these days do push themselves to the limit, physically and mentally, to achieve their goals, and not only in competitive sports. You know, it could be raising money for a charity or just achieving something for personal satisfaction. But whatever you choose to do, whether it's running across a desert or winning a sailing race, there's a lot of hard work involved to get yourself in top physical and mental shape, and success only comes through thorough training. That's the same whether you're an Olympic champion or just taking part in the local fun run.

Of course, physical strength is part of it. I don't think I'd have gone into my sport if I didn't have the physical build for it. But when you're nearly two metres tall and weigh 100 kilos, there's not much chance of being a champion jockey or a sprinter. But I'm sure that I'd still have excelled at something, even if I'd been shorter and slimmer, because that's just in me as a person.

People also ask me if you need to start young to get really good. Well, I'd say, if you're involved in sports as a kid, then the training becomes part of your life and you learn a kind of strategy for success, whatever it is you're trying to do. But there's no reason why someone who starts doing physical activity as an adult shouldn't find the same level of motivation.

You need to make sure you've got a goal – something to aim for – and it has to be something which you really can achieve, something that's within your capabilities. But, of course, it's also got to be a challenge or else you'll have nothing to work towards.

And then people say, 'But what if you're trying really hard but just not getting anywhere?' Well, it could be that you've set yourself the wrong goals or it could just be impatience. The important thing is to aim to make progress in small stages. Each week you should be getting closer to your target. But if you expect too much too soon, you're almost bound to be disappointed.

So keep at it but vary your schedule. If you do the same things every day, you're tempted to make comparisons too soon. Apart from anything else, training becomes tedious if there's no variety in it. And you need time off from it too. At least one day a week, do something else, something completely unrelated.

There's no point in worrying too much about how things are going. You need to review your goals regularly so that you know whether you're getting fitter or faster or stronger or whatever. But you should also be able to relax and enjoy yourself, otherwise what's the point? That's why short-term goals are useful – you know, for example, I'm going to be running five miles a day in two months' time, although my ultimate goal might be running a marathon next year.

But you've got to have one clear goal – like that marathon – and friends can be useful too. Training with a friend means that you've got someone to share the ups and downs with and it's also much harder to give up if there's someone else involved. To be honest, training can be a lonely business and there will be setbacks, so you need to enlist the support of those around you.

So before I go on to types …

Module 5

Vocabulary development 1 p. 42

1a
1	science	7	linguistics
2	scientist	8	linguist
3	genetics	9	archaeology
4	genetic	10	archaeologist
5	psychology	11	astronomer
6	psychological	12	astronomical

1b 1 person 2 subject 3 adjective

1c
1	psychological	4	linguistic
2	genetics	5	archaeological
3	astronomers	6	scientific

2 science, scientist, scientific
genetics, geneticist, genetic
psychology, psychologist, psychological
linguistics, linguist, linguistic,
archaeology, archaeologist, archaeological
astronomy, astronomer, astronomical

Note: It is very important that you stress words correctly in English. If you stress the wrong syllable, people may not understand you. Check in a good dictionary (e.g. *The Longman Exams Dictionary*) if you are unsure which syllable is stressed.

3
1	the latest	5	at the forefront of
2	as a consequence of	6	getting better and better
3	packed with	7	in the widest sense
4	hard to put down	8	to great effect

4 1 e 2 c 3 g 4 h 5 f 6 a 7 b 8 d

5
1 B (similar **to**, the same as)
2 A (**accept** something, **agree to** something)
3 D (**do** research or **carry out** research)
4 A (*Appeared* is usually followed by a *to*- infinitive.)
5 C (You are **working on** a problem if you are trying to solve it.)
6 B (You put *whereas* between two clauses in a sentence.)
7 D (= without saying anything)
8 B (**present** someone with a prize)

Language development 1 pp. 43–44

1
1	does the bank close	6	He'll
2	I'll get	7	I'm meeting
3	I'm going to complain	8	are you going to tell
4	It's going to	9	Will you
5	Are you doing	10	will win

2
1	will discover	5	will have been
2	will be working	6	will go out
3	will have finished	7	will be going/am going
4	will be painting	8	will have left

3
1 will let, find out
2 finish/have finished, shall we go
3 Do you want, leave
4 is, will start
5 are, is going to have/is having/will have
6 stops, don't we go

4 1 A 2 C 3 C 4 A 5 A 6 B 7 C 8 B

5
1	who/that	4	than	7	in
2	to	5	other	8	which/that
3	as	6	if/whether		

Expert language
mustn't it?

Writing p. 45

1 **1** someone you know
  2 formal
  3 why medical research is important, why other types of research are also important, student's own idea

2a/b *Sample answer*

Scientific research is very important but it is very expensive and somebody has to pay for it.

The scientists who study diseases and find cures for them are obviously doing a very important job and should have financial support. Another important group of scientists are the ones who develop new drugs. The work they do in helping to find new types of treatment for diseases is also very significant.

Medical research, however, isn't the only important type of scientific research. For example, the scientists who develop new types of crops for agriculture help farmers to feed the world's growing population and that is extremely valuable work. Also, scientists who study things like DNA are likely to find out things about the world that can benefit everybody in the future.

In my opinion, the benefits of scientific research can be difficult to predict. For example, some people think that exploring outer space is a waste of money but I don't agree. Scientists discover many things when they are planning space missions and those things can be useful on Earth too, so, in my view, it is worth spending money on them.

Listening p. 46

1b **1** 3   **2** 1, 2   **3** 8

2 **1** China
  2 The Naked Face
  3 95/ninety-five
  4 mirror
  5 uncomfortable
  6 personal
  7 managers
  8 chin, lips (in either order)
  9 make-up
  10 nodding, smiling (in either order)

Expert language
1 5, 6   **2** 10

Vocabulary development 2 pp. 47–48

1a **1** remote control   **5** text message
  2 DVD player   **6** viewfinder
  3 keyboard   **7** lens
  4 optical mouse   **8** earphones

1b **1** ringtone **5** website   **9** call
  2 software **6** broadcast **10** zap
  3 channels **7** download
  4 focus   **8** images

2 **Correct order:**
  1 a **2** d **3** f **4** b **5** e **6** c

Complete conversation:
Peter: I think the computer is the most important thing ever invented. If you have a computer, you can do so many things that you couldn't do before. Computers and the internet have changed the way people live.
Ingrid: Yes, that's **true**. But I don't think computers have changed our lives as much as cars. The car is a more important invention, **in** my opinion. It's easy to live without a computer but you can't live without a car, can you?
Peter: No, I suppose **not**. Life would be **much** slower and more difficult without them. But I think other things are more important. What **about** fire, for example? I mean, that's something that changed the history of the whole human race.
Ingrid: Yes, you **are** right – I hadn't thought of that. I'm not sure if fire is a thing that we invented, though. It's a natural phenomenon. People discovered it. **Don't** you agree?
Peter: Yes, I suppose **so**. Well, writing then – writing was invented. That was a really important invention, I think.
Ingrid: I couldn't agree **more**. Without writing we wouldn't be able to live like we do today. The whole of our civilisation is based on things which are written down. Maybe it is the most important invention.

3 **1** a engine; b machine
  2 a electric; b electrical
  3 a appliance; b device
  4 a technician; b mechanic
  5 a discover; b invent
  6 a fix; b correct

4 **1** impression   **5** anxiety
  2 entertainment   **6** development
  3 products   **7** immediately
  4 successful   **8** sale

Expert language
new technology/technologies, new invention, constant stream, home entertainment, new products, everyday lives, great anxiety, digital television

Language development 2 p. 49

1a **3** myself   **6** themselves   **9** each
  4 by   **7** yourself   **10** ✓
  5 ✓   **8** ✓

1b **2** blame yourself   **6** looked at herself
  3 write it (yourself)   **7** concentrate
  4 known each other/one   **8** like each other/one
    another   another
  5 relax

2a **1** b **2** d **3** a **4** e **5** f **6** c

2b **1** how to use   **3** what to do
  2 where I put   **4** why he spoke

3 **1** you enjoy yourself at
  2 you hurt yourself
  3 repaired my bicycle on my
  4 know how to use
  5 have forgotten what Mike
  6 sure who to ask
  7 went by myself
  8 know what to say
  9 been talking to each
  10 you draw this yourself/you do this drawing yourself

Reading pp. 50–51

1 **1** negative meaning (It means you try to be very clever but it doesn't work as well as a simpler solution.)

2b **1** Companies should pay more attention to what customers want when they design new products.

3a **2** it
3 he doesn't seem convinced/something's not quite right

3b/c **2** D **3** A **4** B **5** F **6** E

Expert language
whose job, that comes with it, people who invent

Audio script

Hello. My name's Lillian Scott and the subject of tonight's talk is the skill of face-reading. The idea that you can tell a person's character from the shape of their face is not a new theory. In fact, it goes back centuries but it's only now that people are studying it more seriously. The idea has reached us in Europe via Australia and New Zealand but the skill was originally developed in China. I go into this in some detail in the book I've written on the subject.

It took a long time to find a title for the book. I wanted to call it *Face to Face* but apparently, there's already a book with that title, so that wasn't allowed. In the end, someone suggested *The Naked Face*, which sounded good because I wanted to focus on things which everyone can see but which we tend not to notice. So we went for that.

The book begins by describing how the face works. For example, there are 14 bones in the face with around 95 muscles working around them. This means that we can do all sorts of things with our faces, revealing a great deal about ourselves in the process, because our faces are changing all the time as we speak, as we react towards the world around us.

And you can observe this in your own face. I mean, when people look in a mirror, they tend to adopt a particular facial expression – the one they think looks best. They try to do the same thing when posing for photographs but usually without success because you can't actually see what you look like till later. That's why people are always saying, 'I look awful in that photo,' when to the rest of us they look perfectly normal. And of course, seeing yourself on video can be quite an uncomfortable experience because then you see all your changes of expression and so on.

And then some people think they have a best side, don't they, which they always turn towards the camera. And of course, each side is always different. It's a fact that's puzzled scientists for years but it is true. Some face-reading experts say that people generally want to show the right side of their face to the world because they feel the left is the personal side – you know, they want to keep it to themselves.

So, what character traits can you see in people's faces? I'll give you some examples of things to look out for. Well, good managers generally have wide faces, with the cheekbones wide apart, which is meant to indicate a strong desire to achieve things and meet targets. And that's not the only positive characteristic that you might look out for. Other good signs for success at work are a strong chin, which represents determination, and of course, the shape of the lips has long been associated with that as well.

People often ask me, 'But what about if you don't look like that?' or 'Can you make the most of what you've got in a job interview?' Well, yes, you certainly can – and women especially try to do this. The first thing to remember is that you should look people straight in the eye when you speak, even if it means moving your chair. Some people use make-up or a new hairstyle to emphasise or play down certain facial features but it's best to get professional advice because too much or badly applied make-up, for example, would be a mistake. It actually puts people off.

But basically, it's more a question of how you behave at interviews. If you're tense, your face is likely to look tight and unrelaxed and people will think that's also your character. Whereas if you keep nodding and smiling to show that you're really interested in what they're saying, people tend to like you better.

I'll stop there because I can see that some of you have questions. So we'll …

Module 6

Vocabulary development 1 pp. 52–53

1a **1** ambition
2 replacement
3 confidence
4 popularity
5 determination
6 bravery
7 creativity
8 loneliness

1b

-ence	-ity	-ion
confidence	popularity creativity	ambition determination

-ment	-ness	-ery
replacement	loneliness	bravery

Note: This exercise will help you to see patterns in word formation. Some suffixes are used only for nouns, some only for adjectives, etc. When you learn new words, pay particular attention to word stress – mark the syllable which is stressed. Check in a good dictionary if you are not sure. Look for pronunciation patterns as well as spelling patterns.

2a **1** determi*na*tion, satis*fac*tion, fasci*na*tion
2 crea*ti*vity, popu*la*rity, depen*da*bility, adapta*bi*lity

2b C

3 **1** in **2** in **3** out of **4** by **5** by **6** on **7** by **8** in

4a **1** performance
2 scholarship
3 audition
4 opportunity
5 debut
6 role
7 offer
8 impact
9 launch
10 records

4b give + performance, win + scholarship, go for + audition, give + opportunity, make + debut, play + role, take up + offer, make + impact, launch + a product (perfume), break + record

5 1 has risen to
2 gave an exceptional performance
3 stands out as
4 feel homesick
5 by the popularity
6 turned down
7 lacks patience
8 set off from
9 been a very ambitious
10 has no intention of leaving

Language development 1 p. 53–54

1a 2 D
3 ND (… perfume, which was called *Glow*, quickly …)
4 D
5 D
6 ND (… Lopez, whose success as a singer has been phenomenal, has …)
7 D
8 D

1b 5 Where are the tickets for *Cats* ~~that~~ I bought this morning?
8 The song ~~which~~ we enjoyed most at the Eurovision Song Contest was the Hungarian one.

2 Karaoke, **(1 e)** *whose popularity has spread throughout the world in recent years*, originated in Japan. *Kara* is an abbreviation of the word **(2 g)** which/that means 'empty' in Japanese (***karappo***)/***karappo***, which means 'empty' in Japanese and *oke* is short for *okesutura*, or orchestra. Usually, a recorded song consists of both vocals and a musical accompaniment. However, recordings of songs **(3 c)** which/that consist only of the accompaniment are called *karaoke*.

For almost 30 years Japanese people, **(4 h)** who have always enjoyed singing after work and at parties, have been picking up microphones and singing karaoke. Family karaoke sets, **(5 d)** which display the words and scenes of a song on a monitor, are extremely popular in Japan. Apparently, they also help children **(6 f)** who/that have reading problems to learn to read more quickly.

In Japan, **(7 b)** where houses and flats are often built very close together, noise can be a problem. So special places for people **(8 a)** who/that wanted to sing karaoke started to appear in the towns and countryside. The first 'karaoke box' appeared in a rice field near Kansai as early as 1984.

3a 2 The musical, starring the members of a pop band, was a huge success at the box office.
3 The singer, appearing first at the festival, will record her next album in London.
4 One day I saw a busker playing four instruments at the same time.
5 The band's second album, featuring songs written by the drummer, was fantastic.
6 The vocalist, singing in Spanish for the first time, received a standing ovation.

3b A The rock concert, who was held last night in the college hall, (held last night in the college hall) was a great success. Jeff Stone, who was constantly cheered and applauded by his fans, (constantly cheered and applauded by his fans) amazed …
He played a number of old favourites, which included 'Red Rose' and 'Road to Heaven', (including 'Red Rose' and 'Road to Heaven') and sang …
… the people who were sitting in the front seats (the people sitting in the front seats) jumped up …

B Beethoven's seventh symphony, which was performed by the University Orchestra (performed by the University Orchestra), lacked …

… the musicians who were playing in the strings section of the orchestra (playing in the strings section of the orchestra) appeared …

4 2 Formal: That's the person to whom I spoke on the phone earlier.
Informal: That's the person (who/that) I spoke to on the phone earlier.
3 Formal: Bill is the sound technician for whom we work.
Informal: Bill is the sound technician (who/that) we work for.
4 Formal: They are redecorating the hall in which the concert will take place.
Informal: They are redecorating the hall (which/that) the concert will take place in.
5 Formal: Is this the CD on which you recorded the album?
Informal: Is this the CD (which/that) you recorded the album on?
6 Formal: Are these the tickets for which we paid so much money?
Informal: Are these the tickets (which/that) we paid so much money for?

5 1 of
2 an
3 well
4 than
5 what
6 however/though
7 in
8 with

Expert language
A booklet containing

Writing p. 55

1 1 in a student magazine; readers of this magazine
2 to describe a concert you went to in an interesting and informative way for readers
3 You must say a little about the musicians and the music they played; also whether you think the concert was successful (and why).
4 the review will be read by students, so the style should be fairly informal and include your personal opinions.

2 Review 1: All eight features should be ticked.
Review 2: 4, 6
Review 1 is, of course, much better. In fact, Review 2 is not a review of a concert at all. The writer has simply written about his/her favourite band!

3a

1 The Flaming Lips don't disappoint their British fans
It was obvious from the start that the Flaming Lips concert at the Brighton Centre was going to be different. When Wayne Coyle floated over the heads of the audience inside a huge plastic bubble, everyone knew this ~~is~~ **would be** a night to remember.

The Flaming Lips ~~are~~ **have been** putting on shows like this since the band was formed in 1983 in Oklahoma. They love to surprise their fans with special effects and surrealistic costumes. Wayne Coyle, the band's charismatic vocalist, loves to give people a good time.

In Brighton, the Flaming Lips played that old favourite *Yoshimi Battles the Pink Robots*, as well as *The Yeah Yeah Yeah Song*. The audience danced and sang along with the band, going wild with excitement when the Flaming Lips began to play *Mr Ambulance Man*.

The concert was a huge success. When I left, it seemed that the world had suddenly become more interesting – and more fun. If you love rock music, go and see them. They won't be in the UK for long!

[180 words]

2 I like music and I love going to concerts. Last month I went to two concerts.

A band I really like is called Blue Dream. ~~You have~~ **Have you** heard of them? They are an exciting band from the USA. Blue Dream play back-to-basics blues. They have a ~~hugely~~ **huge** number of rock fans from all over the world. The band consists of Tom and Sylvie Gray, and they ~~are using~~ **use** just guitar and drums to accompany ~~the most~~ **most of** their songs.

They suddenly became famous two years ago. Before that, nobody knew anything about them. Tom and Sylvie always wear blue and black clothes when they perform. Three of the best Blue Dream songs were recently rewritten for performance with an orchestra. I read ~~at~~ **in** a student magazine that a ballet company is going to dance to these songs at an Opera House ~~I'm wondering~~ **wonder** what the audience will think. They normally go and see *Swan Lake*!

I would like to go to that concert.

[160 words]

Listening p. 56

2a 1 B 2 B 3 C 4 C 5 A 6 B 7 A

<table>
<tr><td>Expert language</td></tr>
<tr><td>1 confident, surprised, satisfied
2 foolish, unimpressed, angry, frightening, disappointed, jealous</td></tr>
</table>

3
1	for real	4	hard work
2	a load of rubbish	5	to tears
3	bit	6	to spot

Vocabulary development 2 p. 57

1
1	art exhibition	4	TV show
2	street performance	5	film
3	play		

2

C	O	M	P	O	S	E	R
A	E	E	L	M	I	V	E
S	O	Q	C	W	S	N	V
T	S	I	H	N	T	B	I
V	C	L	A	P	A	H	E
O	R	M	P	U	G	P	W
D	I	E	T	C	E	L	X
U	P	B	E	P	R	O	S
P	T	E	R	F	O	T	T

1	cast	4	review	7	chapter
2	script	5	plot	8	stage
3	composer	6	clap		

3a 1 d 2 h 3 e 4 g 5 c 6 b 7 a 8 f

3b
1	detective	5	talented
2	complicated	6	open-air
3	popular	7	oil
4	abstract		

4
1	D	5	D (collocation)
2	C (bargain **for/over**, profit **by**)	6	B
3	B	7	C
4	A	8	A

<table>
<tr><td>Expert language</td></tr>
<tr><td>a great deal about (question 6)</td></tr>
</table>

Language development 2 pp. 58–59

1
1	isn't interested in
2	is capable of becoming
3	is no connection between
4	is responsible for choosing
5	a quick solution to
6	good at remembering
7	is no comparison between
8	a sudden increase in
9	difficulty (in) understanding
10	were disappointed to miss/about missing/that you missed/ to have missed

2a 1 c 2 f 3 d 4 b 5 g 6 e 7 a

2b 1 Since David Blaine is now a celebrity, he is used to ~~be~~ **being** approached by people on the street in the USA.
2 He stopped appearing in public with his friend Leonardo DiCaprio because he couldn't ~~to~~ get used to the way people always called him 'Leo's friend'.
3 David Blaine is used to ~~be~~ spending a lot of time preparing for his difficult and often dangerous feats.
4 He once tried to hold his breath underwater for longer than the world record of 8 minutes 58 seconds. In training for this, he had to ~~getting~~ **get** used to slowing down his heartbeat so that his body used less oxygen.
5 Although it was very unpleasant at first, David Blaine is now ~~use~~ **used** to being attacked in the press by other illusionists and entertainers.

3
1	to	4	to	7	when
2	for	5	all	8	of
3	my	6	who/that		

<table>
<tr><td>Expert language</td></tr>
<tr><td>6 who/that</td></tr>
</table>

Reading pp. 60–61

2 Paragraph 1: It's unusual because it's crowded with people and has free events, puppet shows, samba bands, etc.
Paragraph 2: The museum is now trendy but didn't use to be; the location used to be a well-off suburb, but is now a poor district.
Paragraph 3: A new director was appointed to revive the museum.
Paragraph 4: The free evening events are aimed at getting people who wouldn't usually go to a museum to visit.
Paragraph 5: Visitor numbers have gone up and people who don't normally visit museums have started to do so.

3 1 B 2 C 3 C 4 D 5 A 6 B

<table>
<tr><td>Expert language</td></tr>
<tr><td>devoted to</td></tr>
</table>

Audio script

I = Interviewer, P = Peter

I: Last year, in a television series called *Faking it*, various people were given four weeks to learn the skills of a new profession. Peter Harris, a painter and decorator from Liverpool, was one of them and he joins me in the studio today. Peter, welcome.

P: Hi.

I: So why were you selected to take part in the programme, Peter?

P: Well, one day, I got a phone call from someone asking me if I'd like to take part. They'd called lots of decorating companies all over the country looking for someone willing to spend four weeks learning to be an artist – you know, instead of painting walls and doors, you'd learn how to do abstract art. And the cameras would be there to see how you got on. But they couldn't get anyone to volunteer. At first I thought it must be one of my friends playing a joke on me, so I laughed and put the phone down.

I: Really?

P: But fortunately, they called back and gave me a number at the television company, where I could call them, and that's when I realised it was for real.

I: So what did your friends think?

P: They thought it was funny because I know nothing about art but I think they admired me for giving it a try. Before the filming started, I went down to the local art gallery with them to have a look at some abstract art. To be honest, I thought it was all a load of rubbish but I still wasn't convinced that I'd actually be able to do it.

I: So what happened? How did you learn?

P: Well, at first, I actually found it exciting because I never knew what was happening from one day to the next. But basically, I had lessons. And of course, I found it was harder than you'd think, especially with the cameras watching. But the worst bit was having to film what's called a video diary every evening saying how the lessons had gone and how I was feeling.

I: But you enjoyed it?

P: I began to see that there really is something behind abstract art. People look at a painting and say, 'What is it?' or 'It's just a load of paint thrown about,' but actually, there's a lot more to it than that. I think people laugh at things they don't understand sometimes but that doesn't mean it's no good. The artist wants you to think, you know, which can be hard work!

I: Absolutely.

P: Then, one day, I was just painting freely, you know, experimenting, and suddenly I realised that what I'd painted looked like a wheelchair. I'd had a football accident as a child and I couldn't walk for a while. It was a frustrating and frightening time for me. Suddenly, all those feelings came back to me. It was so unexpected and I realised that a part of me was coming out in the painting. It reduced me to tears.

I: Did other people see the wheelchair?

P: I don't think so but funnily enough, that was one of the pictures that went through to the final programme. The idea was that my paintings would be shown in a gallery alongside lots of real artists' work and a panel of experts would try and say which ones were mine. It was all part of the idea of the television programme. Anyway, I was fairly determined to prove that I could do it. Lots of people were surprised when three out of four experts failed to spot which paintings were mine. But I was delighted.

I: So now you're an artist?

P: Sort of, yeah. Actually, since the show, I've sold about 15 paintings, which has impressed my family more than anything. And I thought the other artists would really hate me because they find it so hard to sell their work but they were fine. No, the only people I didn't like were some of the people who bought my work. They only seemed to be interested in how much it would be worth in the future.

I: Peter, thank you.

Module 7

Vocabulary development 1 pp. 62–63

1 **1** C (You **slice** meat, bread, etc. by cutting it into thin flat pieces. You **chop** into pieces with a sharp knife. You **grate** food such as cheese and vegetables with a **grater**. You **shred** food like cabbage by cutting or tearing it into long thin pieces.)

2 B (You **roast** food, usually with a little oil, in the oven or over a fire. You **bake** cakes, bread, etc. in an oven. You **fry** food in hot oil.)

3 A

4 A (Coffee without sugar has a strong **bitter** taste. Lemons have a **sour** taste. Food which contains lots of spices is **spicy**.)

5 D (Your stomach **digests** the food you eat. You **sip** a liquid if you drink it slowly and in small amounts each time. You **gobble** food **up** if you eat it very quickly.)

6 C (Meat and poultry – chicken, duck, turkey, etc. – are rich in **proteins**. Rice and pasta are rich in **carbohydrates**.)

7 C

8 D (Butter goes **rancid**. Old food which is covered in a green/black substance (mould) has gone **mouldy**.)

9 B

10 D

11 A (**Starch** is a substance found in bread, rice, potatoes, etc. **Calcium** is a substance which helps bones and teeth to grow. **Flour** is the basic ingredient of bread.)

12 B

2a **1** d **2** h **3** f **4** g **5** a **6** b **7** e **8** c

2b **1** got rid of
2 runs
3 turn to
4 come up with
5 came across
6 put on
7 find a way round
8 cut down on

3 **1** B (when compared with the long time they have been eaten)
2 D (You **play** a role.)
3 C
4 D (Plants **belong to** a category/family/species.)
5 A (arrived **in**, appeared **in**, presented **to**)
6 C
7 D
8 A (joined **to**, added **to**, accompanied **by**)

Expert language
have been cultivating

Language development 1 p. 64

1a 2 You can take your own wine to that restaurant.
  3 You shouldn't/ought not to eat junk food every day.
  4 The table is reserved so we can't sit here.
  5 Alice doesn't have to come with us if she doesn't want to.
  6 I think you should/ought to leave your coat in the cloakroom.
  7 Do we have to book a table at that restaurant?
  8 You shouldn't/ought not to eat too much before going to bed.
  9 You can't/mustn't park your car outside the restaurant.
  10 Can we sit at any table we want?

1b 1 had/have/ought
  2 can
  3 allowed/supposed
  4 should
  5 better
  6 should
  7 had
  8 have
  9 ought

2 1 didn't have to take
  2 aren't allowed to smoke
  3 had better wear
  4 must not forget
  5 don't have to accept
  6 shouldn't have gone
  7 had to book
  8 mustn't go

3 1 with
  2 tastes
  3 Like
  4 its
  5 on
  6 being
  7 the
  8 from

Writing p. 65

1 1 You are making a recommendation.
  2 your teacher; formal language
  3 three: different ages, different levels of income, families

2 Introduction: the main local shopping centres
  Shops for older and younger people
  Shops in different price ranges
  A good place for families to go shopping

3 1 a = ii; b = i
  2 a = i; b = ii
  3 a = i; b = ii
  4 a = i; b = ii
  5 a = ii; b = i
  6 a = ii; b = i

4 The student hasn't talked about older people – only her own age group and children.
  She's talked about expensive shops under the 'age' heading, but not under the 'income' heading.
  She's made recommendations about buying children's clothes – but not 'the whole family'.

Listening p. 66

1 eight extracts
2 1 C 2 B 3 C 4 B 5 A 6 B 7 A 8 C

Expert language
1, 3, 4

Vocabulary development 2 p. 67

1 a 1 A; 2 B (**First impression** is a common collocation.); 3 C
  b 1 A ; 2 A; 3B (The clothes a footballer wears are called his **kit**. Soldiers wear **uniforms**. Actors/Actresses wear **costumes**.)
  c 1 C; 2 A; 3 A (**Bright colours** is a common collocation.); 4 C; 5 B (An old person's face is usually **wrinkled**. Writing paper may be **lined**.)
  d 1 C; 2 C; 3 B; 4 A (A **substance** is a chemical or natural material which is either solid or liquid. A **cloth** is a piece of material which is used for cleaning or drying something.)

2 1 a size; b number; c figure
  2 a suit; b match; c fit
  3 a get dressed; b dress; c wear
  4 a put on; b try on; c have on
  5 a take off; b loosen; c undo
  6 a costume; b uniform; c suit

3 1 unusual
  2 choice
  3 impression
  4 comfortable
  5 anxious
  6 foolish
  7 elegance
  8 outfit

Expert language
dressing up, carry (it) off, join in

Language development 2 pp. 68–69

1a 2 a 3 c 4 a 5 c 6 b 7 a 8 b

1b 2 can't belong
  3 may/might not like
  4 must be
  5 may/might have
  6 can't be
  7 must be having
  8 may/might be trying

2 1 must have been upset when she …
  2 might not have realised it was …
  3 can't have taken it because …
  4 might have taken it
  5 must have been worth a lot …
  6 can't have been very pleased …

3 1 … He must to be very hot.
  2 ✓
  3 … He must find **have found** a new job.
  4 ✓
  5 Tina can't have been paid £200 for …
  6 … They must have **be having** another argument!
  7 ✓
  8 … He may be do **doing** overtime at the office, I suppose.
  9 … She may not **have** found a wedding dress that she liked.

4 1 B 2 C 3 A 4 D 5 B 6 C 7 D 8 A

Expert language
might have worn, may be, must have been

Reading pp. 70–71

3a 2 make the mistake → a better idea is; when you do this → be honest with yourself about what you see

3b/c 2 F 3 A 4 E 5 C 6 G

4 1 c 2 b 3 d 4 a

Expert language
yourself (sentences A and B)

Audio script

1 If nice, decent, ordinary food seems a bit boring and tasteless, what about a light serving of cornflake omelette washed down with tomato and banana soup and a glass of delicious Pepsi and milk? After dinner, you can enjoy coffee with a slice of cheese in it. There are recipes for each of these culinary insults – and several hundred more – on the aptly named website, *Utterly Outrageous Recipes*. But the truly amazing thing about these concoctions, which the site's editor has collected from the thousands that were sent in, is just how many of them contain peanut butter – who'd have thought it was so versatile?

2 I don't eat much meat. I mean, you haven't got the real taste we were brought up on, because the food is so heavily processed nowadays. But I'm hardly a vegetarian, either, although I do get through more fruit than I used to. But you can't get by on that alone, can you? I don't think that vegetarians are any healthier than me, actually. It's usually young people, like my granddaughter, who go with it for a couple of years to be like their friends but it's not because they're really against meat on principle or anything, so they don't keep it up.

3

A: What do you think about the large-scale commercial production of organic food?

B: Well, what I say is that when we buy food from people whom we know and who are producing it locally, we're making an investment in our culture, whereas when we're buying it from a big supermarket chain or food corporation, even though it's in the organic section of the supermarket and carries an organic label, it's not the same kind of investment. But to be honest, it's certainly better than buying from somebody who's not taking care of the land at all, so it's a step in the right direction.

4

A: So Graham, which of these series would you recommend for this city?

B: Well, I suppose I'd go for *The Ultimate Guide* if I had to choose one, although I'm rather disappointed by it. I have no argument with the way the city is described and the layout is clear. But apart from one or two excellent diagrams, you couldn't call the book well illustrated. The other two have lovely photography but this one looks a little flat and grey. No, it's the clear and precise information about restaurants which really makes *The Ultimate Guide* stand out, because if you're really going to use a guidebook, that's what you need.

5

A: Which pizza do you want? There's Margherita or Four Seasons.

B: I always go for the plain one when I'm eating out because until they bring it, you don't know what the topping's like.

A: Don't be daft! Four Seasons always has the same things on it – it'll be like the ones I buy in the supermarket.

B: Mmm ... This advertisement doesn't tell you much. The good thing about going to a pizzeria is that there we'd be able to see what people at other tables were having.

A: Look, it's going to take them half an hour to deliver it, so if you want a pizza, we'd better get on the phone and order one.

6 Do you feel that your current job doesn't allow you to fulfil your potential? If so, you are not alone. According to a recent survey, nearly half of all full- and part-time workers feel the same way. Time for a change? A lot of people seem to think so. In the UK, more than one million people a month look for jobs through recruitment sites on the internet. With such demand, it's not surprising that sites which aim to put job hunters together with job offers have sprung up in their thousands.

7

A: Scientists at a week-long conference in Birmingham have been served smoked salmon-flavoured ice cream with every meal, in an attempt to persuade them that savoury ice cream could be the food industry's next big marketing opportunity. Dr Tony Blake, the scientist behind the experiment, explains:

B: Your brain is conditioned, when you see something that looks like ice cream, to expect the sweet and fruity taste that ice cream usually has. To change that, you have to educate people to try things several times. In my research, I've shown that after about eight helpings, your brain adjusts and you begin to get a taste for it. I'm hoping that commercial interest will now follow.

8 I'm talking to the chefs all the time. I am a very important critic for the restaurant but the staff have also got very good at it too. There's a constant atmosphere of inquiry and constructive criticism with regard to the food we serve. It's not about consistency. It doesn't have to be the same from day to day. You know, one chef's bean soup is going to be very different from another's because one of them is coming from an Italian viewpoint, the other from an Indian one, or whatever. I feel all the time that I'm having this collaboration with some real perfectionists and you know, that's really stimulating.

Module 8

Vocabulary development 1 p. 72

1a Eyes: stare at someone
Hands: clutch something, push something into someone's hand, tap someone on the shoulder
Feet: dash, get to your feet, give something a kick, slip (on a wet surface)
Head: give someone a nod

1b Eyes: glance at someone, wink at someone
Hands: grab something, shake someone's (hand), wave at someone
Feet: jump up, tap your (feet), trip over something
Head: shake your (head)

2

1	get	4	celebrate	7	go	
2	be	5	have	8	break	
3	fall	6	make			

3a

1	relatives	5	colleagues
2	flatmate	6	best friend
3	acquaintance	7	partner
4	fiancée	8	workmates

3b 1 ✗ 2 ✓ 3 ✗ 4 ✓ 5 ✓ 6 ✓ 7 ✗ 8 ✓

4
1 B (phrasal verb: **chat someone up**)
2 D (A **tour** involves visiting several places. A **trip** involves going out or away.)
3 C
4 C (phrasal verb meaning 'the result was')
5 B (**part** = role, **play** = a piece of drama, **show** = a piece of entertainment (singing/dancing, etc.) at the theatre or on TV)
6 D (You **reach/arrive at** a destination. You **achieve/manage to do** something.)
7 C (fixed expression)
8 A

Expert language
unexpectedly, unhurt

Language development 1 pp. 73–74

1 2 I asked her why ~~had she gone~~ **she had gone** there. (WO)
  3 She replied she ~~wants~~ **wanted/had wanted** to improve her English. (T)
  4 I asked her if she ~~will~~ **would** go to London with me in the summer. (T)
  5 She said she had spent some time there the ~~last~~ **previous** year. (WW)
  6 I asked her why ~~didn't she want~~ **she didn't want** to go there again. (WO)
  7 She ~~said~~ **told** me it had rained all the time she was there (WW).
  8 I said we could ~~bring~~ **take** umbrellas with us. (WW)

2a 1 advised   4 admitted   7 threatened
  2 said   5 accused   8 suggested
  3 refused   6 agreed

2b 2 g: Sue apologised (to me) for missing my birthday party.
  3 i: Richard promised to be/that he would be at the wedding.
  4 j: Maria warned me not to go out with Ken because he was dangerous.
  5 c: Denise offered to help me write the invitations.
  6 e: Keith threatened to tell my father if I went to the Oasis Club again.
  7 d: Eve denied inviting/that she had invited my ex-boyfriend to her party.
  8 b: Ruth suggested asking/that I (should) ask Dave out on a date.
  9 f: Maureen advised me to/that I should break off my engagement.
  10 h: Rob accused me of telling him a lie.

3 1 promised not to tell anyone
  2 insisted on buying
  3 whether he could have
  4 why he hadn't arrived
  5 accused Simon of breaking his
  6 warned Paul not to
  7 invited David to
  8 admitted that they hadn't

4 1 for   4 place   7 than
  2 in   5 what   8 from
  3 other   6 neither

> **Expert language**
> We **had** each **sent** … ; … neither of us **had** ever **been** on one before … ; … she**'d come** straight from the office and there **hadn't been** time to change …

Writing p. 75

1a 1 your teacher
  2 neutral, quite formal

2a 1 B 2 A 3 A 4 C 5 A 6 B 7 A

2b *Suggested answers*
  Paragraph 1: Introduction
  situation now: many young people live with their parents
  Paragraph 2: Advantages of living at home
  Advantage(s): feel comfortable; cost of living is expensive
  Example(s): don't need to cook/wash clothes/pay rent
  Paragraph 3: Disadvantages of living at home
  Disadvantage(s): don't become mature or independent living at home
  Example(s): people who go away from home say they start to think for themselves/face problems
  Paragraph 4 (my own idea): young people should stay at home if they want but should try to be more independent;

Example(s): young people living at home should go on holiday without their parents

3 All features should be ticked.

Listening p. 76

1a what it was like to grow up with a twin sister

2 1 C 2 H 3 D 4 A 5 E

> **Expert language**
> I was being compared

3 1 mix   4 bond   7 drove
  2 fiercely   5 turn to   8 gang up on
  3 recipe   6 lumped

Vocabulary development 2 pp. 77–78

1 1 weekly   3 boring   5 unusual
  2 truth   4 expectations   6 glamorous

2a 1 making models   4 gardening
  2 stamp collecting   5 trainspotting
  3 bird-watching   6 board games

3 1 lawn mower   4 anorak
  2 dice   5 magnifying glass
  3 (tube of) glue   6 (pair of) binoculars

  Note: In the exam, it is better to try to describe something using the words you know than to stop speaking. The words and phrases in this exercise will help you to do this.

4 1 spend
  2 down (wind down = relax)
  3 feet (*Put your feet up* is an expression.)
  4 up (take up = start a new hobby)
  5 passing
  6 on
  7 up (springing up = appearing)
  8 give (give someone a call = telephone someone)

Language development 2 pp. 78–79

1 1 have been able to   7 were able to/could
  2 being able to   8 will be able to
  3 was able to   9 haven't been/won't be able to
  4 could
  5 couldn't/wasn't able to   10 can
  6 to be able to

2 2 managed to light   6 succeeded in winning
  3 succeeded in beating   7 managed to play
  4 know how to speak   8 didn't know how to use
  5 will manage to climb

3 1 you be able to take   5 did you manage to make
  2 isn't capable of swimming   6 succeeded in passing
  3 know how to play   7 wasn't able to take
  4 could sing better   8 managed to put up

4 1 as   4 could   7 able
  2 For   5 few   8 between
  3 who/that   6 way

> **Expert language**
> would complete, could afford to travel, could see

Reading pp. 80–81

1 **1** Katie Holleran: accountant, Kevin Shaw: builder, Karen Hallstrom: salesperson, Joe Campilos: office worker

3 **2** C **3** A **4** B **5** D **6** A **7** C **8** D **9** A **10** B

Audio script

1 It used to be funny having a twin sister at school. People would mix us up, which was a laugh. Sometimes we wouldn't bother to correct them but we never actually misled anyone intentionally. But we never thought the same way about things and we used to argue at least once a day. We even had fights too. Sharon's bossier than me but I'm physically stronger, so I'd normally win. We were both fiercely independent but that didn't stop people either buying us identical birthday presents, which was dull, or one to share between us, which was a recipe for disaster! I didn't mind but it used to infuriate her.

2 I used to enjoy sharing a bedroom with Katie because it was our own private space where we could go and be alone. We did argue now and again, and we had different ideas about music and clothes, but I'd definitely say we were closer than normal sisters would be. There was a real bond between us – even though she didn't always keep my secrets when I asked her to, so I could never trust her 100 percent. Even now, people tend to ask us to do things together, like being flower girls at a wedding recently. I always feel part of something when Katie's there, which is nice.

3 According to my mum, I was surprised when she told me that Emily and I were identical twins. I must have been about six at the time and I hadn't really thought about it before but I was happy enough. As kids, Emily and I were very much in tune with each other. It made me feel special. We'd have the same ideas about most things – clothes, music, boys – and although we always tried to be individuals, it never really worked because we were a team. Even now, Emily is the first person I'll turn to if I'm feeling down because I know I can rely on her.

4 I always found it hard being a twin because it meant I had to share everything, including a bedroom! I'm the oldest by ten minutes but people just lumped us together. We both had our own tastes in clothes and we'd do our hair differently but people still got us confused, which used to irritate me a lot. Although we spent most of our time together, Amy was never my best mate or anything. I'd talk to my other friends more than I chatted to her because they tended to listen to me more. Even now, compared to me, she's rather a quiet person, and I suppose that was why.

5 Compared to me, Lucy was really messy as a kid and it drove me mad. It would always be me who had to tidy up our bedroom because she'd left her clothes all over the floor. Luckily, we didn't have lessons together at school and we tried to keep out of each other's way. Going shopping together was a real pain because we never wanted the same things. Even now, I'm happiest in T-shirts and casual trousers, while she prefers dressing up in skirts and dresses. We'd only really get on when we used to gang up on our older brother, Jamie, who we had frequent disagreements with.

Module 9

Vocabulary development 1 p. 82

1a **1** e, up (save up for something)
2 d, up (keep up with something)
3 a, back (pay back money)
4 f, up (set up a business)
5 b, on (take on staff)
6 c, out (take out money)
7 h, for (pay for something)
8 g, out (write out a cheque)

2 **1** withdraw, account **4** worthless, auction
2 inherited, invest, donate **5** turnover, bankrupt
3 market, shares **6** living, inflation

3a **1** donation **5** volunteer **9** fund
2 distribution **6** inform **10** contribute
3 suffer **7** support
4 poverty **8** collection

3b **1** d **2** f **3** b **4** g **5** h **6** c **7** e **8** a

3c **1** volunteers **5** set up **9** collect
2 raise **6** poverty **10** distribute
3 relieve **7** take
4 making **8** donations

4 **1** C **2** B **3** A **4** B **5** B **6** C **7** A **8** D

Expert language
inadequate, upmarket

Language development 1 pp. 83–84

1a **1** opens **5** pays **9** were
2 will close **6** would be **10** didn't give
3 would put **7** are
4 asks **8** makes

1b **1** b **2** b **3** c **4** a **5** b **6** c **7** a **8** b **9** c **10** c

2 **1** as long as/if/provided that **4** unless
2 Even if **5** as long as /if/provided
3 as long as/if/provided that
that

3 **1** had invested, would have made
2 had supported, wouldn't have closed down
3 hadn't sold, would have lost
4 wouldn't have set up, had listened
5 hadn't left, would have given
6 would have given, had asked
7 wouldn't have been able, hadn't borrowed
8 would have bought, had known

4 **2** If I had gone into business with my best friend, I might/would be rich and successful today.
3 If friends hadn't supported me when I lost my home and job, I would be a beggar on the street today.
4 If my brother had taken the advice of his teachers, he wouldn't have apartments in New York and London today.
5 If Julia wasn't/weren't a really good journalist, she wouldn't have won the *Journalist of the Year* award recently.
6 If the government had helped the survivors of the earthquake, large numbers of people wouldn't be homeless today.

5 **1** would have sent (her) some
2 wouldn't be very/so rich
3 as long as you obey
4 harder, you would get
5 if you don't listen
6 wouldn't speak German so
7 provided (that) you don't
8 earlier, you wouldn't feel
9 even if you work
10 unless you get/have

Writing p. 85

2a yes

2b four paragraphs

2c **1** to my mind **3** finally
2 apart from **4** way I see it

2d a large quantity of = many (f)
Initially = In the beginning (c)
communicate = keep in touch (d)
possessed = had (b)
perform = do (a)

2e **Best buy**

I have bought many things in my life, but to my mind the best thing of all is my phone.

In the beginning, I bought my phone so that I could keep in touch with my friends and family. I knew also that I could use it to go online and to take photos. And apart from that, I'll admit that I wanted the latest phone because all my friends had one! I totally love my phone because, thanks to all the apps I've downloaded, it is so much more useful than I expected it to be. I use my phone to keep track of how much exercise I do, its alarm clock wakes me up in the morning and finally, the money app helps me look after my money.

I'm much more organised now that I have my phone. The way I see it, it has changed my life. I couldn't live without it!

Listening p. 86

2a/b
1 C **2** A **3** A **4** B **5** C **6** C **7** B

Expert language
'd ever bought, 'd never won

Vocabulary development 2 p. 87

1a **1** D **2** C **3** B **4** A **5** C **6** A **7** D **8** C **9** B **10** D
11 A **12** B

2 **1** B (**out of** stock = not **in** stock; on sale = available to be bought in a shop; If something is **for sale**, it is simply available to be bought.)
2 A (You follow a **recipe** when you are cooking something. The doctor gives you a **prescription** for some medicine. You buy a **ticket** for the theatre.)
3 D (You talk about a **reduction in price** or when a shop sells something **at a discount** if it sells it cheaper than the normal price.)
4 A (You pay e.g. a lawyer's or doctor's **fee**.)
5 C (A doctor has **patients**. A bank or lawyer has **clients**. **Shoppers** simply means 'people who shop'.)
6 C (A Mercedes is a **make** of car. You read the **label** on a jar of food or on an item of clothing for information about that product.)
7 B

8 D (If you want information about a college or university, you read its **prospectus**. A **brochure** usually gives information about different holidays. A **directory** is normally a list of names, addresses or facts.)
9 C
10 B

Language development 2 pp. 88–89

1a **1** is (singular) **9** were (plural) (*premises* = the building that a shop, restaurant or company uses)
2 buy (plural)
3 was (singular)
4 is (singular)
5 think (plural) **10** are (plural)
6 has (singular) **11** have (plural)
7 spend (plural) **12** has (singular)
8 doesn't (singular)

1b **Noun + singular verb:** money, furniture, economics, everybody, politics, the United States
Noun + plural verb: people, the police, the majority of, premises, trousers, a number of

1c **1** have **4** has/have **7** have
2 are **5** are **8** is/has been
3 was **6** has

2b **2** Both Taylor Swift and George Clooney were born in the USA.
3 One of them was born in the 60s.
4 One of them has parents in show business.
5 None of them comes from Canada.
6 Both Victoria Beckham and George Clooney are married.
7 Victoria Becham and Taylor Swift are songwriters.
8 One of them has a child.
9 Neither Taylor Swift nor George Clooney has a daughter.
10 None of them is a TV presenter.
11 One of them got married in 2014.
12 Both Victoria Beckham and Taylor Swift are singers.

3 **1** ... because ~~it~~ **there** was a lot of traffic.
2 ✓
3 ... 'Is ~~it~~ **there** a post office near here?' 'Yes, ~~it's~~ **there's** a post office ...'
4 ✓
5 ~~It~~ **There** used to be a ...
6 ✓
7 Did you know ~~there's~~ **it's** my birthday today?
8 ~~There's~~ **It's** nearly two in the morning.
9 ... how far is ~~there~~ **it** to the airport ...

4 **1** there's no need/there isn't any need
2 it was unusual for Jack
3 did it take (you) to
4 it doesn't matter
5 is there nothing on
6 there's a problem with
7 there's too much fog
8 it lovely seeing/to see
9 there be a (long/big) queue
10 there was a (big) storm

Reading pp. 90–91

1a a

3a/b **2** A **3** F **4** E **5** B **6** G

Expert language
1 however, But
2 What's more

Audio script

I = Interviewer, M = Mandy

I: My guest today is Mandy Pagham, who, five years ago, won a million-pound prize after buying a single lottery ticket. Mandy, it must have been an incredible moment!

M: Well, at the time it was wonderfully exciting, of course. Although I'd bought the occasional ticket before, I'm not someone who usually gambles, so it wasn't as if I'd been building up my hopes or anything. I was just standing in a newsagent's shop with my friend Louise, who used to buy a ticket every week, and she just said; 'Go on, buy one – you never know, you might be lucky.' So that's what I did.

I: So how did you feel when your number was read out on the television?

M: Well, I wasn't even watching; I was helping my mum in the kitchen. I'd said to my dad, you know, 'Oh, check this ticket for me, will you?' and he'd laughed and said something about 'wasting my money'. And then a few minutes later, he walked slowly into the kitchen, as white as a sheet. I mean some people would've been jumping up and down and shouting but he was sort of speechless. So, it was a few minutes before we realised what had happened.

I: And when you did?

M: Well, we didn't know what to do at first, but you know, everyone at the TV station was very kind and helped us to cope. Then I went up to London to collect the cheque and so had my photo in the newspapers, although I never talked to any reporters. But that's when all the problems started. I mean, if I'd known, I'd have insisted on keeping my privacy but I was just too thrilled to think straight, I'm afraid.

I: So it was a problem, everybody knowing?

M: Oh yes. I mean, suddenly, we had phone calls from cousins we hadn't heard from in years, which was nice in a way, and all sorts of people I didn't know started coming up to me in the street for a chat and I thought, 'Gosh, this is what it must feel like to be rich and famous!' because you don't know whether people really like you or not. So that's when I started to have doubts about it all.

I: I see. So did people ask you for money?

M: Not friends and family, no. I bought presents for all the people I felt close to, including the friend, Louise, who I'd been with when I bought the ticket – I bought her a really nice necklace. But I lost her as a friend. She was jealous, I suppose, because it could so easily have been her. Anyway, she was very nice about it but we just drifted apart. I think she just didn't want to be with me anymore. But the worst bit was the begging letters.

I: Did nobody warn you about that?

M: Oh yes, we'd been told to expect them but it was still upsetting. People I'd never heard of started writing me letters, telling me all these terribly sad stories and asking me for money. I mean, the lottery people said, 'They're mostly untrue, throw them away – don't even open them.' I'm sure they were right but I read them nonetheless. And there were so many that it really began to get me down. I mean, I didn't regret winning the money but I did begin to think that it wasn't fair that I should have it. And that's when I made my decision.

I: To give it away?

M: Not all of it. I bought the things I wanted to buy – a house, a car, all the things people spend half their lives working for, so I'm certainly feeling the benefit of it now – and there's still a bit in the bank. But about half of it, I gave to charity. And I told everyone what I was doing, you know, gave newspaper interviews, let the whole world know that I wasn't enormously rich anymore, I was just myself – and fortunately, I have no regrets.

I: Mandy, thank you for joining us today.

Module 10

Vocabulary development 1 p. 92

1a
1	adventure holiday	4	safari
2	skiing holiday	5	camping holiday
3	package holiday	6	city break

2 *Suggested answers*
beach holiday: a mask and snorkel, sunglasses, suntan lotion, a swimming costume, a wide-brimmed hat
camping holiday: an airbed, antiseptic cream, a family tent, insect repellent, a sleeping bag, a thermos flask,
safari: a camera with telephoto lens
skiing holiday: skis and ski boots, a warm anorak and bobble hat
trekking holiday: an airbed, insect repellent, a one-man tent, a pair of strong walking boots, plasters, a rucksack, a sleeping bag, a walking stick, a wide-brimmed hat

3a
1	flight	5	insurance
2	reservation	6	work permit
3	passport	7	credit cards, currency
4	inoculations		

3b
2	make a reservation	6	apply for a work permit
3	apply for a passport	7	accept credit cards,
4	have inoculations		change currency
5	take out insurance		

4
1 A (phrasal verb meaning 'be educated and cared for as a child until grown up')
2 A (You **gather** or **find out** information.)
3 C (phrasal verb meaning 'discover by chance')
4 A (*Vast* is the only word which collocates with *absolutely*.)
5 A
6 C (idiomatic expression)
7 B (You travel **on foot**, **on horseback**, **by camel** and **by bike**.)
8 B

Expert language
brought up, came across

Language development 1 pp. 93–94

1
1	suffer	4	is being built
2	has just been	5	will be finished
3	decreased	6	apply

2
1 Passengers are kindly requested to keep their seat belts fastened during take-off.
2 Smoking has been banned on all flights, in accordance with recent regulations.
3 Hand luggage must be put under your seat or in the compartment above the seat.
4 Information about the flight can be obtained from the personnel on board.
5 All our flight assistants have been trained to deal with emergency situations.
6 Every effort will be made (by our staff) to ensure that passengers have a pleasant trip.

Answer key

3   **2**   I was given a loan of £2,000 (by the bank).
     3   A complimentary bowl of fruit is offered to every guest.
     4   Travellers have been promised cheaper flights for years.
     5   You will be shown the city's main attractions (by one of our guides).
     6   The first prize in the competition was awarded to Peter.

4a **1**   a be one of the most beautiful cities in the world
           b Prague is one of the most beautiful cities in the world
     2   a to be going on strike next week
           b that airport workers are going on strike next week
     3   a is expected to introduce new measures to boost tourism
           b that the government will introduce new measures to boost tourism
     4   a is thought to have been abducted
           b is thought that the missing tourist has been abducted

4b **1** to be   **5** to have made
     2 is not known   **6** to leave
     3 is thought   **7** to be staying
     4 was involved   **8** to have flown

5   **1** were given directions by   **7** are believed to have cancelled
     2 were included in   **8** are given to the passengers
     3 were made to
     4 is going to be published/will be published   **9** aren't/are not allowed to use
     5 is said to be
     6 haven't/have not been developed   **10** we were welcomed by

Writing p. 95

1   **1** suggest some accommodation
     2 informal
     3 three parts, to write about expensive, reasonable and cheap accommodation

2a yes

2b **1** c   **2** a   **3** b

2c *Suggested answers*
    Dear Madam = Hi/Hello
    I'd like to apologise = Sorry
    Some research has been done = I've done some research
    least expensive = cheapest
    satisfactory = OK/all right
    trust = hope

2d Hi,
    Great to hear from you! Sorry for not replying sooner but I was away for the weekend.
    I've done some research and I think these three might suit your cousin.
    The five-star Victoria Hotel is in the centre of town and has some family rooms. It's the most expensive but it's in a good location and has the best reviews online. The family rooms have a double bed and a sofa that converts into another one. The restaurant is expensive but breakfast is included in the price.
    Green Court Self-Catering Apartments is the cheapest but it looks OK. The accommodation is basic but it's clean and not too far from town. Obviously, they'd need to buy their own food but there's a supermarket next door and a couple of pizza places on the same road.
    There's a mid-price Travellers' Home Hotel near the motorway. It's about five miles from the centre but has a swimming pool and a children's play area. Although it's the least convenient, it's perhaps the most family-friendly. It only has a café but there are three restaurants in the same area.
    I hope this helps!

Listening p.96

2a/b

1	*The Service Guide*	**4**	smile	**8**	wake-up call
2	name	**5**	red flag	**9**	blue arrow
3	greet	**6**	smoking	**10**	taxi
		7	car		

Expert language
1 2 (should), 3 (should), 4 (mustn't), 6 (should), 7 (should), 8 (should)
2 10 (may)

3 **1** b   **2** e   **3** a   **4** d   **5** c

Vocabulary development 2 pp. 97–98

2a **un-:** unacceptable, unattractive, unavoidable, unbelievable, undamaged, unlike, unlikeable, unlimited, unpopular, unsuitable
    dis-: disagreeable, disapprove, dishonest, dislike, dissatisfied
    mis-: misbehave, misinterpret, misunderstand
    -less: careless, harmless, hopeless, thoughtless, useless

2b **1** dissatisfaction   **6** disapproval
     2 misunderstood   **7** dishonesty
     3 unpopular   **8** misinterpreted
     4 unattractive   **9** hopelessly
     5 unbelievably   **10** unavoidable

3   **1** a good time   **4** had a really good
     2 John having a party   **5** something to eat
     3 a quick look at   **6** lot of work to

Language development 2 pp. 98–99

1a **1** were   **3** had gone   **5** could see
     2 could   **4** would stop **6** would

1b **1** had told   **3** would build   **5** would talk
     2 could   **4** hadn't been   **6** had seen

2 *Suggested answers*
    2 I wish he would turn down his music/turn his music down.
    3 If only I'd gone to bed earlier.
    4 If only I'd studied harder.
    5 If only it would stop raining.
    6 I wish I could go to the (rock) concert (on Monday).
    7 I wish my sister didn't live so far away (from me).

3   **1** said   **3** were   **5** hadn't said
     2 didn't open   **4** learnt   **6** phoned

4   **1** is time we called/to call   **6** time we set off
     2 would rather you didn't   **7** I could have gone
     3 wish I hadn't told   **8** as if I am/were/was
     4 only your friend could go   **9** is time you told
     5 wish you would stop   **10** would rather you'd asked

5   **1** who/that   **4** how   **7** to/until/till
     2 than   **5** let/allow   **8** have/get
     3 like   **6** have/need

Reading pp. 100–101

2 **2** C   **3** B   **4** C   **5** D

3 **1** C   **2** A   **3** B   **4** A   **5** C   **6** D   **7** B   **8** D   **9** C   **10** A

Expert language
are affected, are designed, is built, creativity is required

Audio script

OK, I don't want to spend too long on this but we've got quite a few new members of staff with us this month, and some of you who've been here a while are going to be taking on new duties. So, the purpose of this meeting is just to quickly run through some of the training points that can get forgotten in busy periods. They're all written in this booklet called *The Service Guide*, which you all have a copy of, but I'll just remind you anyway.

First of all, I'd like to talk about the reception desk. Now, whether you're actually staffing the desk or not, most of you will work in reception at some time or another and in busy times, any of you may be asked to help out there, so it's imperative that you know not just the basic procedures but also our customer service policy.

The company regards the reception desk as one of the most important places in the hotel. It's where people arrive, where they have direct contact with staff and where they go if they want help or if they want to complain.

So, first and foremost, remember the three golden rules: Firstly, if you can, always address guests by name – this is quite often written on credit cards and booking documents – or type in the room number and it'll come up on the screen.

Secondly, it's important not to keep people waiting. If you have to, greet them and apologise for the delay, tell them how long you're going to be – anything rather than just ignoring them as they're waiting.

Thirdly, remember to smile no matter how tired or harassed you're feeling or how horrid guests might be. We're there for them and we want them to feel welcome, whoever they are.

Now, most guests have two main points of contact with the reception desk. When they check in and when they leave. So, I'll go through those two procedures in detail.

When guests first arrive, check whether or not they have a booking – most will have – and the list of guests expected will show up on the screen with their room allocation. Check this first. Room allocations change according to when departing guests check out and how this fits in with the cleaning rota. So, make sure that there is a red flag against the room number on screen as this will indicate that cleaning is complete and the room is free. Most rooms are non-smoking and any guests requiring a smoking room will usually need to have booked this in advance. Check this with them and make sure the room allocated is correct.

Before handing over the key, there are a number of other questions to ask. Firstly, establish whether the guest has a car in the underground parking area and if so, make a note of the registration number. Ask for the guest's credit card and take an imprint, explaining that this is a deposit against payment. And finally, check whether the guest requires a wake-up call in the morning and enter the details in the database. Then, if all is well, hand over the room key and call a porter to show the guest to the room.

So, that's check-in. Although there are busy periods for this, it's not as bad as checking out. Most people check out just after breakfast and this is when queues can occur. For normal checking out, the main thing is to make sure that there are no outstanding room service, bar or restaurant accounts. A blue arrow will appear on the screen if this is the case or a green flag if there are no other payments to go on the bill.

Remember that guests who are leaving often ask for information about the hotel and may ask you to book a taxi for them. No matter how busy it gets, you must try to be as helpful as possible because how they were treated on departure often leaves a lasting impression on people.

Now, I hope you're all familiar with the procedure for settling accounts …

Module 11

Vocabulary development 1 p. 102

1a *Suggested answers*
   Positive: creative, easy-going, generous, intellectual, open-minded, punctual, sensible, sensitive, sociable, witty
   Negative: arrogant, irritable, mean, moody, pessimistic, suspicious, vain
   It depends: ambitious, impulsive

1b 1 ambitious, arrogant, intellectual
   2 creative, sensitive, witty
   3 irritable, mean, pessimistic
   4 easy-going, generous, open-minded
   5 moody, suspicious, vain

2						
1	with	**5**	to	**9**	in
2	about	**6**	in	**10**	between
3	in	**7**	of	**11**	in
4	about	**8**	with	**12**	in

3a 1 pessim<u>i</u>stic, enthusi<u>a</u>stic, art<u>i</u>stic, hist<u>o</u>ric
   2 cheer, <u>cheer</u>ful; del<u>i</u>ght, del<u>i</u>ghtful; <u>won</u>der, <u>won</u>derful; <u>beau</u>ty, <u>beau</u>tiful; dis<u>grace</u>, dis<u>grace</u>ful
   3 a<u>maze</u>, a<u>maz</u>ing; con<u>fuse</u>, con<u>fus</u>ing; frust<u>rate</u>, frust<u>rat</u>ing; <u>satisfy</u>, <u>satisfy</u>ing; em<u>bar</u>rass, em<u>bar</u>rassing

3b 1 C   **2** C

4			
1	unfortunate	**5**	variety
2	entertainer	**6**	anxiety
3	seriously	**7**	ability
4	illness(es)	**8**	confidence

Expert language
are encouraged to do

Answer key

Language development 1 pp. 103–104

1
1 because (R)
2 Even though (C)
3 in order to (P)
4 as (R)
5 due to (R)
6 so as to (P)
7 despite (C)
8 so that (P)

2
1 Despite
2 although/even though
3 as/because/since
4 Despite
5 so that/in order that
6 Despite
7 in order to/so as to
8 so that/in order that

3
1 A lot of male athletes at university wouldn't train with me **because/since** I was too fast for them.
2 I'm successful in athletics **due to** the tremendous support I receive from my husband and family.
3 **Even though** I love eating out and trying new dishes, I often discuss my diet with my dietician.
4 Every year I go to a camp in Albuquerque in the USA **in order to** train (there).
5 I want to spend some time in the USA **so as to** be able to/ **so that** I will be able to run on the road circuit.
6 I love running on roads and mountain trails **because of** the sense of freedom I feel.
7 **Since/Because** I live a fulfilled life, I'm not concerned about my athletics career ending.
8 After athletics, I'd do something else **so that** I could continue to channel my energy and ambitions.

4
1 part
2 out
3 more
4 such
5 all
6 as
7 that/when/ after
8 so

Expert language
took part, were, led

Writing p. 105

1
1 your own opinion
2 formal
3 three

2 1 A 2 C 3 B

3–5

Many people believe that they can only be successful if they earn a lot of money and own lots of luxury goods. Clearly, this is not true.

Obviously, we need some money to pay for things like rent and food but other things are more important when it comes to happiness. (1) **For example**, a strong network of friends and a good relationship with our family members is vital if you want to be happy.

(2) **Furthermore**, being fit and healthy is definitely much more important than being surrounded by wealth. If you're ill, you can't enjoy your wealth anyway, so you won't be happy.

Finally, you are more likely to feel happy if you choose a job or a course of study you enjoy. (3) **Some people argue that** you should choose the highest-paid careers but surely, the happiest people do something they love, rather than something that is well paid.

(4) **In my opinion**, lots of possessions and a well paid job may make your life comfortable but they do not make you happy.

Listening p. 106

2a 1 A 2 A 3 C 4 B 5 C 6 C 7 A 8 B

Expert language
1 4 and 8 **2** 7 **3** 6

Vocabulary development 2 pp. 107-108

1
1 vegetarian (**vegetation** = trees, bushes and plants in a particular place)
2 raw (Vegetables which are **raw** are uncooked.)
3 illnesses (An **illness** is a health problem that makes you feel ill. A **disease** is a specific illness that has a medical name.)
4 stressful (A person feels **stressed**.)
5 nutritious (Food which is **edible** can be eaten – it is not poisonous.)
6 pace (**Pace of life** is an expression)
7 surgery (Businesspeople work in an **office**.)
8 wards (**dormitory** = a large room in a school or hostel where several people sleep)
9 treat (You can say you have been **cured** if you are no longer ill after a course of treatment.)
10 injured (Soldiers are **wounded** in a battle.)
11 have (You **have an operation**. The surgeon **operates** on you.)
12 infected

2a
1 have
2 feel
3 make
4 catch
5 break
6 sprain
7 take
8 give

2b
2 have an operation
3 made a quick recovery
4 catch a cold/flu
5 have an injection
6 sprained your ankle
7 take an X-ray

3b
1 show
2 while
3 there are
4 kind of
5 could be
6 on the other hand
7 like
8 Personally
9 However
10 would choose

Language development 2 pp. 108-109

1a
1 We have such a beautiful view from our window.
2 It is such a nice day that I want to go swimming.
3 I have never eaten such delicious food before.
4 Why is it so important to take exercise?
5 This documentary is so boring that I think I will fall asleep.
6 He has so much money that he can buy anything he wants.
7 We had such good weather on holiday that we stayed another week.
8 You should not eat so many hamburgers.

1b
1 such a
2 such a
3 so few
4 so
5 such
6 so
7 much
8 so

2
1 too
2 enough
3 very
4 enough
5 too
6 too
7 enough
8 very

3
1 so
2 very/so
3 so
4 too
5 enough
6 such
7 enough
8 too
9 so
10 enough

4
1 as
2 as
3 such as/like
4 like
5 like
6 such as
7 as
8 like

5
1 aren't strong enough
2 such a good pianist (piano player)
3 works as a doctor in
4 was so loud (that) we
5 enjoyed ourselves so much (that)
6 are too unfit to
7 were so many people at
8 as if they were
9 as if it's/it is going
10 so difficult/hard for you to

Reading pp. 110–111

2 Question 1: paragraph 4 ('coming up with an entire health package for somebody')

Question 2: paragraph 1 (the rich and famous, e.g. supermodels and pop singers)

Question 3: paragraphs 2, 3 (always been sporty; 'convinced that fitness is the basis of a full and happy life')

Question 4: paragraph 6 (he's a partner 'I see myself more as a training partner')

3 1 B 2 D 3 A 4 B 5 C 6 C

Expert language
Paragraph 4: 'After leaving school'

4 1 looked set to
2 gave Matt a taste of
3 coincided with
4 comes as no surprise

Audio script

1 It's not unusual to feel angry or be at the receiving end of someone else's temper several times a day, especially at work. Understanding what triggers an angry response, whether in yourself or in others, helps you to avoid upsetting situations, however, and this means you're less likely to become a victim of your emotions. There are plenty of courses in conflict management which can help you; just try a quick search on the web to find one. But if dealing with the general public is part of your job, do encourage your employer to take responsibility for this training. After all, it's as much for their benefit as yours.

2 I stayed in an expensive hotel last autumn and had a couple of minor complaints about the service. For once, there wasn't one of those irritating feedback forms to fill in, so I wrote a letter once I was home, pointing out my dissatisfaction and saying how things could be improved. While the original faults were not serious enough to make me mad, when the hotel failed to respond to my letter, I did get cross. So I called to see why the letter had been ignored and the extraordinary response from the voice at the other end was, 'Was it clear that your letter needed a reply?' I was speechless!

3 The directness and honesty of children can be a source of deep embarrassment to their parents. Children lack the ability to be tactful, often hurting the feelings of ageing relatives by coming out with things like, 'I've already got three of those,' when they open a present. But wouldn't it be great to say what you really feel sometimes? I put it to psychologist Tamara Fenton that perhaps if only we could acquire a little of that childish directness and care a little less about what people thought of us, we'd be far better off.

4
A: Here we are – the restaurant's just through this doorway.
B: Oh dear! There's only a couple of people in there! I don't know if I fancy that. Look, there's something I want to talk to you about but it's personal – I don't want anyone else to hear. They don't even have any music. Can't we go somewhere livelier?
A: All right. Is it something serious?
B: I'll tell you when we're sitting down. How about the pizzeria opposite the station? At least they've got piped music.
A: Yeah, OK – if that's what you prefer.

5 Laughter occupies a special place in human social life and it's a fascinating feature of our biology. Scientists have studied all kinds of emotions and behaviour but few have done research into laughter. Generally, we associate laughter with pleasure, happiness and joy but in some cultures it's also a sign of embarrassment or even fear. In fact, only 10–20 percent of laughter is a response to humour. Most of the time, it's a message we send to other people – it can be communicating a joyful mood, a willingness to be friends but it can also be unkind and of course, you can always tell if it is.

6 It all started in a second-hand bookshop, when I spotted a copy of Fiona Harrold's *Be your own life coach*. It was less than a pound and I thought it would be a laugh to read a self-help book – something to chat to my friends about. The friendly orange cover promised to show me how to take control of my life and achieve my wildest dreams. But the truth is, with a few easy exercises and a few uplifting words, that book has helped me feel that I can take on the world. I know people will smile at this but I have nothing but praise for it.

7 Of course I love the club. It was part of my life for 20 years and I wish them nothing but success but I'm moving on. I've got a place to study for a sports science degree and I start at the end of the month. It's a three-year course and I'm looking forward to it immensely because it sounds like fun. Who knows if I'll go back into football at the end of it? I'm an optimist, so I make a point of never saying never but that's why my horizons have no limit.

8 I hadn't intended to buy another car. After all the trouble I'd had with the previous one, I said I'd settle for public transport in future, however inconvenient it was. Then I saw Betsy. She was parked outside a friend's house, with 'For Sale' written in the window. Twenty-five years old, light blue and irresistible. Other cars are faster, warmer, more economical and easier to drive but just walking past mine makes me smile and when I turn the key and hear the purr of her engine, well, I'm queen of the road!

Module 12

Vocabulary development 1 p. 112

1a 1 judge
2 witness
3 police officer
4 jury
5 lawyer
6 defendent
7 lawyer
8 reporters

1b 1 c 2 e 3 g 4 d 5 b 6 h 7 a 8 f

1c **verb + noun collocations:** commit + crime, reach + verdict, pass + sentence, win + case(s), break into + house, steal + jewellery, give + description, arrest + criminal
other useful crime expressions:
the defendant: is **on trial** for murder; **pleads guilty/ innocent** to the charge (of murder); has a **long record** of **minor offences**, acted in **self-defence**
the police: have **found fingerprints**; have **got a DNA sample** (from ...); found evidence at the **scene of the crime**
the judge: will **sentence him to several years in prison/life imprisonment**

2 1 A (phrasal verb meaning 'discover by chance')
2 B (If you **hang out** somewhere, you are spending time there for no real purpose.)
3 D
4 A
5 C (**theft** = stealing something; **burglary** = breaking into a house and then stealing things; **fraud** = obtaining money illegally in a deceitful way; **forgery** = copying a document/painting/money illegally)
6 B
7 C (You are: **arrested for a crime/charged with a crime** by the police. Later, in court, you are: **convicted of the crime** (if they find you guilty)/**sentenced to X years in prison.**)
8 A (**regarded as**, **viewed as**, **considered to be**)

Expert language
came across, hanging out, looked upon

Language development 1 pp. 113–114

1 1 in order to
2 such
3 before
4 While
5 and
6 However
7 because
8 if
9 After
10 which (*who* is also possible)

2 1 Being out of work, Simon spent all his time reading books.
2 Hearing the telephone ring, he put down his book and got up to answer it.
3 Feeling annoyed at the interruption, he picked up the telephone and shouted 'yes' as loud as he could.
4 Realising that the caller had hung up, he put the receiver down again.
5 Not having been out all day, he got ready to go for a walk.
6 On reaching the door, he heard the telephone ring again.
7 Running to the phone, he picked up the receiver and heard the voice of his girlfriend who asked what the matter was.
8 Despite feeling rather guilty, he couldn't help smiling.

3 1 **As soon as** Peter (had) arrived at his brother's house, he realised something was wrong.
2 **Even though** it was a hot day, all the doors and windows were closed.
3 Peter was sure Tom was at home **as** he had phoned him an hour before.
4 **Opening** the front door, he went inside **and** looked in all the rooms.
5 **If** Tom had gone out, he would have left a note.
6 His brother was a sensible man **who** always told others what his plans were.
7 **As** Peter was climbing the stairs, the doorbell rang.
8 He rushed down the stairs **so** quickly **that** he almost fell.
9 **Seeing** his brother on the doorstep, he gave a cry of relief.
10 Tom laughed **and** told Peter that the police had arrested him in the afternoon **because** they had mistaken him for an escaped bank robber!

4 1 in
2 was
3 so
4 addition
5 such
6 as
7 when
8 from

Expert language
old-fashioned

Writing p. 115

1 1 someone you don't know
2 formal
3 why you loved the book, a brief summary of the plot and why you think it is relevant to children now

2a–c

My favourite childhood book was *The Secret Garden* by Frances Hodgson Burnett. I loved it because it took me into a world that was completely different from my own. I was a 21st-century boy ⟨living⟩ in a city-centre flat, while the book is about a girl living in the countryside 100 years ago.

The Secret Garden's main character is ten-year-old Mary, who is sent to live with an uncle when her ⟨parents⟩ die. Living in a remote house with only his servants, the uncle is a miserable man. He leaves Mary to look after herself, so **(1) not surprisingly**, she is lonely and unhappy. ⟨Gradually,⟩ she explores the area around the house and she finds the secret garden of the title. Over the course of the book, she makes friends, learns how to care for other people and becomes a ⟨happier,⟩ healthier child.

Although it was written a long time ago, **(2) as far as I'm concerned**, today's children will still find the story engaging. There is an element of ⟨mystery⟩ which keeps you reading and the themes of the need for parental love and the importance of friendship are, **(3) without doubt**, always ⟨relevant.⟩

3 1 yes 2 yes 3 yes

Listening p. 116

1 1 question 10
2 questions 3 and 4

2 1 modern languages
2 teacher
3 exhausting
4 romantic
5 history of science
6 (new) planet
7 clothes
8 events
9 plot
10 500/five hundred words

Expert language
9 (When planning a novel …), 10 (When she's working on a book …)

Vocabulary development 2 p. 117

1a Television: commercials, documentary, editor, newscaster, presenter, reporter, viewers, weather forecast
Newspapers: article, circulation, editor, gossip column, reporter, small ads, tabloid, weather forecast
The internet: download, editor, log on, server, surf, weather forecast, web page

1b 1 circulation
2 article
3 surf
4 tabloid
5 weather forecast
6 download
7 commercials
8 small ads
9 editor
10 newscaster

2a 1 on
2 up
3 around
4 on
5 of
6 into
7 for
8 up
9 out
10 on

2b 1 picked up
2 going in for
3 talked me into doing
4 get on (well)
5 going on
6 took on
7 hang around with
8 get out of

3 1 A
2 D
3 C (fixed expression: *to take place*)
4 A (collocation)
5 B
6 B (**Reduce** is a transitive verb: somebody **reduces** something. **Decline** is intransitive and does not need an object. **Retired** refers to a person not to the influence. It is important to read the whole sentence here.)
7 A

8   D (***spectators*** = people who watch a game or event; ***passers-by*** = people in the street who see something happen by chance; ***observers*** = people who see or notice something)

Expert language
for instance, such as

Language development 2 pp. 118–119

1a
1	to buy	5	to go
2	replacing	6	to give
3	to write	7	cutting
4	to be updated	8	to be rewritten

1b
1	to take	5	to go
2	feeding/to be fed	6	washing/to be washed
3	testing/to be tested	7	to help
4	replacing/to be replaced	8	cleaning/to be cleaned

2a
1	having/getting	4	have/get	8	done/redecorated
2	them	5	have/get	9	had
3	will	6	it	10	was
		7	have/get		

2b
2	have/get your eyes tested	5	have/get a swimming pool built
3	have/get it serviced	6	have/get the chimney cleaned
4	had my teeth checked		

3
1	her house broken into	6	needs knocking
2	had your photograph	7	car washed
3	house needs to be	8	need to go
4	having/getting my computer repaired	9	just had my new watch
5	have central heating put in	10	having her new fridge delivered

4
1	however	5	such
2	between	6	with
3	what	7	way
4	there	8	that/which

Reading pp. 120–121

2 1   Main points: lots of young people want to work in television; most people in the UK spend a lot of time in front of the TV; we rely on TV for our knowledge of the world; TV can influence what we buy, read etc.; unlike other influences on us, TV isn't interactive; TV could have a better influence but at present doesn't

2   generally bad

3   1 C   2 E   3 G   4 B   5 F   6 D

Expert language
A   **Despite** this, …
B   There is, **however**, …
D   **But** equally, …
E   **But** most of the time, …
F   **But** the reality …

4   1 B   2 C   3 D   4 B   5 A   6 C   7 D

Audio script

Hi there. My name's Laura Reddington and I've come along to answer questions sent in by listeners about my life and work.

Firstly, Sue from London asks if I have always been interested in books. Well, yes, Sue, I have – although not necessarily English literature because my degree was actually in modern languages. But, I always thought it would be wonderful to be a writer, however, I also knew it'd be very time-consuming and I didn't see that as a good career move when I was younger. I considered journalism, even publishing, but in the end I got a good job as a teacher and that tended to come first. So, this ambition to be a writer was, sort of, on hold whilst I did other things.

Now, Bill from Edinburgh asks if I regret not starting earlier. In a way, but maybe novelists shouldn't write until they've had a bit of experience of the world. Being out at work, you meet all sorts of people, see how they behave in different situations. I loved it and found it very satisfying, but also very exhausting. After 20 years, I'd had enough. That's when I decided to try my hand as a writer, because I was looking for a new challenge.

My first thought was that I needed to make a living, so I tried romantic fiction – without success, I might add. I thought it would be easy money because those novels sell in their millions. But, although I made up some great characters, the stories didn't work well. I just hadn't found the right thing and so my work wasn't published. It took something a little deeper and darker, I suppose, to bring out my talent as a writer. It turned out that a historical thriller was just the thing for me.

Sandra from Dublin asks how I got the idea for my first one. Well, Sandra, I've always loved history and I could see from other novels that were doing well that the history of science interested people. I'm a fan of astronomy myself and I've always read widely on the subject. I was looking through my books one day when I came across the story of a man who thought he'd found a new planet. I realised this was going on at about the same time as a famous murder case in London. So I thought I could mix the two stories together to make a sort of detective novel.

People ask me if I did lots of research for that book. Yes, I needed to get the historical details correct – you know, have people wearing the right clothes for the period and things like that. But then there are no records of what actually happened to people from day to day and, of course, the murder mystery was never actually solved in real life. So, I made up most of the events I describe. In a novel, it all needs to seem real to the reader but people aren't actually checking the historical facts.

Another question: Bill from Canada asks about the actual writing. How do I go about it? Well, that book took two years to write. I know some people can sit down and just write – you know, the inspiration just comes and until they've finished, they don't know how it will end. But for me, it's all about planning. Once I'd got all the plot clear in my mind, I was able to work the characters out in detail. Only then did I sit down and concentrate on the actual writing. Some writers do a lot of rewriting but once the ideas are in place, I just write – I know that some writers manage a thousand words a day, and I have done 750 on occasion, but usually around 500 words is the right amount for me. I keep reading through it, changing little things as I go, but most of it just flows from my brain to the page.

Practice exam

Reading and Use of English

Part 1 p.122

1 C   2 B   3 C   4 B   5 A   6 D   7 B   8 C

Part 2 p. 123

9	BECAUSE	12	FROM	15	WHO
10	USED	13	HOW	16	LET
11	SO	14	OF		

Part 3 p. 124

17	MEMBERSHIP	21	UNLIKE
18	BENEFICIAL	22	FITNESS
19	EXPLANATION	23	INCREASINGLY
20	GROWTH	24	ESPECIALLY/SPECIALLY

Part 4 p.125

25 MOST EXCITING (ONE/THAT) I HAVE/MOST EXCITING (ONE) (THAT) I'VE

26 IS SAID TO HAVE GIVEN

27 TAKE ADVANTAGE OF

28 WERE PREVENTED FROM COMPLETING

29 GET MY MOTORBIKE SERVICED

30 HE COULD HAVE SPOKEN

Part 5 pp. 126–127

31 C   32 B   33 A   34 B   35 A   36 D

Part 6 pp. 128–129

37 E   38 A   39 C   40 B   41 F   42 D

Part 7 pp. 130–131

43 C   44 D   45 A   46 A   47 B   48 D   49 A   50 D
51 C   52 B

Writing

Part 1 p. 132

1   *Model answer*

Wherever we go, we are exposed to advertising – whether on television, our mobiles or on billboards. It is part of daily life but can encourage people to live beyond their means.

Advertising's principal role is to inform. Without it, sellers would not be able to communicate with customers and share information about products. With such a range of products on the market, consumers need to understand and compare products to make informed decisions.

However, sometimes advertising persuades us to make the wrong decision. With so much clever wording, it is sometimes difficult to separate fact from fiction. Customers must learn to read between the lines so they are not tricked by advertisers or encouraged to spend money they cannot afford.

Interestingly, advertising is also an art form. Advertisers grab our attention using incredibly creative and amusing ideas which entertain us. However, this only serves to persuade us more that we cannot live without their products.

Advertising has a very prominent role in the world today. It can be useful if it is informative. However, to suggest that you won't be successful or happy if you don't buy the product is irresponsible.

Part 2 p. 123

2   *Model answer*

My ideal friend

If you could combine the best qualities of the people you know into the ideal friend, what would they be? Most humans are sociable and enjoy spending time with other people but what do we look for and how do we choose our friends?

For me, an ideal friend is someone who has a sense of humour, is interesting and supportive. A person who has the ability to see the funny side of things is much better company than someone who complains a lot. Equally, an interesting person is always a good companion because they have lots to talk about and they are curious about the world. But we have to be realistic: life isn't always fun and there are times when we need to share our worries with someone who will listen, be sympathetic and perhaps give good advice.

On balance, I think the most important quality in a friend is that they are supportive. By sharing feelings and understanding each other's characters, you can build a genuine friendship that will last for years; and hopefully, have a laugh along the way!

3   *Model answer*

Great value, great location!

I recently spent a weekend at Silver Sun Hotel with a group of friends. In such an expensive and enormous city, the hotel, which is centrally located next to the station, was a great find and met all our expectations.

We were very satisfied with our rooms, which, although small and a little old-fashioned, had everything we needed and were very warm and clean. The staff in reception were incredibly helpful, giving us lots of sightseeing tips and advice on how to get great discounts around the city.

We booked our rooms on the hotel's website at a very good price, so we were very pleasantly surprised that a simple breakfast of bread rolls and coffee was included. Overall, for a central hotel with clean rooms, I think the Silver Sun is excellent value for money. My only criticism is that there is a daily charge to use wi-fi.

The hotel is ideal for budget travellers who want a base while they explore the city. It is unsuitable for disabled and elderly travellers as there isn't a lift to the bedrooms which are all on the upper floors.

4   *Model answer*

Hi Alex,

Good to hear from you! Your project sounds interesting. Actually, we've got a public holiday next week, so this is good timing!

We only have eight public holidays in the UK. Traditionally, they're called bank holidays because they are days when banks are closed. In England and Wales we don't have a national day but Scotland and Northern Ireland do.

Most of our public holidays fall on a Monday, which means we get a long weekend off. People often hang out with friends or take the opportunity to visit family. For example, on August Bank Holiday, people might have a barbecue or go to the beach. There are always news stories about long queues of traffic if the weather's good! And nowadays, with so many cheap airlines, some people fly off for a short break.

There should definitely be more – people always want more holidays! I'd like another in autumn as it's a long time between August Bank Holiday and the next one on 25 December.

I'd better go now – I've got to finish an essay for tomorrow's deadline! Just get in touch if you need more information.

Love,
Fran

Listening

Part 1 p. 124

1 B 2 A 3 B 4 C 5 B 6 C 7 C 8 A

Part 2 p. 125

9	uncle	14	back
10	the past	15	1650
11	London	16	sentimental
12	stable	17	clean
13	sensitive hands	18	conservationist

Part 3 p. 126

19 B 20 E 21 H 22 D 23 F

Part 4 p. 127

24 A 25 C 26 C 27 B 28 A 29 A 30 B

Audio script

Part 1

1 Basically, I was looking for somewhere to get away from it all and relax because the last few months have been so hectic at work, but I didn't want to feel cut off because it's nice to meet people on holiday, too. The complex sounded exactly what I was looking for – there were ten villas with a shared swimming pool and a restaurant but each one had its own private sitting-out area. What I wasn't prepared for, however, was the fact that the place was popular with young families. So it was very noisy during the day and extremely dull in the evening.

2
A: How did you get on at the dentist's?

B: I'm afraid it's a bit of a long story. I got held up on the motorway, so I was 15 minutes late for the appointment. Anyway, the next patient had gone in, so I'd missed it, which is fair enough, but then the receptionist said I'd have to pay anyway. I'm afraid after rushing like mad trying to get there on time, I was a bit stressed out and I just lost my temper. I feel awful about it now because I really shouted at her in front of a waiting room full of people. It made me feel better at the time, though.

3
A: I feel sorry for Mandy, really – I mean, she spent hours preparing that report and no one thought to tell her that the policy had changed.

B: Well, you know, she's invited to all the meetings …

A: Come on, if we went to all the meetings we're invited to, none of us would ever get anything finished.

B: Well, even if you're not there, the minutes are circulated by email, you know, so I don't believe that she wasn't told. Either she wasn't listening or she hadn't checked her inbox.

A: I guess so, but I still feel sorry for her.

4 Want to feel more confident in the gym? Swap your baggy T-shirt and track pants for racy sportswear that will make you look great. Our new autumn range of stretchy tops in bright colours is stylish and comfortable, as well as allowing you to move freely. Our hard-wearing weatherproof jackets hold warmth in and keep the rain out, without making you look like a shapeless ball of plastic, and our must-have footwear, equally good for running or working out in the gym, wouldn't look out of place in the office.

5 A listener, Mary, writes from Oxford to ask: 'What's the best age to introduce a child to computers?' Well, Mary, recent research suggests that this can be a positive move for kids as young as three. It can enhance language and creative skills and give them a headstart in understanding technology. But that doesn't mean sticking the child in front of a screen and leaving them to it. Get a chair that's the right height and keep each session to half an hour or less – more than enough time in one position for growing bones and a vulnerable spine. And sit with them; then you can answer any questions they might have.

6 There can't be many people around who haven't read at least one book by David Granham. His blend of subtle characterisation and superb plot lines makes his thrillers almost universally popular. But if you haven't sampled one yet, his latest offering, *The Colne Verdict*, is not the place to start. Although fans will find all the usual ingredients in place and the writing is up to his usual standard, my impression is that the formula is beginning to wear a little thin, as if perhaps he's getting a little bored with it himself and needs to try something a little different.

7
A: And next we have a call from Sally, who works in a bank. Go ahead, Sally.

B: Hello, yes … I work in a big office and my department has hired and lost eight secretarial staff in as many months. I wouldn't say our salary structure was poor, and the hours and conditions are fairly standard, so what is driving new recruits away? As a section leader, I'm involved in recruitment discussions but I'm at a loss to know how to reverse the situation.

A: Right, well, let's ask our expert, Tom Willis, what he …

8
A: I made a reservation for this evening. The names's Walters.

B: Mmm … Ah, yes, here we are. The front row of the stalls and I think you've also booked dinner in the restaurant upstairs before the performance.

A: That's right – a table for two. What time is dinner served?

B: From 6.30 onwards, but we recommend that you take your seats in the auditorium by about 7.25 because the curtain goes up at 7.30, so it's best not to leave it too late.

A: Oh, right. My wife's just gone to freshen up in our hotel room. It's only across the street but I hope she's not long.

Part 2

Hi there! My name's Peter Denison and I make my living repairing old clocks and watches. I'm here to tell you about my work.

People assume that my interest in clocks and watches must come from a family tradition but that's not the case. Actually, my father was a farmer who preferred animals to machinery, perhaps because my grandfather was a vet. But growing up, I was always fixing bikes and taking things like radios to bits. I remember going to see an uncle whose garage was full of tools and machines. I used to spend all day in there with him while my cousins were playing football. I guess he saw that I was interested and encouraged me.

Then, one day, when I was 14, I took my parents' clock to bits and discovered that clocks are actually beautifully made inside. It never worked again but I'd made a thrilling discovery and that's when I decided to specialise in timepieces. For me, clocks are something which connect us with the past. I like old things that haven't been altered or modernised but still work perfectly.

Later, I did a course in what's known as horology at a college in Birmingham. I did well and went on to get a job with a top firm of jewellers in London afterwards. I was employed as what's called an improver, doing all sorts of repair work for two years. It was excellent experience but I didn't like city life, so eventually, I decided to go home and set up my own workshop in the country.

I began working in a corner of an old factory. Other craftsmen used the rest of the building, so it was relatively cheap. Actually, I've spent my entire adult life working on my own in little rooms. I had a garden shed at one point, then a little office behind a shop and my current workshop is in a converted stable. My workspace is made up of hundreds of little drawers and each piece of equipment has its place, so it's not as untidy as it might appear.

People often ask me what qualities you need for this kind of work. Well, good eyesight, sensitive hands and a lot of patience are essential. Repairing a woman's watch the size of a small coin can be like doing micro-surgery and I work with my shoulders hunched forward, an eyeglass in my eye, just a few centimetres away from the watch or clock mechanism. Fortunately, my eyes are still sound but like a lot of watchmakers, I do find I get back problems.

So what type of clocks do I mostly work with? Well, old ones if I can – from the period between 1850 and 1950, although occasionally, I'll get one going back to 1750 and that's a real thrill for me. The oldest I've worked on was an Italian night clock dating from 1650. A lamp shone behind the clock face so that the time was reflected onto the wall – a lovely piece of craftsmanship.

People always ask me whether most things can be fixed and the answer is: 'Yes, as long as they were well made originally.' People are very sentimental about old clocks. They're often inherited, you know, handed down through the generations. But people generally don't bring them in to me until they break or stop working properly. In the old days people knew they needed to clean working things but now it doesn't occur to people. It needs doing at least once every three years.

So what do I get out of the job exactly? I often think of myself as a conservationist because I'm devoted to repairing things and keeping old things going. Working with your hands doesn't seem to be as valued in modern society as it once was, which is a shame. The environment is very important to me and I try to grow my own vegetables and keep hens for eggs. So it's not just the clocks.

So before I go on to show you an example ...

Part 3

1   I've been here about five years. At first I wasn't sure that I'd made the right choice because it was quite a while before I got to know the neighbours. For me, it was a question of position. I work from home, so it wasn't that I had to travel in to work or anything but I wanted to be able to pop to the post office and get in a few basic provisions without wasting half my day. All the bigger flats I looked at were a bus ride away from the shops. I don't have a car and I didn't like the idea of being cut off, so I settled for less space.

2   I'm so close to the station you can hear the trains from my flat. I didn't realise that until I moved in, but I've got used to it now. I came here when I retired. I used to have a much larger place but no longer needed the space. What attracted me was the fact that there's a man on the door downstairs who checks who's coming in and what's going on – being on your own at my age, that's a comfort. I thought he'd also do little maintenance jobs for me, but that's not part of his job, apparently. Fortunately, I made friends with a nice couple downstairs who help me out when anything needs doing.

3   I was looking for somewhere close to my work because I didn't want to waste time travelling back and forth, so I wasn't really looking in this area at all. Then a colleague, who lived in the block, told me that this place was free. As soon as I saw how much space you got for your money, I jumped at the chance. I'd been looking at places with tiny rooms just because they were on good bus routes. It was only after I'd moved in that I realised how good the local shops are and what a nice part of town it is. You really feel safe walking round here – even late at night.

4   When I first saw this flat, I was put off by the fact that it's on a very busy road. It's the main commuter route into the city centre. But actually, I bought it from a friend, who introduced me to the people upstairs. They were very welcoming and convinced me that it really wasn't a problem. I liked the idea of being close to such nice people, so I decided that, although I'd have liked bigger rooms, it was probably a good buy. It was only later that I discovered how good the local shops are and that the block itself is well maintained by the security guard who lives on the ground floor.

5   My last flat was very convenient, handy for the shops and well connected for public transport. But the building itself was falling to pieces and I got fed up trying to get the owner to do something about it. So, I moved out to this place instead because there's a caretaker who's paid to keep the place in order. I wasn't looking for much bigger rooms but actually, I've had no trouble using the space and the other residents turned out to be really friendly. It gives you a nice feeling of security to know that if you have a problem, you can always pop next door for help.

Part 4

I = Interviewer, G = Grant

I: My guest today will soon be joining a very small and very special group of people. Ever since the idea of space tourism was first seriously considered in the late 1990s, some people have had their name on the waiting list, as they saved up the fee. One of those people is Grant Sowerby, who is just about to leave on the trip of a lifetime. He'll be spending ten days on a space station as it orbits the Earth. Grant, welcome.

G: Hi.

I: What are you most looking forward to about the flight?

G: There'll be so many experiences in those ten days that it's hard to know which will be the greatest moment. But I guess the launch is what I'm looking forward to most. There can't be many things as exhilarating as being in a rocket as it flies out of the atmosphere. The first experience of weightlessness and seeing the Earth from outside the atmosphere, those are going to be incredible too, but maybe not quite so thrilling.

I: Don't you feel scared at all?

G: I wouldn't be human if I didn't. Because I'm not a military pilot or even a professional test pilot – this isn't something I do every day, you know. But I've done months of training alongside real astronauts, so I hope I'm up to the challenge.

I: Will you have specific responsibilities on the flight?

G: Very much so. The spaceship is extremely small and so every seat has a set of controls in front of it. I'll be handling the systems that are controlled from the right-hand seat – for example, radio, TV and some of the navigation systems. The flight commander sits in the centre and can take over from me on those functions if necessary but hopefully, I'll be a fully-functioning member of the crew.

I: And was the training difficult?

G: Some of the survival training – you know, when we're prepared for an unexpected landing in the sea or in an extreme winter climate – has been physically very challenging. Much worse than the training for weightlessness, although that was pretty tough too.

I: Some people are completely against the idea of tourists going into space. Do you see this trip as a holiday?

G: Actually, I see it very much as a life experience. People use the term 'space tourism' to describe what I'm going to do but actually, it's a bit misleading. I've been training flat-out for 12 months and I'll be working flat-out every day that I'm up there. So, I'm going to need a real holiday when I come back.

I: What sort of things will you be doing?

G: I'll be looking at different ways of measuring the energy an astronaut uses during a space flight and how that affects the muscles. But the astronauts all tell me that the one thing they wished they'd had more of up there is free time. So I'm going to make sure that I have some, at least.

I: And what advice do you have for other people who fancy a trip into space?

G: Well, the price is a bit steep at the moment, which cuts a lot of people out, and then you've got to go through months of training. I mean, not everyone's up to that, physically, nor can they spare the time, and it can be frustrating for people. I mean, I was fortunate because if you don't make it through the training, basically, they don't let you go.

I: Right.

G: The best advice I can give is to say, 'Just keep patient.' I mean, space travel's going to become far more accessible sooner or later, and I reckon it's going to be sooner than people think. I'm confident that with so many companies keen to organise trips, this market's going to open up considerably. I couldn't tell you what it might cost but I'm confident that within ten years, I'll be able to buy a ticket and fly up there again without having to go through such a complicated training procedure.

I: Grant, thank you. And best of luck with the flight.

G: Thanks.

Pearson Education Limited
Edinburgh Gate
Harlow
Essex CM20 2JE
England
and Associated Companies throughout the world.

www.pearsonelt.com

© Pearson Education Limited 2015

The right of Nick Kenny and Richard Mann, to be identified as authors of
this Work has been asserted by them in accordance with the Copyright,
Designs and Patents Act 1988.

All rights reserved; no part of this publication may be reproduced,
stored in a retrieval system, or transmitted in any form or by any means,
electronic, mechanical, photocopying, recording, or otherwise without
the prior written permission of the Publishers.

First published 2003
Third edition published 2015
ISBN: 978-1-4479-8062-9
Set in Amasis and Mundo Sans
Printed in Slovakia by Neografia

Acknowledgements
*We are grateful to the following for permission to reproduce copyright
material:*
(Key: b-bottom; c-centre; l-left; r-right; t-top)

123RF.com: Denis Tabler 81tr, Filip Fuxa 30tc, Hongqi Zhang 10c, Luis
Santos 81bl, Oleg Doroshenko 12, sauletas 27br, Sergey Novikov 23;
Alamy Images: Adrian Sherratt 68, Archive Photos 26cl, Blend Images
21bl, DP RM 81tl, dpa picture alliance 10t, Heritage Image Partnership Ltd
24, Holger Burmeister 116, JTB MEDIA CREATION, Inc. 100c, Juice Images
21bc, 104, justin barton 11, Tetra Images 21br; **Corbis:** Bettmann 26tl,
Colin Monteath / Hedgehog House 27bl, Gail Mooney 26tc, Underwood
& Underwood 26tr; **Fotolia.com:** Monkey Business 9, 139b; **FotoLibra:**
Jeff Greenberg 100b; **Getty Images:** Andrew Goodman 88b, Carl Court
AFP 40, Dan Regan 59, Hulton Archive 93, JEWEL SAMAD / AFP 88t,
Jupiterimages 60, NCP / Star Max / GC Images) 88tc, Peter Macdiarmid 28;
Pearson Education Ltd: Ann Cromack. Ikat Design 22; **PhotoDisc:** Doug
Menuez 27tr; **Photolibrary.com:** Andres Rodriguez 108c; **Rex Features:**
111; **Shutterstock.com:** Adriano Castelli 26c, bestimagesevercom 45,
Catalin Petolea 115, Christopher Kolaczan 27c, CreativeNature.nl. 27tl,
Darren Baker 14b, Elaine Nash 30tl, Felix Mizioznikov 46c, gorillaimages
38, Jason Stitt 46cl, John Kropewnicki 36tl, Juan Carlos Zamora 35, KPG_
Payless 139c, Lex-art 71, lightpoet 39, Martin Novak 140c, Mikhail Pogosov
36tr, Minerva Studio 15t, Monkey Business Images 76, racorn 46cr, Richard
Carey 78, Stefan Schurr 108t, StockLite 91, tarasov 63, Tyler Olson 140b,
Vittorio Bruno 30tr, YanLev 107; **Sozaijiten:** 81br; **The Kobal Collection:**
Saul Zaentz Company 50

All other images © Pearson Education

Every effort has been made to trace the copyright holders and we
apologise in advance for any unintentional omissions. We would be
pleased to insert the appropriate acknowledgement in any subsequent
edition of this publication.

Illustrated by David Semple 33, 47, 62, 87, 106, 112